# SMP AS/A2 Mathematics

D0434102

# Core 1
## for Edexcel

CAMBRIDGE
UNIVERSITY PRESS

**The School Mathematics Project**

**SMP AS/A2 Mathematics writing team** David Cassell, Spencer Instone, John Ling, Paul Scruton, Susan Shilton, Heather West

**SMP design and administration** Melanie Bull, Carol Cole, Pam Keetch, Nicky Lake, Jane Seaton, Cathy Syred, Ann White

The authors thank Sue Glover for the technical advice she gave when this AS/A2 project began and for her detailed editorial contribution to this book. The authors are also very grateful to those teachers who commented in detail on draft chapters.

PUBLISHED BY THE PRESS SYNDICATE OF THE UNIVERSITY OF CAMBRIDGE
The Pitt Building, Trumpington Street, Cambridge, United Kingdom

CAMBRIDGE UNIVERSITY PRESS
The Edinburgh Building, Cambridge CB2 2RU, UK
40 West 20th Street, New York NY 10011–4211, USA
477 Williamstown Road, Port Melbourne, VIC 3207, Australia
Ruiz de Alarcón 13, 28014 Madrid, Spain
Dock House, The Waterfront, Cape Town 8001, South Africa

http://www.cambridge.org/

Typesetting and technical illustrations by The School Mathematics Project

The authors and publisher are grateful to London Qualifications Limited for permission to reproduce questions from past Edexcel examination papers. Individual questions are marked Edexcel. London Qualifications Limited accepts no responsibility whatsoever for the accuracy or method of working in the answers given.

# Using this book

Each chapter begins with a **summary** of what the student is expected to learn.

The chapter then has sections lettered A, B, C, … (see the contents overleaf). In most cases a section consists of development material, worked examples and an exercise.

The **development material** interweaves explanation with questions that involve the student in making sense of ideas and techniques. Development questions are labelled according to their section letter (A1, A2, …, B1, B2, …) and answers to them are provided.

**D** Some development questions are particularly suitable for discussion – either by the whole class or by smaller groups – because they have the potential to bring out a key issue or clarify a technique. Such **discussion questions** are marked with a bar, as here.

**K** **Key points** established in the development material are marked with a bar as here, so the student may readily refer to them during later work or revision. Each chapter's key points are also gathered together in a panel after the last lettered section.

The **worked examples** have been chosen to clarify ideas and techniques, and as models for students to follow in setting out their own work. Guidance for the student is in italic.

The **exercise** at the end of each lettered section is designed to consolidate the skills and understanding acquired earlier in the section. Unlike those in the development material, questions in the exercise are denoted by a number only.

**Starred questions** are more demanding.

After the lettered sections and the key points panel there may be a set of **mixed questions**, combining ideas from several sections in the chapter; these may also involve topics from earlier chapters.

Every chapter ends with a selection of **questions for self-assessment** ('Test yourself').

Included in the mixed questions and 'Test yourself' are **past Edexcel exam questions**, to give the student an idea of the style and standard that may be expected, and to build confidence. Occasionally, exam questions are included in the exercises in the lettered sections.

A calculator is not required for 'Test yourself' questions in this book (in line with the current examination requirements for this module); but a scientific or graphic calculator may be appropriately used elsewhere; there are many opportunities to use a graph plotter or a spreadsheet facility.

# Contents

# 1 Linear graphs and equations

In this chapter you will
- revise work on linear graphs and their equations
- change a given linear equation to a different form
- solve problems by using intersecting linear graphs
- revise and extend work on simultaneous equations

## A Linear graphs (answers p 162)

**K** On any part of a straight line graph, the gradient is the ratio $\dfrac{\text{increase in } y}{\text{increase in } x}$.

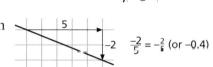

$$\frac{6}{2} = 3$$

A gradient can be a fraction. It is negative if the line goes down as it goes to the right (since the increase in $y$ is negative).

$$\frac{-2}{5} = -\frac{2}{5} \text{ (or } -0.4)$$

**K** Lines that have the same gradient are parallel.

**A1** Give the gradients of each of these straight lines. Draw sketches if you need to. Are any of the lines parallel?

    **A** The line from $(2, 1)$ to $(4, 6)$      **B** The line from $(-4, -2)$ to $(-1, -5)$

    **C** The line from $(-1, 0)$ to $(2, -1)$      **D** The line from $(-3, -3)$ to $(1, 7)$

**K** An equation of the form $y = mx + c$ is a straight line.
$m$ is the gradient and $c$ is the $y$-intercept.
The $y$-intercept is the value of $y$ where the line cuts the $y$-axis.

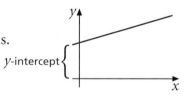

**A2** Draw these straight lines on squared paper.

    **(a)** $y = 2x + 4$      **(b)** $s = -2t + 7$      **(c)** $y = 3x - 5$      **(d)** $y = 5$

**A3** A graph has the equation $3x + 4y - 24 = 0$.

    **(a)** Substitute 0 for $x$ in the equation.
        Solve the equation you get.
        What point does this tell you the graph goes through?

    **(b)** Substitute 0 for $y$ in the equation.
        Solve the equation you get.
        What point does this tell you the graph goes through?

The results from question A3 tell you where the graph cuts the axes, enabling you to sketch the graph.

A sketch graph is not drawn on graph paper, but key points are labelled.

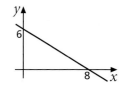

**A4** Use the above method to sketch a graph of each of these equations.

(a) $2x + 5y - 20 = 0$  (b) $7x + 4y - 28 = 0$  (c) $2x - 4y + 8 = 0$

(d) $4x - 3y - 12 = 0$  (e) $6x + 5y + 30 = 0$  (f) $x + 5y + 5 = 0$

**A5** Sketch graphs of these.

(a) $3x + 7y = 21$  (b) $5x + y = -5$  (c) $2x - 2y = -9$

**A6** A straight line goes through $(0, 8)$ and $(6, 0)$. Write its equation in the form $ax + by = c$, where $a$, $b$ and $c$ are constants.

You will often find it useful to change the equation of a linear graph into an equivalent form, as in the following example.

---

### Example 1

Find the gradient of the straight line graph $4x + 5y - 3 = 0$.

### Solution

*Make y the subject of the equation.* $\qquad\qquad 5y = -4x + 3$

$$y = -\tfrac{4}{5}x + \tfrac{3}{5}$$

*Look at the coefficient of x.* $\qquad\qquad$ So the gradient is $-\tfrac{4}{5}$.

---

**A7** Write each of these equations in the form $y = mx + c$.

(a) $3x + y - 2 = 0$  (b) $x - 2y + 6 = 0$  (c) $3x + 5y - 2 = 0$

**A8** Sort these into three sets of parallel lines, giving the gradient for each set.

$\qquad 3x - y - 4 = 0 \qquad y = -\tfrac{1}{2}x + 2 \qquad y = 3x + \tfrac{1}{2} \qquad y = -3x + 4$

$\qquad y = 7 - \tfrac{1}{2}x \qquad 3x + y - 7 = 0 \qquad y = -\tfrac{1}{2} + 3x \qquad y = -2 - 3x$

**A9** There are some pairs of **perpendicular** lines here (one line at right angles to the other).

(a) Record the gradients of each pair of perpendicular lines. Describe how the gradients in any pair are related.

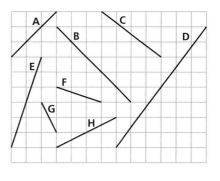

(b) What is the gradient of any line perpendicular to a line that has gradient $\tfrac{2}{3}$?

(c) What is the gradient of any line perpendicular to a line with gradient $-4$?

(d) If two lines with gradients $p$ and $q$ are perpendicular, what is the value of $pq$?

**K** If two lines with gradients $m_1$ and $m_2$ are perpendicular,
$m_2 = -\dfrac{1}{m_1}$  or  $m_1 m_2 = -1$.

**A10** Which of these lines are perpendicular to one another?
  **A** The line from $(1, 3)$ to $(7, 4)$  **B** The line from $(0, 0)$ to $(5, 4)$
  **C** The line from $(4, 2)$ to $(8, -3)$  **D** The line from $(0, 0)$ to $(12, 2)$

**A11** Which of these lines are perpendicular to one another?
  **A** $y = 2x + 4$  **B** $5x + y = 2$  **C** $y = -\frac{1}{2}x - 3$  **D** $y = \frac{1}{5}x - 2$
  **E** $y = \frac{3}{4}x$  **F** $y = 3 - 2x$  **G** $y = \frac{1}{2}x + 5$  **H** $3x + 4y - 1 = 0$

**A12** Can you think of any perpendicular lines for which the
  rule $m_1 m_2 = -1$ will not work?

---

**Example 2**

Identify any parallel or perpendicular lines among these.
**A** $y = 3x + 2$  **B** $3y = 2x$  **C** $3x - y - 5 = 0$  **D** $3x + 2y = 5$

**Solution**

*Write the equations in the form $y = mx + c$.*
A $y = 3x + 2$
B $y = \frac{2}{3}x$
C $y = 3x - 5$
D $y = -\frac{3}{2}x + \frac{5}{2}$

*Examine the x-coefficients (gradients).*
A and C are parallel (with gradient 3).
B and D are perpendicular because $\frac{2}{3} \times -\frac{3}{2} = -1$.

---

**Example 3**

Sketch the graph of $\dfrac{x}{2} + \dfrac{y}{3} = 5$.

**Solution**

*Multiply through by 6 to avoid the fractions.*    $3x + 2y = 30$

*Find where the graph cuts the x-axis (where $y = 0$) by substituting 0 for y.*
$$3x + 0 = 30$$
$$x = 10$$
So the graph cuts the x-axis at $(10, 0)$.

*Similarly for the y-intercept substitute 0 for x.*    $0 + 2y = 30$
$$y = 15$$
So the graph cuts the y-axis at $(0, 15)$.

*Sketch the graph and label key points.*

---

## Exercise A (answers p 162)

**1** Which of the following graphs are parallel to the graph of $5x + 6y = 15$?

$$y = \tfrac{5}{6}x - 15 \qquad \frac{x}{6} + \frac{y}{5} = 1 \qquad y = -\tfrac{5}{6}x + 4 \qquad y = 30 + \tfrac{5}{6}x$$

**2** Draw a sketch of each of these graphs.

(a) $y = 2x - 7$       (b) $7x + 6y - 42 = 0$       (c) $2x - 3y = 12$

**3** There are three sets of parallel lines here.
Match them up and say what the gradient is for each set.

A $x + 7y = 1$      B $y = -\tfrac{2}{7}x + 3$      C $\dfrac{x}{7} + y = 3$      D $2y = 7x - 3$

E $2x + 7y = 1$      F $2y - 7x - 1 = 0$      G $x + 7y + 2 = 0$      H $\dfrac{x}{2} - \dfrac{y}{7} + 3 = 0$

**4** For each of these equations,

     (i) rearrange it into the form $y = mx + c$

     (ii) give the gradient

     (iii) give the intercept on the $y$-axis

(a) $3x + y + 7 = 0$      (b) $x + 2y - 8 = 0$      (c) $4x + 5y + 1 = 0$

(d) $3x - 2y - 6 = 0$      (e) $-7x + 2y + 3 = 0$      (f) $-4x - 6y + 9 = 0$

**5** What is the gradient of a straight line of the form $ax + by + c = 0$,
where $a$, $b$ and $c$ are constants?

**6** Which of these lines are parallel to the line $y = 4x - 2$?

$$y = 2 - 4x \qquad y = 4x + 8 \qquad 4x + y + 6 = 0 \qquad -8x + 2y - 7 = 0$$

**7** Which of these lines are parallel to the line $2x + 3y = 4$?

$$3x - 2y + 1 = 0 \qquad y = \tfrac{2}{3}x + 6 \qquad 4x + 6y + 3 = 0 \qquad y = -\tfrac{2}{3}x$$

**8** Which of these lines are perpendicular to the line $y = 3x + 1$?

$$y = \tfrac{1}{3}x - 1 \qquad 6x - 2y + 3 = 0 \qquad y = -\tfrac{1}{3}x + 2 \qquad x + 3y = 1$$

**9** Which of these lines are perpendicular to the line $5x - 3y + 2 = 0$?

$$-3x - 5y + 1 = 0 \qquad 3x - 5y - 10 = 0 \qquad y = 6 - \tfrac{3}{5}x \qquad y = \tfrac{3}{5}x + 4$$

**10** A triangle has vertices $A$ $(-2, 1)$, $B$ $(-1, -4)$ and $C$ $(9, -2)$.
Find the gradients of its sides $AB$, $BC$ and $CA$.
What does this tell you about the triangle?

**11** A quadrilateral has vertices $A$ $(1, 4)$, $B$ $(4, 2)$, $C$ $(9, 3)$ and $D$ $(3, 7)$.
Find the gradients of its sides $AB$, $DC$, $AD$ and $BC$.
What special kind of quadrilateral is it?

## B Finding the equation of a linear graph (answers p 163)

Here a straight line with gradient 3 goes through the point (1, 2).

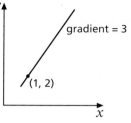

**D** **B1** Give the coordinates of three other points on the line.

**B2** What do you think the line's equation is?

Although you can probably spot the equation mentally in a simple case like this, it is a good idea to have a written method that also works for less obvious equations.

One such method is as follows.

Consider the standard form of a straight line $y = mx + c$.

Substitute the values given above.

$$2 = 3 \times 1 + c$$
$$2 = 3 + c$$
$$c = -1$$

So the line's equation is $y = 3x - 1$.

This is a satisfactory method. However the following approach has the advantage of leading to a general formula that allows you to deal with some problems in a more direct way.

Here again is the line with gradient 3 going through (1, 2).

The point labelled $(x, y)$ is any point (a 'general point') on the line.

Whatever the value of $y$, the height of the triangle is $y - 2$.
Similarly the base of the triangle is $x - 1$.

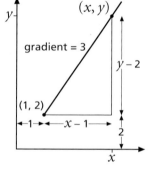

*Since the gradient is 3,*    $\dfrac{y - 2}{x - 1} = 3$

*Multiply both sides by $(x - 1)$.*    $y - 2 = 3(x - 1)$
$$y - 2 = 3x - 3$$
$$y = 3x - 1$$

**K** In general, a straight line with gradient $m$ passing through the point $(x_1, y_1)$ has the equation $\dfrac{y - y_1}{x - x_1} = m$ or $y - y_1 = m(x - x_1)$.

**B3** Use this formula to find the equation of each of these straight lines, in the form $y = mx + c$.

(a) Passing through (3, 2) with gradient 4

(b) Passing through (2, 4) with gradient −1

(c) Passing through (−2, −5) with gradient 3

(d) Passing through (−6, 1) with gradient $\frac{1}{4}$

(e) Passing through (−3, 2) with gradient $-\frac{1}{2}$

## Example 4

Find the equation of the line that passes through $(2, 3)$ and $(4, 8)$.

### Solution

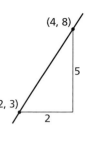

*Find the height and width of the triangle made between the points.*

$$\text{gradient} = \tfrac{5}{2}$$

*Substitute this gradient and one of the points in the formula $y - y_1 = m(x - x_1)$; here the point $(2, 3)$ has been chosen.*

$$y - 3 = \tfrac{5}{2}(x - 2)$$
$$y - 3 = \tfrac{5}{2}x - 5$$
$$y = \tfrac{5}{2}x - 2$$

**Alternative solution** (without use of the formula above)

*Again, from the dimensions of the triangle,* $\quad \text{gradient} = \tfrac{5}{2}$

So the required line has the form $y = \tfrac{5}{2}x + c$.

*Substitute the values of the point $(2, 3)$.*

$$3 = \tfrac{5}{2} \times 2 + c$$
$$3 = 5 + c$$
$$c = -2$$

So the required line is $y = \tfrac{5}{2}x - 2$.

## Mid-points

If a straight line is drawn between the points $(1, 2)$ and $(5, 8)$ it is easy to see that their mid-point (the point halfway between them) is $(3, 5)$.

Adding the two given $x$-coordinates and dividing by 2 gives the $x$-coordinate of the mid-point; similarly with the $y$-coordinates.

The mid-point of the points $(x_1, y_1)$ and $(x_2, y_2)$ is $\left( \dfrac{x_1 + x_2}{2}, \dfrac{y_1 + y_2}{2} \right)$.

## Example 5

Find the equation of the perpendicular bisector of the line segment between $P\,(12, 9)$ and $Q\,(16, 15)$.

### Solution

*The perpendicular bisector is the line perpendicular to PQ going through the mid-point of PQ.*

The mid-point is $\left( \dfrac{12 + 16}{2}, \dfrac{9 + 15}{2} \right)$, which is $(14, 12)$.

The gradient of $PQ$ is $\tfrac{6}{4}$, which is $\tfrac{3}{2}$.
So the perpendicular bisector has gradient $-\tfrac{2}{3}$.

*Use the gradient and point P in the formula $y - y_1 = m(x - x_1)$.*

$$y - 14 = -\tfrac{2}{3}(x - 12)$$
$$y - 14 = -\tfrac{2}{3}x + 8$$

*This gives the equation of the required line.* $\quad y = -\tfrac{2}{3}x + 22$

**Exercise B** (answers p 163)

**1** Find the equation of each of these straight lines in the form $y = mx + c$.

    **(a)** Passing through $(7, 2)$ with gradient 3

    **(b)** Passing through $(3, 0)$ with gradient $\frac{1}{2}$

    **(c)** Passing through $(-1, -1)$ and parallel to $y = 2x + 5$

    **(d)** Passing through $(-2, 4)$ and parallel to $3x + 2y + 7 = 0$

**2** Find the equation of each of these straight lines in the form $y = mx + c$.

    **(a)** Passing through $(6, 4)$ and $(12, 6)$     **(b)** Passing through $(-2, 5)$ and $(4, -1)$

**3** Find the mid-point of each of these line segments.

    **(a)** From $(1, 6)$ to $(7, 2)$   **(b)** From $(-3, 1)$ to $(5, 3)$   **(c)** From $(-3, -5)$ to $(4, -1)$

**4** Find the equation of each of these straight lines in the form $y = mx + c$.

    **(a)** Perpendicular to the line $y = 4 - 2x$, passing through $(0, 0)$

    **(b)** Perpendicular to the line $3x + 4y = 5$, passing through $(3, -2)$

    **(c)** Perpendicular to the line $y = 2.5x + 0.5$, passing through $(-1, -2)$

**5** For each pair of points,

    **(i)** find their mid-point

    **(ii)** find the equation of the line passing through them

    **(iii)** use Pythagoras's theorem to find the length of the line segment between them, leaving as exact values any square roots that don't 'work out'

    **(a)** $(4, 4)$ and $(6, 10)$    **(b)** $(4, -2)$ and $(8, 4)$    **(c)** $(-4, 5)$ and $(-1, 2)$

**6 (a)** Find the equation of the line passing through $(-4, -3)$ and $(2, 1)$.

    **(b)** Given that this line also passes through the point $(a, 5)$, find $a$.

**7** $(-1, 2)$ is the mid-point of line segment $AB$. $B$ is the point $(2, -0.5)$. What is point $A$?

**8** A line segment is drawn from $(1, 2)$ to $(6, 4)$. Find the equation of a line that goes through its mid-point and is perpendicular to it.

## C Problem solving with linear graphs (answers p 163)

Electricity companies send out bills every three months (every quarter).

    **C1** Company P simply charges £0.09 per unit of electricity used.

        **(a)** Write a formula for $C$, the cost in £, in terms of $E$, the number of units used in the quarter.

        **(b)** Draw axes like these. Go up to 1000 units and £100. Draw a graph of company P's formula and label it.

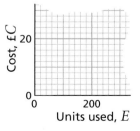

**C2** Company Q has a different way of charging each quarter. The table shows examples of amounts charged.

| Units used, $E$ | 100 | 500 | 700 | 1000 |
|---|---|---|---|---|
| Cost, £$C$ | 22 | 50 | 64 | 85 |

(a) Draw a graph of this data on the same grid and label it Q.

(b) Write a formula for $C$ in terms of $E$ that fits this information.

(c) If you had to describe company Q's way of charging each quarter using words rather than a formula, what would you say?

Linear graphs like those you have drawn for C1 and C2 can help you see real-life problems clearly and make comparisons.

**C3** For each of the following customers, use your graphs to decide which of the two electricity companies would give better value and what would it charge.

(a) A customer who uses 300 units a quarter

(b) One who uses 750 units a quarter

(c) One who uses 900 units a quarter

With some website research, comparing different suppliers' costs this way can save a consumer a lot of money.

## Exercise C (answers p 163)

**1** A couple opening a restaurant want some publicity leaflets printed.
Printer R quotes '£50 one-off charge plus £0.02 per leaflet'.
Printer S uses the formula $C = 0.05n + 40$, where $C$ is the cost in £s and $n$ is the number of leaflets.

(a) On a grid with $n$ on the horizontal axis, draw graphs of what the printers charge.

(b) The couple plan to spend £65 on as many leaflets as possible.
Which printer should they choose and how many leaflets should they order?

**2** Oil is being pumped out of a tank at a constant rate.
This graph shows the volume, $V$ litres, of oil in the tank at a time $t$ seconds from when the pumping starts.

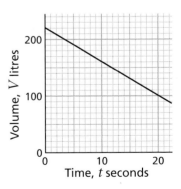

(a) At what rate, in litres per second, is oil leaving the tank?

(b) Write a formula for $V$ in terms of $t$.
Substitute $V = 0$ into your formula and solve the equation to find when the tank will be empty.

(c) Use this information to complete the graph accurately on graph paper.

(d) A second tank is having oil pumped steadily out of it at the same time. The formula for the volume of oil it holds is $V = 250 - 8t$. Work out when it will be empty and draw its graph on the same grid.

(e) When will the two tanks hold the same amount?
What is this amount?

**3** At a certain place in a cave, a stalactite and a stalagmite start to form.

The stalagmite grows up from the floor at 0.3 cm per year.

stalactite

**(a)** Write a formula for the height $H$ cm of its tip above the ground after $t$ years.

The stalactite grows down from the ceiling at 0.2 cm per year.
The ceiling is 320 cm above the floor at this place.

stalagmite

**(b)** Write a formula for the height $H$ cm of the stalactite's tip above the ground after $t$ years.

**(c)** Draw graphs of these formulas on the same grid.
(You will need several hundred years on the horizontal axis.)

**(d)** From the graphs, when will the two tips be 100 cm apart?

**(e)** When will the stalactite and stalagmite touch?
How high above the floor will the point of contact be?

**4** A school band makes a CD and investigates the cost of having copies made with a coloured design printed on them.

Company X quotes £110 for 20 copies or £190 for 100 copies.

Company Y quotes £50 for 10 copies plus £2 for each additional copy.

**(a)** For each company, find a linear formula for the cost £$C$ of $n$ copies. Draw or sketch graphs if it helps.

**(b)** Use the formulas to decide which company is cheaper for

**(i)** 50 copies        **(ii)** 80 copies

## D Solving simultaneous linear equations

Problems that involve finding where the graphs of two linear equations intersect can be dealt with by solving a pair of simultaneous equations.
This can be quicker and is more accurate than using the graphs.

There are several methods for solving a pair of simultaneous equations.
Which is best depends on the form of the equations.

The symbol $\Rightarrow$ appears in the examples on the opposite page.
It is used to connect two mathematical statements when the second one follows mathematically from the first (that is, the first statement **implies** the second).
In practice you can think of it as meaning 'So …'.

The symbol $\therefore$ ('therefore') is used in a similar way.

## Example 6

Find where these two linear graphs intersect.

$$3x + 4y = 26$$
$$7x - y = 9$$

**Solution** (by equating coefficients)

*Note the coefficient of y in the first equation.*
*Multiply the second equation by 4 to get the 'same size' coefficient.*

$$3x + 4y = 26$$

$$28x - 4y = 36$$

*Add the previous two equations together.*

$$31x = 62$$
$$\Rightarrow \quad x = 2$$

*Substitute this in the simpler equation.*

$$14 - y = 9$$
$$\Rightarrow \quad y = 5$$

So the point of intersection is $(2, 5)$.

*Check by substituting your values for x and y into the original equations.*

$$\text{LHS} = 3\times 2 + 4\times 5 = 26, \text{ which equals RHS}$$
$$\text{LHS} = 7\times 2 - 5 = 9, \text{ which equals RHS}$$

## Example 7

Find where these two graphs intersect.

$$y = 7 - 3x$$
$$2x + 5y = 9$$

**Solution** (by equating coefficients)

*In the first equation get the x and y terms on the left-hand side.*
*Multiply this equation by 5.*
*Here is the second equation.*
*Subtract it from the multiplied first equation.*

$$3x + y = 7$$
$$15x + 5y = 35$$
$$2x + 5y = 9$$
$$13x = 26$$
$$\Rightarrow \quad x = 2$$

*Substitute into the first given equation.*

$$y = 7 - 6 = 1$$

So the graphs intersect at $(2, 1)$.

*Check by substitution into the formulas for the graphs.*

**Solution** (by substitution)

*Here are the two given equations again.*

$$y = 7 - 3x$$
$$2x + 5y = 9$$

*The first one states that the expression $7 - 3x$ is equal to y.*
*So replace y in the second equation by this expression.*
*Simplify.*

$$2x + 5(7 - 3x) = 9$$
$$2x + 35 - 15x = 9$$
$$\Rightarrow \quad -13x = -26$$
$$\Rightarrow \quad x = 2$$

*Then find y as in the previous method.*

You have just seen two methods for solving simultaneous equations. There is a third method that is particularly suited to intersecting graphs that are in the form $y = \ldots$

---

### Example 8

Find the point of intersection of these graphs.
$$y = 2x - 1$$
$$y = 4 - x$$

**Solution** (by equating the expressions for $y$)

At the point of intersection, both graphs have the same $y$ value.
Therefore the expression for $y$ in the first graph must
equal the expression for $y$ in the second graph.

$$2x - 1 = 4 - x$$
$$\Rightarrow \quad 3x = 5$$
$$\Rightarrow \quad x = \frac{5}{3}$$

Substitute into the simpler equation.

$$y = 4 - \frac{5}{3} = \frac{7}{3}$$

So the point of intersection is $(\frac{5}{3}, \frac{7}{3})$.

---

The following example is not about graphs (though it could be solved by drawing a pair of intersecting graphs). It is still suited to the 'equating the expressions for $y$' approach (though here expressions for $h$ are equated).

---

### Example 9

A snail climbs up from the bottom of a garden wall at 0.5 cm per minute. Starting at the same time from a point 3.24 metres up the wall, a millipede walks down the wall at a steady rate of 4 cm per minute. When are the two at the same level, and what is that level?

**Solution**

Define the 'unknowns'.

Let $h$ be the height up the wall in centimetres.
Let $t$ be the time in minutes from the start.

Express each creature's height in terms of time.

$h = 0.5t$ (snail)
$h = 324 - 4t$ (millipede)

When they are at the same height,
$$0.5t = 324 - 4t \qquad \text{(snail's } h = \text{millipede's } h\text{)}$$
$$\Rightarrow \quad 4.5t = 324$$
$$\Rightarrow \quad t = 72$$

Substitute in the snail's formula.

$$h = 0.5 \times 72 = 36$$

After 72 minutes they are both 36 cm from the bottom of the wall.

---

### Exercise D (answers p 164)

**1** Solve the following pairs of equations using the 'equating coefficients' method.

(a) $3p + q = 19$
$5p + 2q = 32$

(b) $5a + 3b = 8$
$3a - b = 9$

(c) $2h + 3j = 1$
$7h + 4j = -16$

**2** Solve the following pairs of equations using the 'substitution' method.

(a) $y = 2x$
$3x + y = 15$

(b) $3x + 2y + 12 = 0$
$y = x - 1$

(c) $q = 2p - 6$
$3p - 2q = 11$

**3** Solve the following pairs of equations using the 'substitution' method. Where necessary, first make $y$ the subject of one of the equations.

(a) $y = 5x$
$7x - 3y + 4 = 0$

(b) $x + y + 1 = 0$
$2x + 3y - 1 = 0$

(c) $y - x + 8 = 0$
$5x + 4y + 5 = 0$

**4** Solve these pairs of equations by 'equating the expressions for $y$'.

(a) $y = 2 - \frac{1}{3}x$
$y = 3(x - 1)$

(b) $y = \frac{2}{3}x$
$y = 2(2 - x)$

(c) $s = 2t - 3$
$s = 1 + \frac{1}{2}t$

**5** Solve these pairs of equations by 'equating the expressions for $y$'. Where necessary, first make $y$ the subject of one of the equations.

(a) $x + y = 1$
$y = 2x - 14$

(b) $y = 1 - 3x$
$y = 5(1 + x)$

(c) $y - x = 1$
$y = 4x + 10$

**6** Find the point of intersection of each pair of straight lines. Choose an appropriate method in each case.

(a) $y = 2x - 7$
$\frac{x}{3} + \frac{y}{5} - 3 = 0$

(b) $3x + 5y = 25$
$2x + 6y = 26$

(c) $y = 2x + 1$
$7x + 10y = 64$

**7** What happens when you try to solve the following simultaneous equations? Give a graphical explanation in each case.

(a) $y = 2 - \frac{2}{3}x$
$2x + 3y = 18$

(b) $y = -5 - \frac{5}{3}x$
$5x + 3y + 15 = 0$

(c) $x - 2 - \frac{1}{2}y = 0$
$y = 2x + 5$

**8** The straight lines represented by these equations form a triangle.

$y = 4x - 17$ $\qquad\qquad$ $y = 2x + 4$ $\qquad\qquad$ $2x + 3y = 5$

Find the coordinates of the vertices of the triangle.

**9** Plumber A makes a £40 call-out charge and then charges £40 per hour. Plumber B makes a £29 call-out charge and then charges £44 per hour.

(a) For each plumber, write a formula for $C$, the total cost in £s, in terms of $t$, the time worked in hours.

(b) Find the length of job for which both plumbers charge the same amount.

(c) Which plumber is cheaper for jobs that take longer than the length of time you found for (b)?

**10** Obtain an exact answer to exercise C question 2 (e) using simultaneous equations.

**11** Obtain an exact answer to exercise C question 3 (e) using simultaneous equations.

## Using a computer

In AS mathematics you need to solve simultaneous equations on paper.
But for real-life problems people often use computers.

You can do this with
Microsoft® Excel's Solver tool,
which is available as an add-in.
Here it has been set up for question
1 (a) of exercise D.

| | A | B | C | D |
|---|---|---|---|---|
| | Equations | | | |
| 1 | p | q | 3p + q | 5p + 2q |
| 2 | | | =3*A2+B2 | =5*A2+2*B2 |
| 3 | | | | |

Solver will put the solutions in these blank cells.

**Solver Parameters**

First equation

Set Target Cell: $C$2

Equal To: ○ Max ○ Min ● Value of: 19

By Changing Cells:

$A$2:$B$2

Subject to the Constraints

Second equation

$D$2=32

Buttons: Solve, Close, Guess, Options, Add, Change, Reset All, Delete, Help

Computers can solve larger groups of simultaneous equations, not just pairs.
Their immense equation-solving power is put to good use in, for example,
weather forecasting.

## Key points

- For any part of a straight line graph, the gradient is the ratio $\dfrac{\text{increase in } y}{\text{increase in } x}$. (p 6)

- An equation of the form $y = mx + c$ is a straight line,
  where $m$ is the gradient and $c$ is the $y$-intercept. (p 6)

- Lines that have the same gradient are parallel. (p 6)

- If two lines with gradients $m_1$ and $m_2$ are perpendicular,
  $m_2 = -\dfrac{1}{m_1}$ or $m_1 m_2 = -1$. (p 8)

- A straight line with gradient $m$ passing through the point $(x_1, y_1)$ has
  the equation $\dfrac{y - y_1}{x - x_1} = m$ or $y - y_1 = m(x - x_1)$. (p 10)

- The mid-point of the points $(x_1, y_1)$ and $(x_2, y_2)$ is $\left( \dfrac{x_1 + x_2}{2}, \dfrac{y_1 + y_2}{2} \right)$. (p 11)

- The point of intersection of two graphs is found by treating their equations as
  simultaneous equations and solving them. (pp 14–16)

## Mixed questions (answers p 164)

**1** A quadrilateral is formed by the lines $y = 3x - 4$, $y = -\frac{1}{3}x$, $y = 3x + 5$ and $y = 7 - \frac{1}{3}x$. What special type of quadrilateral is it?

**2** A quadrilateral is formed by the lines $y = 0$, $3x + 5y = 15$, $x = 0$ and $3x + 5y = 30$.

(a) What special type of quadrilateral is it?      (b) Find its vertices.

**3** The straight line $l_1$ has equation $4y + x = 0$.
The straight line $l_2$ has equation $y = 2x - 3$.

(a) On the same axes, sketch the graphs of $l_1$ and $l_2$. Show clearly the coordinates of all points at which the graphs meet the coordinate axes.

The lines $l_1$ and $l_2$ intersect at the point $A$.

(b) Calculate, as exact fractions, the coordinates of $A$.

(c) Find an equation of the line through $A$ which is perpendicular to $l_1$.
Give your answer in the form $ax + by + c = 0$, where $a$, $b$ and $c$ are integers.     Edexcel

**4** The straight line $l_1$, with equation $y = \frac{3}{2}x - 2$ crosses the $x$-axis at the point $P$.
The point $Q$ has coordinates $(5, -3)$.

(a) Calculate the coordinates of the mid-point of $PQ$.

The straight line $l_2$ is perpendicular to $l_1$ and passes through $Q$.

(b) Find an equation for $l_2$ in the form $ax + by = c$, where $a$, $b$ and $c$ are integer constants.

The lines $l_1$ and $l_2$ intersect at the point $R$.

(c) Calculate the exact coordinates of $R$.     Edexcel

**5** A triangle has vertices $A$ (1, 1), $B$ (1, 11) and $C$ (7, 13).

(a) Find the equation of the side $AC$.

(b) From the mid-point of $AB$ a perpendicular to $AC$ is drawn, meeting $AC$ at $P$.
Find the equation of the perpendicular and hence the coordinates of $P$.

(c) From the mid-point of $BC$ a perpendicular to $AC$ is drawn, meeting $AC$ at $Q$.
Find the equation of this perpendicular and hence the coordinates of $Q$.

(d) Show that the line segment $PQ$ is half the length of $AC$.

**6** A quadrilateral is drawn with its vertices at the points shown.

(a) Find the equations of its diagonals $AC$ and $BD$, and hence find their point of intersection.

(b) Give the mid-points of the four sides.

(c) A new quadrilateral is formed by joining the four mid-points. Work out the gradient of each side of this new quadrilateral.

(d) What do your answers to (c) tell you about this new quadrilateral?

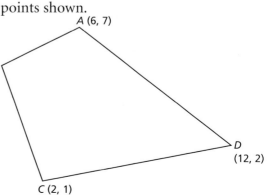

A (6, 7)

B (0, 5)

D (12, 2)

C (2, 1)

**7** Find the equation of the line that goes through the origin $(0, 0)$ and is perpendicular to the line $8x + 6y - 50 = 0$.

Find where these two lines intersect and hence find the perpendicular distance of the line $8x + 6y - 50 = 0$ from the origin.

**8** Determine, with reasons, whether the following points all lie on the same straight line.

$(-3, -3)$   $(2, -1)$   $(9, 2)$

**9** The line segment $PQ$ has $y = 2x + 2$ as its equation.
The point $P$ is at $(0, i)$ and the point $Q$ is at $(j, 8)$.

(a) Find the values of $i$ and $j$.

The point $R$ is at $(-8, 6)$.

(b) Show that triangle $PQR$ has a right angle at $P$.

(c) Find the perimeter of triangle $PQR$, expressing your result in the form $a\sqrt{b}$, where $a$ and $b$ are integers and $b$ is as small as possible.

**10** In a triangle, a median is a line from a vertex to the mid-point of the opposite side.

(a) Find the equations of the three medians of the triangle with vertices $A\,(11, 1)$, $B\,(9, 9)$ and $C\,(1, 5)$.

(b) Show that these medians intersect at a single point, giving its coordinates.

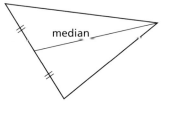

**\*11** The diagram shows a kite. $A$ is the point $(2, 9)$. $C$ is the point $(8, 1)$.

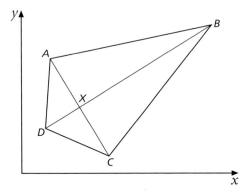

(a) Find the coordinates of $X$, where the diagonals intersect.

(b) Find the equation of the diagonal $DB$.

$D$ is the point $(1, p)$ and $B$ is the point $(q, 11)$

(c) Find $p$ and $q$.

(d) Show that $\angle ADC$ is a right angle.

(e) Find the area of the kite.

## Test yourself (answers p 165)

None of these questions requires a calculator.

**1** Write the equations of the following lines in the form $y = mx + c$.

(a) $5x + y = 4$    (b) $x - 2y + 6 = 0$    (c) $x + 2y = 3$    (d) $y - 6 = 2(x + 4)$

**2** The line $y = 3x + 4$ is drawn. State whether each of the following lines is parallel to it, perpendicular to it, or neither.

(a) $3x + y = 2$    (b) $y = 2 - \frac{1}{3}x$    (c) $3x - y - 7 = 0$    (d) $x + 3y - 2 = 0$

**3** A straight line goes through the points $(2, 3)$ and $(6, 2)$.

(a) What is its gradient?

(b) Give its equation in the form $y = mx + c$.

**4** Give the equation of the line joining the origin to the mid-point of $(5, 3)$ and $(-1, 7)$.

**5** Find the length of the line joining $(1, -2)$ and $(-1, 1)$, leaving your answer as an exact value.

**6** Line $l$ has the equation $y = 6x + 1$.

(a) Give the equation of the line through $(1, 0)$ parallel to $l$.

(b) Give the equation of the line through $(3, -1)$ perpendicular to $l$.

**7** Solve the following pairs of simultaneous equations by an appropriate method.

(a) $4x + 5y - 6 = 0$
$y = x + 3$

(b) $y = x + 1$
$7x + 3y = 0$

(c) $y = 3 - x$
$3x + 5y - 12 = 0$

(d) $y = 2x + 5$
$y = -3x$

(e) $3x + 5y = 30$
$5x + 3y = 42$

(f) $y = \frac{2}{3}x - 1$
$y = \frac{3}{2}x + 4$

**8** The points $A (-2, 4)$, $B (6, -2)$ and $C (5, 5)$ are the vertices of triangle $ABC$ and $D$ is the mid-point of $AB$.

(a) Find an equation of the line passing through $A$ and $B$ in the form $ax + by + c = 0$, where $a$, $b$, and $c$ are integers to be found.

(b) Show that $CD$ is perpendicular to $AB$.                                        Edexcel

**9** The points $A$ and $B$ have coordinates $(4, 6)$ and $(12, 2)$ respectively. The straight line $l_1$ passes through $A$ and $B$.

(a) Find an equation for $l_1$ in the form $ax + by = c$, where $a$, $b$ and $c$ are integers.

The straight line $l_2$ passes through the origin and has gradient $-4$.

(b) Write down an equation for $l_2$.

The lines $l_1$ and $l_2$ intersect at the point $C$.

(c) Find the exact coordinates of the mid-point of $AC$.                          Edexcel

# 2 Surds

In this chapter you will
- learn how to manipulate surds and express them in different ways
- solve problems, leaving your solutions in surd form

## A Understanding surds

$\sqrt{a}$ means the positive square root of $a$ and it can be written as $\sqrt{a}$ or $\sqrt{a}$.
$\sqrt{a+b}$ is not the same as $\sqrt{a}+b$.
For example, $2\sqrt{16}+9 = \left(2 \times \sqrt{16}\right)+9 = 2 \times 4 + 9 = 17$
However, $2\sqrt{16+9} = 2\sqrt{25} = 2 \times 5 = 10$

A **rational** number is one that can be expressed in the fractional form $\dfrac{a}{b}$, where $a$ and $b$ are integers. Examples are $\frac{3}{4}$ and $-\frac{4}{3}$.

An **irrational** number cannot be expressed in fractional form.
The square roots of all positive integers (except the perfect squares 1, 4, 9, 16, …) are irrational. Examples are $\sqrt{3}$ and $\sqrt{7}$.

A number that involves an irrational root is said to be in **surd form**.
Examples are $2\sqrt{3}$ and $\sqrt{7}+1$.

We use surd form when we want to be **exact**.
For example, the length of a diagonal of a unit square is exactly $\sqrt{2}$, but any decimal approximation of this value (such as 1.414) is not exact.

---

**Example 1**

Find in surd form the perimeter of isosceles triangle $ABC$.

**Solution**

By Pythagoras, the length of $AB$ is $\sqrt{2^2 + 3^2} = \sqrt{4+9} = \sqrt{13}$.
So the perimeter is $6 + \sqrt{13} + \sqrt{13} = 6 + 2\sqrt{13}$.    *This is an exact value.*

---

**Exercise A** (answers p 166)

**1** Each of these is a rational number. Express each one as an integer, fraction or decimal.

(a) $\sqrt{49}$

(b) $-\sqrt{81}$

(c) $\sqrt{\dfrac{1}{9}}$

(d) $6\sqrt{9}$

(e) $\sqrt{100} \times 4$

(f) $\sqrt{100 \times 4}$

(g) $\sqrt{\dfrac{25}{4}}$

(h) $\dfrac{\sqrt{25}}{4}$

(i) $\sqrt{9}+7$

(j) $\sqrt{9+7}$

(k) $\sqrt{0.16}$

(l) $\left(\sqrt{7}\right)^2$

(m) $\left(\sqrt{3}\right)^4$

(n) $\left(2\sqrt{3}\right)^2$

(o) $2\sqrt{0.09}$

(p) $\sqrt{0.000001}$

**2** A rectangle has a length of 10 cm and a width of 3 cm.
In surd form, find the length of one of its diagonals.

**3** Write each of these in the form $p\sqrt{3}$ where $p$ is an integer.

   **(a)** $\sqrt{3} + \sqrt{3}$    **(b)** $6\sqrt{3} - 2\sqrt{3}$    **(c)** $\left(\sqrt{3}\right)^3$    **(d)** $\left(\sqrt{3}\right)^5$    **(e)** $\left(2\sqrt{3}\right)^5$

**4** An isosceles triangle has a base length of 4 cm and a height of 5 cm.
Show that the perimeter of the triangle is $4 + 2\sqrt{29}$ cm.

**5** A square has vertices with coordinates $(2, 1)$, $(4, 2)$, $(5, 0)$ and $(3, -1)$.
Show that the perimeter of this square is $4\sqrt{5}$.

**6** In triangle $PQR$, $PQ = 4$ cm, $QR = 1$ cm,
$\angle PQR = 90°$ and $\angle QPR = \alpha°$.
Find the exact value of $\cos \alpha°$.

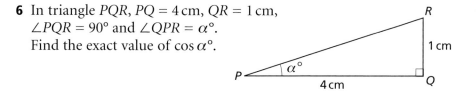

**7** The shaded square has been constructed by
joining the mid-points of a larger square.
Find the perimeter of the larger square in surd form.

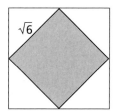

## B Simplifying surds (answers p 166)

**B1** Without using a calculator, decide which of these statements are true.

   **A** $\sqrt{4} \times \sqrt{25} = \sqrt{100}$    **B** $\dfrac{\sqrt{36}}{\sqrt{9}} = \sqrt{4}$    **C** $\sqrt{50} + \sqrt{50} = \sqrt{100}$

   **D** $\sqrt{2} \times \sqrt{18} = \sqrt{36}$    **E** $\sqrt{150} - \sqrt{50} = \sqrt{100}$    **F** $\dfrac{\sqrt{200}}{\sqrt{2}} = \sqrt{100}$

**B2** Prove that each of these statements is true for all $p$ and $q$.

   **(a)** $\sqrt{p^2} \times \sqrt{q^2} = \sqrt{p^2 \times q^2}$      **(b)** $\dfrac{\sqrt{p^2}}{\sqrt{q^2}} = \sqrt{\dfrac{p^2}{q^2}}$

**B3** How could you use the statements in B2 to prove that, for all $a$ and $b$,

   **(a)** $\sqrt{a} \times \sqrt{b} = \sqrt{ab}$      **(b)** $\dfrac{\sqrt{a}}{\sqrt{b}} = \sqrt{\dfrac{a}{b}}$

**B4** How would you show someone that, in general, $\sqrt{a} + \sqrt{b}$ is not equivalent to $\sqrt{a + b}$ ?

**K** In general $\quad \sqrt{a \times b} = \sqrt{a} \times \sqrt{b}$

and $\quad \sqrt{\dfrac{a}{b}} = \dfrac{\sqrt{a}}{\sqrt{b}}$

When working in surd form, it is important to be able to manipulate expressions so they are as simple as possible. You can use the above rules to simplify many expressions.

---

**Example 2**

Simplify the product $\sqrt{3} \times \sqrt{2}$ .

**Solution**

$\sqrt{3} \times \sqrt{2} = \sqrt{3 \times 2} = \sqrt{6}$

---

**Example 3**

Express $\sqrt{18}$ in terms of the simplest possible surd.

**Solution**

*Begin by writing 18 as a product where one of the numbers is a square number.*

$\sqrt{18} = \sqrt{9 \times 2} = \sqrt{9} \times \sqrt{2} = 3\sqrt{2}$

---

**Example 4**

Simplify the quotient $\dfrac{\sqrt{6}}{\sqrt{2}}$ .

**Solution**

$\dfrac{\sqrt{6}}{\sqrt{2}} = \sqrt{\dfrac{6}{2}} = \sqrt{3}$

---

**Example 5**

Express $\sqrt{\dfrac{2}{9}}$ in terms of the simplest possible surd.

**Solution**

$\sqrt{\dfrac{2}{9}} = \dfrac{\sqrt{2}}{\sqrt{9}} = \dfrac{\sqrt{2}}{3}$ or $\frac{1}{3}\sqrt{2}$

---

**Example 6**

Expand and simplify $\sqrt{2}\left(\sqrt{2} - \sqrt{7}\right)$.

**Solution**

$\sqrt{2}\left(\sqrt{2} - \sqrt{7}\right) = \sqrt{2} \times \sqrt{2} - \sqrt{2} \times \sqrt{7}$
$= 2 - \sqrt{14}$

---

**Example 7**

Expand and simplify $\left(\sqrt{3} + 1\right)\left(3\sqrt{3} - 5\right)$.

**Solution**

$\left(\sqrt{3} + 1\right)\left(3\sqrt{3} - 5\right) = \sqrt{3} \times 3\sqrt{3} - \sqrt{3} \times 5 + 3\sqrt{3} - 5$
$= 9 - 5\sqrt{3} + 3\sqrt{3} - 5$
$= 4 - 2\sqrt{3}$

*You can set your working out in a table.*

| $\times$ | $\sqrt{3}$ | $1$ |
|---|---|---|
| $3\sqrt{3}$ | $9$ | $3\sqrt{3}$ |
| $-5$ | $-5\sqrt{3}$ | $-5$ |

---

**Exercise B** (answers p 166)

**1** Simplify these products, writing your answers as simply as possible.

(a) $\sqrt{5} \times \sqrt{2}$  (b) $\sqrt{2} \times \sqrt{8}$  (c) $2\sqrt{7} \times \sqrt{3}$  (d) $5\sqrt{3} \times 2\sqrt{2}$

**2** Express each of the following in the form $a\sqrt{b}$ in terms of the simplest possible surds.

(a) $\sqrt{8}$  (b) $\sqrt{54}$  (c) $\sqrt{32}$  (d) $\sqrt{50}$

(e) $2\sqrt{150}$  (f) $5\sqrt{99}$  (g) $3\sqrt{200}$  (h) $2\sqrt{128}$

**3** Simplify these, writing your answers as simply as possible.

(a) $\dfrac{\sqrt{6}}{\sqrt{3}}$  (b) $\dfrac{\sqrt{27}}{\sqrt{3}}$  (c) $\dfrac{3\sqrt{14}}{\sqrt{2}}$  (d) $\dfrac{3\sqrt{24}}{\sqrt{6}}$

**4** Express each of the following in terms of the simplest possible surds.

(a) $\sqrt{\dfrac{4}{7}}$  (b) $\sqrt{\dfrac{3}{25}}$  (c) $3\sqrt{\dfrac{16}{5}}$  (d) $4\sqrt{\dfrac{7}{4}}$  (e) $3\sqrt{\dfrac{11}{81}}$

**5** (a) Express each of these in the form $k\sqrt{3}$.  (i) $\sqrt{12}$  (ii) $\sqrt{75}$

(b) Hence write $\sqrt{75} - \sqrt{12}$ in the form $n\sqrt{3}$ where $n$ is an integer.

**6** Express each of the following in the form $a\sqrt{b}$ in terms of the simplest possible surds.

(a) $4\sqrt{3} + \sqrt{12}$  (b) $\sqrt{45} - \sqrt{20}$  (c) $\sqrt{200} + 9\sqrt{2} - \sqrt{72}$

(d) $\dfrac{\sqrt{10} \times \sqrt{60}}{\sqrt{75}}$  (e) $\dfrac{\sqrt{108} - \sqrt{48}}{\sqrt{3}}$  (f) $\dfrac{2\sqrt{14} \times 4\sqrt{6}}{\sqrt{7}}$  (g) $\dfrac{\sqrt{98} + \sqrt{50}}{3\sqrt{2}}$

**7** A rhombus has diagonals that measure 14 cm and 2 cm.
Show that the length of one of its edges is $5\sqrt{2}$ cm.

**8** Expand the brackets and write each result in terms of the simplest possible surds.

(a) $\sqrt{3}\left(\sqrt{3} + 3\sqrt{5}\right)$  (b) $\sqrt{10}\left(\sqrt{30} - \sqrt{2}\right)$

**9** Expand the brackets and write each result as simply as possible.

(a) $\left(\sqrt{2} + 9\right)\left(3\sqrt{2} - 1\right)$  (b) $\left(\sqrt{2} + \sqrt{3}\right)\left(\sqrt{5} - \sqrt{2}\right)$

(c) $\left(\sqrt{5} + 6\right)\left(4 - 3\sqrt{5}\right)$  (d) $\left(\sqrt{3} + 7\right)^2$

**10** Expand the brackets and write each result as simply as possible.

(a) $\left(5 + \sqrt{11}\right)\left(5 - \sqrt{11}\right)$  (b) $\left(5 + 2\sqrt{3}\right)\left(5 - 2\sqrt{3}\right)$

(c) $\left(\sqrt{5} - \sqrt{7}\right)\left(\sqrt{5} + \sqrt{7}\right)$  (d) $\left(2\sqrt{5} + 1\right)\left(2\sqrt{5} - 1\right)$

**11** Expand the brackets and write each result as simply as possible.

(a) $\left(\sqrt{a} + b\right)\left(\sqrt{a} - b\right)$  (b) $\left(x + \sqrt{y}\right)\left(x - \sqrt{y}\right)$  (c) $\left(\sqrt{p} - \sqrt{q}\right)\left(\sqrt{p} + \sqrt{q}\right)$

**12** Prove that $\left(a\sqrt{b} + c\sqrt{d}\right)\left(a\sqrt{b} - c\sqrt{d}\right)$ is a rational number for all rational $a$, $b$, $c$ and $d$.

## C Rationalising the denominator

A pair of numbers such as $5 + \sqrt{2}$ and $5 - \sqrt{2}$ is called a pair of **conjugates**.

Another example of a pair of conjugates is $-\sqrt{2} - 3\sqrt{5}$ and $-\sqrt{2} + 3\sqrt{5}$.

The product of any pair of conjugates like these (which involve square roots of rational numbers) is always a rational number.

For example, $\left(5 + \sqrt{2}\right)\left(5 - \sqrt{2}\right) = 25 - 5\sqrt{2} + 5\sqrt{2} - 2$

$$= 23$$

In general $(a + b)(a - b) = a^2 - ab + ba - b^2$

$$= a^2 - b^2$$

You can use this rule to multiply out conjugates.

For example, $(4\sqrt{3} - 1)(4\sqrt{3} + 1) = (4\sqrt{3})^2 - 1^2$

$$= 48 - 1$$

$$= 47$$

It can be useful to eliminate any surds from the denominator of a fractional expression. It often makes the expression simpler and hence easier to use in any subsequent calculation.

### Example 8

Express $\dfrac{12}{5\sqrt{2}}$ in the form $a\sqrt{b}$ , where $a$ and $b$ are rational numbers.

#### Solution

*Multiply top and bottom by $\sqrt{2}$ to give a rational denominator.*

$$\frac{12}{5\sqrt{2}} = \frac{12 \times \sqrt{2}}{5\sqrt{2} \times \sqrt{2}} = \frac{12\sqrt{2}}{10} = \frac{6\sqrt{2}}{5} = \frac{6}{5}\sqrt{2}$$

### Example 9

By rationalising the denominator, simplify $\dfrac{\sqrt{3} - 5}{2\sqrt{3} + 1}$ .

#### Solution

*Multiply top and bottom by $2\sqrt{3} - 1$ to give a rational denominator.*

$$\frac{\sqrt{3} - 5}{2\sqrt{3} + 1} = \frac{\left(\sqrt{3} - 5\right)\left(2\sqrt{3} - 1\right)}{\left(2\sqrt{3} + 1\right)\left(2\sqrt{3} - 1\right)}$$

$$= \frac{6 - \sqrt{3} - 10\sqrt{3} + 5}{12 - 2\sqrt{3} + 2\sqrt{3} - 1} \qquad \text{\textit{The product in the denominator is worked out in full here.}}$$
$$\qquad\qquad\qquad\qquad\qquad \text{\textit{Instead, you could evaluate }} \left(2\sqrt{3}\right)^2 - 1^2 \text{ \textit{to obtain }} 12 - 1 = 11.$$

$$= \frac{11 - 11\sqrt{3}}{11}$$

$$= 1 - \sqrt{3} \qquad\qquad 1 - \sqrt{3} \text{ \textit{is much simpler to use than }} \dfrac{\sqrt{3} - 5}{2\sqrt{3} + 1}.$$

**Example 10**

Rationalise the denominator of $\dfrac{2}{1-\sqrt{5}}$.

**Solution**

*Multiply top and bottom by $1+\sqrt{5}$ to give a rational denominator.*
$$\dfrac{2}{1-\sqrt{5}} = \dfrac{2(1+\sqrt{5})}{(1-\sqrt{5})(1+\sqrt{5})}$$

$$= \dfrac{2+2\sqrt{5}}{-4}$$

*Multiply top and bottom by $-1$ to make the denominator positive.*
$$= \dfrac{-2-2\sqrt{5}}{4}$$

*Divide top and bottom by 2 to simplify.*
$$= \dfrac{-1-\sqrt{5}}{2}$$  *This could be written as $-\tfrac{1}{2} - \tfrac{1}{2}\sqrt{5}$.*

---

**Exercise C** (answers p 167)

**1** Rationalise the denominators of these. Simplify your answers where appropriate.

(a) $\dfrac{7}{\sqrt{6}}$  (b) $\dfrac{12}{\sqrt{3}}$  (c) $\dfrac{1}{\sqrt{5}}$  (d) $\dfrac{1-\sqrt{5}}{\sqrt{2}}$  (e) $\dfrac{8\sqrt{3}-2}{3\sqrt{2}}$

**2** (a) Express each of these in the form $k\sqrt{7}$.  (i) $\sqrt{28}$  (ii) $\dfrac{21}{\sqrt{7}}$

(b) Hence write $\sqrt{28} + \dfrac{21}{\sqrt{7}}$ in the form $n\sqrt{7}$, where $n$ is an integer.

**3** Rationalise the denominators of the following.

(a) $\dfrac{1}{\sqrt{3}+1}$  (b) $\dfrac{5}{\sqrt{6}-1}$  (c) $\dfrac{7}{5\sqrt{2}-1}$  (d) $\dfrac{\sqrt{5}+4}{\sqrt{2}+1}$  (e) $\dfrac{6}{\sqrt{5}+\sqrt{2}}$

(f) $\dfrac{1}{\sqrt{3}+\sqrt{5}}$  (g) $\dfrac{\sqrt{3}}{3+\sqrt{13}}$  (h) $\dfrac{7\sqrt{2}}{3+2\sqrt{2}}$  (i) $\dfrac{\sqrt{10}+1}{\sqrt{5}-\sqrt{2}}$  (j) $\dfrac{\sqrt{11}-\sqrt{10}}{\sqrt{11}+\sqrt{10}}$

**4** Show that $\dfrac{\sqrt{3}+5}{3-\sqrt{3}} = 3 + \tfrac{4}{3}\sqrt{3}$.

**5** Given that $\dfrac{6-\sqrt{7}}{\sqrt{7}-2} = p + q\sqrt{7}$, where $p$ and $q$ are rational, find the value of $p$ and $q$.

**6** Given that $\dfrac{5-\sqrt{3}}{1+\sqrt{3}} = a + b\sqrt{3}$, where $a$ and $b$ are integers, find the value of $a$ and $b$.

**7** Rationalise the denominator of $\dfrac{1}{3\sqrt{2}-4}$ and hence prove that $\dfrac{1}{3\sqrt{2}-4} > 2$.

**8 (a)** Rationalise the denominator of these. **(i)** $\dfrac{5\sqrt{3}}{4+\sqrt{11}}$ **(ii)** $\dfrac{4\sqrt{11}}{\sqrt{3}+1}$

**(b)** Hence simplify $\dfrac{5\sqrt{3}}{4+\sqrt{11}} + \dfrac{4\sqrt{11}}{\sqrt{3}+1}$ as far as you can.

**9** Simplify each of these as far as you can.

**(a)** $\dfrac{6\sqrt{2}}{3+\sqrt{7}} + \dfrac{4\sqrt{7}}{\sqrt{2}-1}$ **(b)** $\dfrac{4\sqrt{5}}{\sqrt{3}-1} - \dfrac{4\sqrt{3}}{\sqrt{5}+1}$ **(c)** $\dfrac{\sqrt{2}}{2+\sqrt{3}} + \dfrac{\sqrt{3}}{1+\sqrt{2}}$

**10** The area of a rectangle is 15 and its length is $2+\sqrt{7}$.

Find its width and write it in the form $a\sqrt{7}+b$.

**11** Triangle $ABC$ has an area of 5.

The length of base $BC$ is $6\sqrt{2}-2\sqrt{3}$.
Find the height of this triangle, measured from base $BC$.
Write your answer exactly, in its simplest form.

**\*12** Rationalise the denominator of $\dfrac{1}{\sqrt{2}+\sqrt{3}+\sqrt{5}}$ .

## D Further problems

**Example 11**

Triangle $PQR$ is isosceles.
$PR = 7\,\text{cm}$ and $QR = 10\,\text{cm}$.

Find the exact area of the triangle.

**Solution**

Since the triangle is isosceles, $QX = \frac{1}{2}QR = 5\,\text{cm}$.

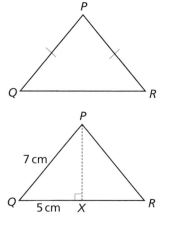

By Pythagoras, the length of $PX$ is $\sqrt{7^2 - 5^2} = \sqrt{49-25}$
$= \sqrt{24}$
$= \sqrt{4} \times \sqrt{6}$
$= 2\sqrt{6}\,\text{cm}$  *Try to write your answer in terms of the simplest possible surds.*

So the area of $PQR$ is $\frac{1}{2} \times 10 \times 2\sqrt{6} = 10\sqrt{6}\,\text{cm}^2$.

The value $\pi$ is an irrational number. All powers of $\pi$ are irrational too.
For example, $\pi^4$ and $\sqrt{\pi}$ are also irrational.

---

**Example 12**

The area of a semicircle is $4\pi$.
Show that the perimeter of this semicircle is $2\sqrt{2}(2 + \pi)$.

**Solution**

The area of the semicircle is $4\pi$.

The area of a semicircle is $\dfrac{\pi r^2}{2}$, where $r$ is the radius, so $\dfrac{\pi r^2}{2} = 4\pi$.

So $\dfrac{r^2}{2} = 4$ and hence $r = \sqrt{8} = 2\sqrt{2}$.

So the diameter is $2 \times 2\sqrt{2} = 4\sqrt{2}$.

The length of the curved part of the semicircle is

$$\frac{\pi \times \text{diameter}}{2} = \frac{\pi \times 4\sqrt{2}}{2} = 2\sqrt{2}\,\pi.$$

Thus the perimeter of the semicircle is

   length of diameter + length of curved part

   $= 4\sqrt{2} + 2\sqrt{2}\,\pi = 2\sqrt{2}(2 + \pi)$ as required.

---

**Exercise D** (answers p 167)

Give an exact answer to each problem.
Use $\pi$ and the simplest possible surds where appropriate.

   **1** Find the length of the line joining the points with coordinates $(-3, -5)$ and $(5, -1)$.

   **2** A rectangle has vertices with coordinates $(0, 0)$, $(6, 4)$, $(4, 7)$ and $(-2, 3)$.
   Find the area of the rectangle.

   **3** A circle has a radius of $3\sqrt{7}$. What is the area of this circle?

   **4** Show that triangle $XYZ$ is a right-angled triangle.

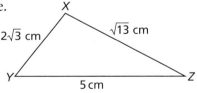

   **5** A circle has an area of $7\pi$.
   What is the circumference of the circle?

**6** The two lines sketched here have equations

$y = \sqrt{2}x + 9$ and $y = 10 - x$.

Find the coordinates of the point of intersection.

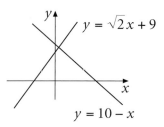

**7** A quarter-circle has an area of $6\pi$.
Show that the perimeter of the
quarter-circle is $\sqrt{6}(4 + \pi)$.

**8** A circle has an area of $50\,\text{cm}^2$.
Show that the radius is $5\sqrt{\dfrac{2}{\pi}}$ cm and the circumference is $10\sqrt{2\pi}$ cm.

**9** The diagram shows a triangle in a semicircle.

2 cm    4 cm

Work out

**(a)** the perimeter of the semicircle    **(b)** the total shaded area

**10** The diagram shows a quarter-circle.
Length $AB$ is 10 cm.

$B$

$A$

Show that the perimeter of the quarter-circle is $5\sqrt{2}\left(2 + \frac{1}{2}\pi\right)$ cm.

---

## Key points

- A root such as $\sqrt{5}$ that cannot be written exactly as a fraction is **irrational**.    (p 22)

- An expression that involves irrational roots is in **surd form**.
  Examples are $3\sqrt{5}$ and $\sqrt{10} - 7$.    (p 22)

- $\sqrt{ab} = \sqrt{a} \times \sqrt{b}$    (pp 23–24)

- $\sqrt{\dfrac{a}{b}} = \dfrac{\sqrt{a}}{\sqrt{b}}$    (pp 23–24)

- The product of the two **conjugates** $\left(a\sqrt{b} + c\sqrt{d}\right)$ and $\left(a\sqrt{b} - c\sqrt{d}\right)$ is always
  a rational number (when $a$, $b$, $c$ and $d$ are rational).
  So, for example, to **rationalise the denominator** of the expression
  $\dfrac{6 + \sqrt{7}}{3 - 7\sqrt{2}}$ you need to multiply the numerator and denominator by $3 + 7\sqrt{2}$.    (p 26)

## Test yourself (answers p 168)

None of these questions requires a calculator.

**1** Points $A$ and $B$ have coordinates $(-2, -1)$ and $(4, 1)$ respectively.
Show that $AB$ has length $p\sqrt{10}$, stating the value of $p$.

**2 (a)** Express each of the following in the form $a\sqrt{2}$.

    **(i)** $\sqrt{18}$                 **(ii)** $\sqrt{50}$

 **(b)** Hence write $\sqrt{18} + \sqrt{50}$ in the form $b\sqrt{2}$.

**3** Express $\dfrac{35}{\sqrt{7}}$ in the form $p\sqrt{q}$, where $p$ and $q$ are integers.

**4** Show that $\dfrac{8}{\sqrt{3}} \times \dfrac{\sqrt{15}}{\sqrt{20}}$ is an integer.

**5** Points $A$, $B$ and $C$ have coordinates $(1, 2)$, $(3, 4)$ and $(9, -2)$ respectively.

 **(a) (i)** In surd form, find the lengths $AB$, $BC$ and $AC$.

    **(ii)** Hence show that $ABC$ is a right-angled triangle.

 **(b)** Find the area of triangle $ABC$.

**6** Given that $(2 + \sqrt{7})(4 - \sqrt{7}) = a + b\sqrt{7}$, where $a$ and $b$ are integers,

 **(a)** find the value of $a$ and the value of $b$.

 Given that $\dfrac{2 + \sqrt{7}}{4 + \sqrt{7}} = c + d\sqrt{7}$, where $c$ and $d$ are rational numbers,

 **(b)** find the value of $c$ and the value of $d$.            *Edexcel*

**7** Express $\dfrac{2\sqrt{2}}{\sqrt{3} - 1} - \dfrac{2\sqrt{3}}{\sqrt{2} + 1}$ in the form $p\sqrt{6} + q\sqrt{3} + r\sqrt{2}$,
where the integers $p$, $q$ and $r$ are to be found.            *Edexcel*

**8** The shape shown is a sector $ABC$ of a circle with centre $A$ and radius $AB$.
The radius of the circle is $8\,\text{cm}$ and the triangle $ABC$ is equilateral.

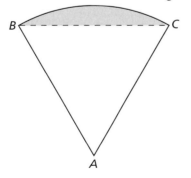

Show that the area of the shaded segment is $16\left(\tfrac{2}{3}\pi - \sqrt{3}\right)\,\text{cm}^2$.

# 3 Quadratic graphs and equations

In this chapter you will learn how to
- multiply out brackets and factorise quadratic expressions
- write a quadratic expression in completed-square form and relate it to the sketch of the corresponding graph, noting the vertex and line of symmetry
- solve a quadratic equation by factorising, completing the square or using the formula
- relate the roots of a quadratic equation to where its graph crosses the $x$-axis
- evaluate and interpret the discriminant of a quadratic expression

## A Expanding brackets: revision

**Example 1**

Multiply out $5x(x-6)$.

**Solution**

$$5x(x-6) = 5x \times x - 5x \times 6$$
$$= 5x^2 - 30x$$

**Example 2**

Multiply out $(3x+2)(x-6)$.

**Solution**

$$(3x+2)(x-6) = 3x(x-6) + 2(x-6)$$
$$= 3x^2 - 18x + 2x - 12$$
$$= 3x^2 - 16x - 12$$

*You can set out your working in a table.*

| $\times$ | $x$ | $-6$ |
|---|---|---|
| $3x$ | $3x^2$ | $-18x$ |
| $2$ | $2x$ | $-12$ |

**Exercise A** (answers p 168)

1 Multiply out each expression.
   (a) $3(4x-7)$  (b) $2x(x+5)$  (c) $-x(3x-1)$

2 Multiply out each expression and write the result in its simplest form. Use a table for each one if you find it useful.
   (a) $(x+5)(x+6)$  (b) $(5+x)(x-3)$  (c) $(2x-5)(x-1)$
   (d) $(7-x)(3x+1)$  (e) $(2-x)(6-x)$  (f) $3(x-5)(x+8)$
   (g) $4(3-x)(3x-7)$  (h) $(x+2)(x-2)$  (i) $(4x+3)(4x-3)$
   (j) $(x+3)^2$  (k) $2(x+11)^2$  (l) $(x-6)^2$

3 Multiply out each expression and write the result in its simplest form.
   (a) $(x+a)(x+b)$  (b) $(x+a)^2$  (c) $k(x+a)^2$
   (d) $(x+a)(x-a)$  (e) $(ax+b)^2$  (f) $(ax+b)(ax-b)$

# B Factorising quadratic expressions: revision

Any expression of the form $ax^2 + bx + c$ (where $a \neq 0$) is called a **quadratic** expression. Sometimes a quadratic expression can be factorised into the product of linear factors.

---

**Example 3**

Factorise $2x^2 - 8x$.

**Solution**

$2x^2 - 8x = 2x(x - 4)$

---

**Example 4**

Factorise $3x^2 + 8x + 5$.

**Solution**

$3x^2 = 3x \times x$

*These two terms must multiply to give 5.*

*$5 \times 1$ and $-5 \times -1$ are the possible products for 5.*

| $\times$ | $x$ | $\phantom{0}$ |
|---|---|---|
| $3x$ | $3x^2$ | |
| | | $5$ |

*These two terms must add to give $8x$.*

| $\times$ | $x$ | $1$ |
|---|---|---|
| $3x$ | $3x^2$ | $3x$ |

This table gives the correct result so the factorisation is $3x^2 + 8x + 5 = (3x + 5)(x + 1)$.

---

**Example 5**

Factorise $18x^2 - 32$.

**Solution**

*Look for any common factors first.*
*$9x^2 - 16 = (3x)^2 - 4^2$ is a difference of two squares so the factorisation is $(3x + 4)(3x - 4)$.*

$$18x^2 - 32 = 2(9x^2 - 16)$$
$$= 2(3x + 4)(3x - 4)$$

*A table confirms this.*

| $\times$ | $3x$ | $-4$ |
|---|---|---|
| $3x$ | $9x^2$ | $-12x$ |
| $4$ | $12x$ | $-16$ |

---

**Exercise B** (answers p 168)

**1** Factorise each expression.

(a) $x^2 + 5x$      (b) $x^2 - 10x$      (c) $3x^2 - 6x$      (d) $4x^2 + 10x$

(e) $12x + 18x^2$      (f) $9x - x^2$      (g) $15x - 9x^2$      (h) $-x^2 + 7x$

**2** Factorise each expression.

(a) $x^2 + 6x + 5$      (b) $x^2 - 6x + 5$      (c) $x^2 + 6x + 9$

(d) $x^2 + 10x + 9$      (e) $x^2 - 9x + 18$      (f) $x^2 + 4x - 21$

(g) $x^2 - x - 12$      (h) $x^2 - 14x - 15$      (i) $x^2 - 10x + 25$

**3** Factorise each expression.

(a) $2x^2 + 5x + 3$      (b) $3x^2 + 16x + 5$      (c) $5x^2 - 8x + 3$

(d) $3x^2 - 20x - 7$      (e) $6x^2 + 27x - 15$      (f) $3x^2 + 11x + 6$

(g) $3x^2 + 19x + 6$      (h) $4x^2 - 22x + 24$      (i) $3x^2 - 22x - 16$

(j) $4x^2 - 4x + 1$      (k) $6x^2 - 29x - 5$      (l) $10x^2 - 29x + 12$

**4** Factorise each expression.

(a) $x^2 - 9$      (b) $x^2 - 100$      (c) $x^2 - 1$

(d) $4x^2 - 25$      (e) $9x^2 - 1$      (f) $32 - 50x^2$

**5** Where possible, factorise each expression fully.

(a) $2x^2 - 3x - 9$      (b) $x^2 - 2x + 7$      (c) $2x^2 - 2x - 60$

(d) $2x^2 + 5x + 1$      (e) $6x^2 + 9x - 15$      (f) $16x^2 - 8x - 3$

(g) $-x^2 - 2x + 15$      (h) $36x^2 - 25$      (i) $45 + x - 2x^2$

**6** (a) Confirm that, when $x = 7$, the value of $x^2 + 10x + 25$ is a square number.

     (b) By factorising, show that the value of $x^2 + 10x + 25$ is a square number for any integer value of $x$.

**7** (a) (i) Find the value of the expression $x^2 + 3x + 2$ when $x = 6$.

         (ii) Write this value as the product of two consecutive numbers.

     (b) Show that the value of $x^2 + 3x + 2$ can be written as a product of two consecutive numbers for any integer value of $x$.

**\*8** (a) Confirm that, when $x = 3$, the value of $16x^2 - 8x + 1$ is an odd square number.

     (b) Show that the value of $16x^2 - 8x + 1$ is an odd square number for any integer $x$.

**\*9** (a) (i) Find the value of the expression $4x^2 - 1$ when $x = 5$.

         (ii) Write this value as the product of two consecutive odd numbers.

     (b) Show that the value of $4x^2 - 1$ can be written as a product of two consecutive odd numbers for any integer value of $x$.

## C Parabolas (answers p 169)

**C1** Use a graph plotter on a computer or graphic calculator to plot the graph of $y = ax^2 + bx + c$ for various values of $a$, $b$ and $c$.
Note the effect of making $a$ negative.

Curves with equations that can be written in the form $y = ax^2 + bx + c$ ($a \neq 0$) are **parabolas**.

The curve seen when a plane cuts a cone like this is a parabola. The Ancient Greek mathematician and astronomer Appollonius (3rd century BCE) was the person who named these curves 'parabolas'.

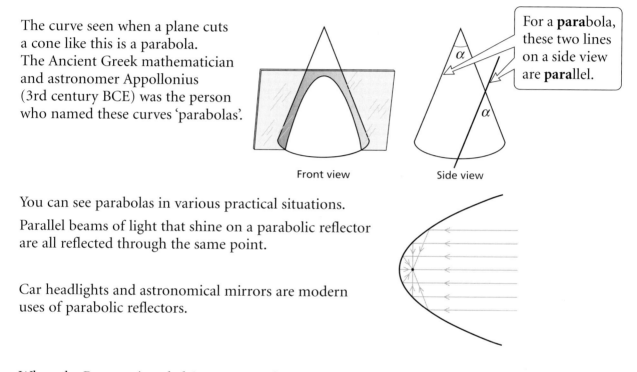

Front view                    Side view

For a **para**bola, these two lines on a side view are **para**llel.

You can see parabolas in various practical situations.

Parallel beams of light that shine on a parabolic reflector are all reflected through the same point.

Car headlights and astronomical mirrors are modern uses of parabolic reflectors.

When the Romans invaded Syracuse on the coast of Sicily in 214 BCE, Archimedes invented various devices to defend the city. These include the famous 'burning mirrors' which are supposed to have set ships on fire. They were made as close as possible to the shape of a parabolic mirror and focused the Sun's rays on to the invading ships.

Hundreds of years later, cannons were becoming widely used in warfare and it was important to be able to judge accurately where a cannon ball would land. Galileo (1564–1642) determined that the path of a cannon ball (and indeed any object moving under gravity such as a golf ball) follows a parabolic curve.

The relationship between parabolic graphs and their equations is an important one.

The parabola with equation $y = x^2$ has a vertical line of symmetry along the $y$-axis and a **vertex** at the origin. The vertex of the graph of $y = x^2$ is a minimum point.

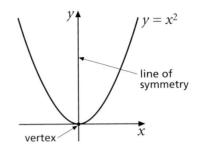

Use a graph plotter to draw the graphs in the problems below.

**C2** (a) Plot the graph of $y = x^2$ and superimpose the graphs of $y = 2x^2$ and $y = \frac{1}{3}x^2$. Describe the relationship between the graphs.

(b) Investigate graphs of the form $y = kx^2$ for both positive and negative values of $k$. How are they related to $y = x^2$?

**C3** Investigate graphs of the form $y = x^2 + q$ for both positive and negative values of $q$. How are they related to $y = x^2$?

**C4** Investigate graphs of the form $y = (x + p)^2$ for both positive and negative values of $p$. How are they related to $y = x^2$?

**C5** Plot the graph of $y = x^2$ and superimpose the graph of $y = (x + 5)^2 + 2$.

(a) What are the coordinates of the vertex of $y = (x + 5)^2 + 2$?

(b) What is the equation of its line of symmetry?

(c) (i) Show that the equation of the graph can be written as $y = x^2 + 10x + 27$.

(ii) Hence write down where the graph crosses the $y$-axis.

**C6** Investigate graphs with equations in the form $y = (x + p)^2 + q$. How are they related to $y = x^2$?

**C7** What do you think is the vertex of the graph of $y = (x - 6)^2 + 9$?

**C8** What do you think is the equation of the line of symmetry of $y = (x + 4)^2 - 3$?

**C9** Investigate graphs of the form $y = 2(x + p)^2 + q$ for both positive and negative values of $p$ and $q$. How are they related to $y = 2x^2$?

**C10** How do you think graphs of the form $y = k(x + p)^2 + q$ are related to $y = kx^2$?

**C11** (a) (i) What do you think are the coordinates of the vertex of $y = 3(x - 2)^2 - 5$?

   (ii) What is the equation of its line of symmetry?

   (b) (i) Show that the equation of the graph can be written as $y = 3x^2 - 12x + 7$.

   (ii) Hence determine where the graph crosses the $y$-axis.

We can work algebraically when translating curves.

For example, the graph of $y = 2x^2$ is translated 3 units to the right and 4 units up.

Using vector notation this translation can be represented by $\begin{bmatrix} 3 \\ 4 \end{bmatrix}$.

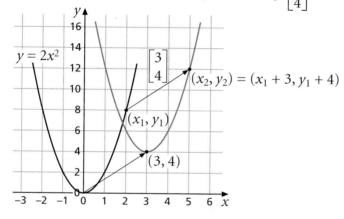

Let $(x_1, y_1)$ be a point on $y = 2x^2$ and let $(x_2, y_2)$ be its image on the translated curve.

Then $(x_2, y_2) = (x_1 + 3, y_1 + 4)$, giving

$\qquad x_1 = x_2 - 3 \qquad$ *from rearranging $x_2 = x_1 + 3$*

and $\quad y_1 = y_2 - 4 \qquad$ *from rearranging $y_2 = y_1 + 4$*

We know that $y_1 = 2x_1{}^2$, so it must be true that

$\qquad y_2 - 4 = 2(x_2 - 3)^2$

and so $y - 4 = 2(x - 3)^2$ is the equation of the transformed curve.

This can be written as $y = 2(x - 3)^2 + 4$.

> So to find the equation of the curve that is the result of translating $y = 2x^2$ by $\begin{bmatrix} 3 \\ 4 \end{bmatrix}$ you can replace $x$ by $(x - 3)$ and $y$ by $(y - 4)$.

**C12** What is the equation of the image of the curve $y = x^2$ after a translation of $\begin{bmatrix} 6 \\ 5 \end{bmatrix}$?

**C13** What is the equation of the image of the curve $y = 2x^2$ after a translation of $\begin{bmatrix} -3 \\ 2 \end{bmatrix}$?

**C14** Which translation will transform the curve $y = x^2$ to $y = (x - 9)^2 + 7$?

**C15** Which translation will transform the curve $y = 3x^2$ to $y = 3(x + 1)^2 - 6$?

**Example 6**

The graph below is a translation of $y = x^2$.

What is its equation in the form $y = ax^2 + bx + c$?

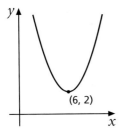

**Solution**

The vertex is (6, 2) so the translation is $\begin{bmatrix} 6 \\ 2 \end{bmatrix}$.

So the equation can be written as

$$y - 2 = (x - 6)^2$$
$$\Rightarrow \quad y = (x - 6)^2 + 2$$
$$= x^2 - 12x + 36 + 2$$
$$= x^2 - 12x + 38$$

So the equation is $y = x^2 - 12x + 38$.

---

**Example 7**

Sketch the graph of $y = 3(x + 2)^2 - 1$, showing the vertex, the $y$-intercept and the line of symmetry.

**Solution**

The equation can be written $y + 1 = 3(x + 2)^2$.

The graph can be obtained by translating $y = 3x^2$ by $\begin{bmatrix} -2 \\ -1 \end{bmatrix}$. So the vertex is $(-2, -1)$ and the line of symmetry is $x = -2$.

When $x = 0$,
$y = 3 \times (0 + 2)^2 - 1 = 11$.
So the $y$-intercept is 11.

---

**Exercise C** (answers p 170)

**1** Which translation will transform the curve $y = x^2$ to $y = (x - 4)^2 - 5$?

**2** Which translation will transform the curve $y = x^2$ to $y = (x + 8)^2 + 1$?

**3** What is the vertex of the graph with equation $y = (x - 5)^2 + 7$?

**4** What is the equation of the line of symmetry for the graph of $y = (x + 2)^2 - 3$?

**5** (a) (i)  Write the equation $y = (x + 7)^2 - 5$ in the form $y = ax^2 + bx + c$.

   (ii) Hence write down the $y$-intercept.

   (b) Sketch the graph of $y = (x + 7)^2 - 5$.
   Show clearly the coordinates of the vertex and the $y$-intercept.

**6** Sketch the graph for each of these equations, showing clearly the vertex and $y$-intercept.

   (a) $y = (x - 2)^2 + 5$     (b) $y = (x - 4)^2$     (c) $y = (x + 6)^2 - 20$

**7** Show that the graph of $y = (x + 3)^2 + 1$ does not cross the $x$-axis.

**8** Each of these graphs is a translation of $y = x^2$.
Find the equation of each one.

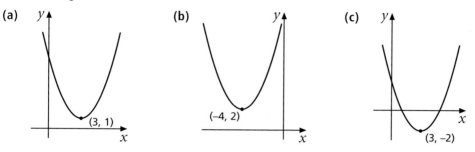

(a) (3, 1)

(b) (–4, 2)

(c) (3, –2)

**9 (a) (i)** Which translation will transform the curve $y = 2x^2$ to $y = 2(x + 1)^2 - 3$?

**(ii)** What are the coordinates of the vertex of $y = 2(x + 1)^2 - 3$?

**(b)** Write $y = 2(x + 1)^2 - 3$ in the form $y = ax^2 + bx + c$.

**(c)** Sketch the graph of $y = 2(x + 1)^2 - 3$, showing clearly the vertex, axis (line) of symmetry and the $y$-intercept.

**10** Sketch the graph for each of these equations, showing clearly the vertex and $y$-intercept.

**(a)** $y = 2(x + 4)^2 + 1$      **(b)** $y = 3(x - 2)^2 - 7$      **(c)** $y = 4(x + 1)^2 - 3$

**11 (a) (i)** Which translation will transform the curve $y = -x^2$ to $y = -(x + 2)^2 + 5$?

**(ii)** What is the vertex of $y = -(x + 2)^2 + 5$?

**(b)** On the same set of axes, sketch the graphs of $y = -x^2$ and $y = -(x + 2)^2 + 5$, showing clearly the vertex of $y = -(x + 2)^2 + 5$.

**(c)** What is the $y$-intercept of $y = -(x + 2)^2 + 5$?

**12 (a)** Show that the expression $-2(x - 3)^2 + 11$ is equivalent to $-2x^2 + 12x - 7$.

**(b)** Sketch the graph of $y = -2(x - 3)^2 + 11$, showing clearly the vertex, axis of symmetry and the $y$-intercept.

**\*13** The parabola with equation $y = x^2$ is stretched by a factor of 3 in the $y$-direction.
Then it is translated by $\begin{bmatrix} 8 \\ 1 \end{bmatrix}$.
Write down the equation of the transformed graph.

**\*14** The parabola with equation $y = x^2$ is reflected in the $x$-axis.
Then it is stretched by a factor of 4 in the $y$-direction.
Finally, it is translated by $\begin{bmatrix} -5 \\ -3 \end{bmatrix}$.
Write down the equation of the transformed graph.

**\*15** Each of these graphs is a sketch of a parabola.
Determine the equation of each one.

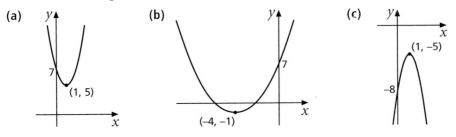

(a) (1, 5)

(b) (−4, −1)

(c) (1, −5), −8

## D Completing the square (answers p 170)

The identity $(x + a)^2 = x^2 + 2ax + a^2$ is useful when dealing with squares.

For example, $(x - 3)^2 = x^2 + 2 \times (-3) \times x + 3^2$
$$= x^2 - 6x + 9$$

The expression $x^2 - 6x + 9$ is called a **perfect square** as it can be written as $(x - 3)^2$.

**D1** Expand each expression.

(a) $(x + 4)^2$      (b) $(x - 9)^2$      (c) $(x + 20)^2$

(d) $(x - 1)^2$      (e) $(x + \frac{1}{4})^2$      (f) $(x - \frac{1}{3})^2$

**D2** Decide which of the expressions below are perfect squares.

A   $x^2 + 10x + 25$     B   $x^2 + 6x + 12$     C   $x^2 - 16x + 64$

D   $x^2 - 2x + 2$     E   $x^2 - 10x - 25$     F   $x^2 - 12x + 36$

G   $x^2 + x + \frac{1}{4}$     H   $x^2 - 7x + 9\frac{1}{4}$

**D3** What values of $k$ make these expressions perfect squares?

(a) $x^2 + 14x + k$      (b) $x^2 + kx + 121$      (c) $x^2 - kx + 64$

**D4** Multiply out the brackets and write each expression in its simplest form.

(a) $(x + 5)^2 - 25$    (b) $(x + 3)^2 - 9$    (c) $(x - 3)^2 - 9$    (d) $(x - 7)^2 - 49$

**D5** (a) Express $x^2 + 6x + 9$ in the form $(x + p)^2$.

(b) Hence express $x^2 + 6x$ in the form $(x + p)^2 + q$.

(c) Hence express $x^2 + 6x + 5$ in the form $(x + p)^2 + q$.

(d) Sketch the graph of $y = x^2 + 6x + 5$.

**D6** (a) Express $x^2 - 14x$ in the form $(x + p)^2 + q$.

(b) Hence express $x^2 - 14x + 50$ in the form $(x + p)^2 + q$.

(c) Sketch the graph of $y = x^2 - 14x + 50$.

Expressions in the form $(x + p)^2 + q$ are said to be in **completed-square form**.

---

**Example 8**

Write $x^2 - 8x + 3$ in completed-square form.
Hence find the minimum value of the expression $x^2 - 8x + 3$.
State the value of $x$ that gives this minimum value.

**Solution**

*Start with the first two terms.*
*The constant inside the brackets is found*
*by halving the coefficient of x.*

$$x^2 - 8x = (x - 4)^2 - 16$$

*Adjust your answer to take into account the*
*constant term.*

$$x^2 - 8x + 3 = (x - 4)^2 - 16 + 3$$

$$\Rightarrow \quad x^2 - 8x + 3 = (x - 4)^2 - 13$$

*You can check this by multiplying out the brackets and simplifying.*

$(x - 4)^2 \geq 0$ for all values of $x$ so the
minimum value of $x^2 - 8x + 3$ is $-13$.

*The minimum value occurs when $(x - 4) = 0$.* The minimum value occurs when $x = 4$.

---

**D7** Write the following in completed-square form.

(a) $x^2 + 14x + 2$       (b) $x^2 - 6x + 12$       (c) $x^2 + 8x - 3$

**D8** (a) Write $x^2 + 2x - 4$ in completed-square form.

(b) Hence sketch the graph of $y = x^2 + 2x - 4$.

**D9** (a) Write $x^2 + 18x + 82$ in completed-square form.

(b) Hence show that $x^2 + 18x + 82 > 0$ for all values of $x$.

**D10** (a) Write $x^2 + 4x + 11$ in completed-square form.

(b) (i) Hence show that the minimum value of $x^2 + 4x + 11$ is 7.

(ii) State the value of $x$ that gives this minimum value.

**D11** (a) Multiply out $(x - \frac{1}{2})^2$.

(b) Hence express $x^2 - x$ in the form $(x + p)^2 + q$.

(c) Write $x^2 - x - 5$ in completed-square form.

**D12** Write the following in completed-square form.

(a) $x^2 + 3x + 1$       (b) $x^2 + 5x + 10$       (c) $x^2 - 9x - 3$

**D13** (a) Write $x^2 - x + \frac{7}{4}$ in completed-square form.

(b) Hence show that the minimum value of $x^2 - x + \frac{7}{4}$ is $1\frac{1}{2}$.

**K** Any quadratic expression can be written in the **completed-square form** $k(x + p)^2 + q$.

The process of writing a quadratic in this form is called **completing the square**.

---

### Example 9

Write $2x^2 + 12x - 1$ in completed-square form.

### Solution

*Write the first two terms as a product of two factors where one factor is the coefficient of $x^2$.*

$$2x^2 + 12x = 2[x^2 + 6x]$$

*Write the expression in square brackets in completed-square form.*

$$= 2[(x + 3)^2 - 9]$$

*Multiply out the square brackets.*

$$= 2(x + 3)^2 - 18$$

*Adjust.*

$$2x^2 + 12x - 1 = 2(x + 3)^2 - 18 - 1$$
$$= 2(x + 3)^2 - 19$$

---

**D14** (a) Write $3x^2 - 12x - 4$ in completed-square form.

(b) Sketch the graph of $y = 3x^2 - 12x - 4$, showing clearly the vertex and the $y$-intercept.

**D15** Write the following in completed-square form.

(a) $2x^2 + 16x + 40$      (b) $3x^2 - 18x - 1$      (c) $2x^2 + 10x - 8$

---

### Example 10

Write $-3x^2 - 6x + 5$ in completed-square form.
Hence find the maximum value of $-3x^2 - 6x + 5$.

### Solution

$$-3x^2 - 6x = -3[x^2 + 2x]$$
$$= -3[(x + 1)^2 - 1]$$
$$= -3(x + 1)^2 + 3$$
$$\Rightarrow \quad -3x^2 - 6x + 5 = -3(x + 1)^2 + 3 + 5$$
$$= -3(x + 1)^2 + 8$$

$-3(x + 1)^2 \leq 0$ for all values of $x$, so the expression $-3x^2 - 6x + 5$ has a **maximum** value of 8.

---

### Exercise D (answers p 171)

**1** Write each of these expressions in completed-square form.

(a) $x^2 + 6x + 10$      (b) $x^2 - 10x + 3$      (c) $x^2 + 18x - 2$

(d) $x^2 - 4x + 13$      (e) $x^2 + 3x - 1$      (f) $x^2 - 5x + 9$

**2 (a)** Show that $x^2 - 12x + 41$ is equivalent to $(x - 6)^2 + 5$.

**(b)** Which of these points is the vertex of the graph of $y = x^2 - 12x + 41$?

$(6, 41)$  $(-6, 5)$  $(-6, 41)$  $(6, 5)$  $(6, -5)$  $(-12, 41)$

**(c)** Show that the graph of $y = x^2 - 12x + 41$ crosses the $y$-axis at $(0, 41)$.

**3** For each equation below,

**(i)** write the quadratic in completed-square form

**(ii)** sketch the corresponding graph, indicating clearly the vertex and $y$-intercept

**(a)** $y = x^2 + 6x + 15$   **(b)** $y = x^2 + 8x - 2$   **(c)** $y = x^2 - 2x + 5$

**(d)** $y = x^2 - 4x - 3$   **(e)** $y = x^2 + 3x + 7$   **(f)** $y = x^2 - 7x - 2$

**4** By completing the square, show that the graph of $y = x^2 - 6x + 13$ does not cross the $x$-axis.

**5 (a)** Express $x^2 + 2x + 5$ in completed-square form.

**(b) (i)** Show that $x^2 + 2x + 5$ has a minimum value of 4.

**(ii)** State the value of $x$ that gives this minimum value.

**6** Show that the graph of $y = x^2 + 4x + 1$ crosses the $x$-axis twice.

**7 (a)** Express $x^2 + 10x + 1$ in the form $(x + p)^2 + q$, finding the values of $p$ and $q$.

**(b)** State the minimum value of the expression $x^2 + 10x + 1$.

**8** By completing the square, show that the graph of $y = x^2 + 4x + 4$ touches the $x$-axis at just one point.

**9** Write each of these expressions in completed-square form.

**(a)** $2x^2 + 4x - 1$   **(b)** $3x^2 - 12x + 13$   **(c)** $5x^2 - 10x - 1$

**(d)** $2x^2 + 16x + 32$   **(e)** $3x^2 + 3x + 5$   **(f)** $4x^2 - 12x - 5$

**10 (a)** Show that $3x^2 + 12x - 7$ is equivalent to $3(x + 2)^2 - 19$.

**(b)** Write down the vertex of the graph of $y = 3x^2 + 12x - 7$.

**(c)** Show that the graph of $y = 3x^2 + 12x - 7$ crosses the $y$-axis at $(0, -7)$.

**(d)** Write down the equation of the line of symmetry of the curve $y = 3x^2 + 12x - 7$.

**11** For each equation below,

**(i)** write the quadratic in completed-square form

**(ii)** sketch the graph, indicating clearly the vertex and $y$-intercept

**(a)** $y = 2x^2 - 12x + 21$   **(b)** $y = 3x^2 + 6x + 3$   **(c)** $y = 4x^2 + 4x + 3$

**12** By completing the square, show that the graph of $y = 5x^2 - 20x + 24$ does not cross the $x$-axis.

**13** For each expression below,

      **(i)** write it in completed-square form

      **(ii)** write down the minimum value of the expression

      **(iii)** state the value of $x$ which gives this minimum value

    **(a)** $3x^2 + 18x + 25$         **(b)** $2x^2 - 4x + 5$         **(c)** $2x^2 + 14x + 1$

**14 (a)** Express $2x^2 + 16x + 3$ in the form $p(x + q)^2 + r$, where $p$, $q$ and $r$ are constants.

    **(b)** State the minimum value of $2x^2 + 16x + 3$.

**15** Two ships set off from different harbours at the same time.

    The distance between the ships is given by the formula $d = t^2 - 8t + 19$, where $d$ is the distance in kilometres and $t$ is the time in hours.

    **(a)** Write the formula in completed-square form.

    **(b)** Hence find the distance between the ships when they are nearest to each other.

    **(c)** How many hours have they been sailing when they are nearest to each other?

**16** Write each of these expressions in completed-square form.

    **(a)** $2x^2 + 3x + 1$         **(b)** $3x^2 - 3x - 2$         **(c)** $4x^2 - 3x - 1$

**17 (a)** By multiplying out the brackets, show that $-2(x + 1)^2 + 5$ is equivalent to $-2x^2 - 4x + 3$.

    **(b)** Write down the vertex of the graph of $y = -2x^2 - 4x + 3$.

    **(c)** State the $y$-intercept of the graph of $y = -2x^2 - 4x + 3$.

    **(d)** Sketch the graph of $y = -2x^2 - 4x + 3$.

**18** For each equation below,

      **(i)** write the quadratic in completed-square form

      **(ii)** sketch the corresponding graph, indicating clearly the vertex and $y$-intercept

    **(a)** $y = -x^2 - 6x + 1$     **(b)** $y = 3 + 8x - x^2$     **(c)** $y = -2x^2 - 12x - 25$

**19 (a)** Find the maximum value of the expression $-3x^2 + 30x - 74$.

    **(b)** What value of $x$ gives this maximum value?

**20** The height of a particular golf ball is given by the formula $h = 30t - 5t^2$, where $h$ is the height in metres and $t$ is the time in seconds.

    **(a)** Write the formula in completed-square form.

    **(b)** Hence find the maximum height of the ball.

    **(c)** After how many seconds does the ball reach its maximum?

# E Zeros of quadratics

The line of symmetry, the vertex and the $y$-intercept are important features of a parabolic graph. Also useful are the points at which the graph crosses the $x$-axis, if it does. The graphs of all quadratic functions of $x$ must cross the $y$-axis but some graphs do not cross the $x$-axis.

The values of $x$ at the points of intersection with the $x$-axis are called the **zeros** of the function because they make the function equal to zero.

---

## Example 11

Find where the graph of $y = 2x^2 + 3x - 2$ crosses the $x$-axis.

### Solution

*On the x-axis the value of y is* 0.

$$2x^2 + 3x - 2 = 0$$
$$\Rightarrow \quad (2x - 1)(x + 2) = 0$$

*Either* $(2x - 1) = 0$ *or* $(x + 2) = 0$.

giving $x = \frac{1}{2}$ and $x = -2$

So the graph crosses the $x$-axis at $(\frac{1}{2}, 0)$ and $(-2, 0)$.

---

## Example 12

Solve the equation $3x^2 + 15x + 18 = 0$.

### Solution

$$3x^2 + 15x + 18 = 0$$

*3 is a common factor of each term so divide each side of the equation by 3.*

$$\Rightarrow \quad x^2 + 5x + 6 = 0$$

*The quadratic factorises.*

$$\Rightarrow \quad (x + 3)(x + 2) = 0$$

*Either* $(x + 3) = 0$ *or* $(x + 2) = 0$.

giving $x = -3$ and $x = -2$

So the solutions are $x = -3$ and $x = -2$.

---

## Example 13

Show that the graph of $y = 12x - 4 - 9x^2$ just touches the $x$-axis at one point.

### Solution

*On the x-axis the value of y is* 0.

$$12x - 4 - 9x^2 = 0$$

*Multiply each side of the equation by* $-1$ *to make the coefficient of* $x^2$ *positive.*

$$\Rightarrow \quad 9x^2 - 12x + 4 = 0$$

*The quadratic factorises.*

$$\Rightarrow \quad (3x - 2)(3x - 2) = 0$$

*There is only one zero, that is when* $(3x - 2) = 0$. giving $x = \frac{2}{3}$

The parabola cannot cross the $x$-axis at just one point, so the graph just touches it at $(\frac{2}{3}, 0)$.

---

**Exercise E** (answers p 172)

**1** Solve each equation.

(a) $x^2 - 4x = 0$         (b) $x^2 + 2x = 0$         (c) $x^2 + 7x + 6 = 0$

(d) $x^2 - 6x + 9 = 0$      (e) $2x^2 - 12x - 32 = 0$      (f) $x^2 - 9x + 18 = 0$

(g) $2x^2 + 5x - 3 = 0$      (h) $3x^2 - x - 2 = 0$       (i) $6x^2 + 33x - 63 = 0$

(j) $5x^2 - 16x + 12 = 0$    (k) $12 - 35x - 3x^2 = 0$     (l) $4x^2 - 20x + 25 = 0$

**2** Find out where the graph of each equation crosses or meets the $x$-axis.

(a) $y = x^2 + x - 12$       (b) $y = x^2 - 9x + 8$       (c) $y = 2x^2 + 13x + 6$

(d) $y = 3x^2 + 19x - 14$    (e) $y = x^2 - 7x$           (f) $y = x^2 - 9$

(g) $y = 2x^2 - 8x + 6$      (h) $y = 3x^2 + 30x + 75$    (i) $y = -2x^2 + 4x + 16$

**3** The graph of $y = x^2$ has been translated to produce each graph below.
Find the equation of each graph in the form $y = ax^2 + bx + c$.

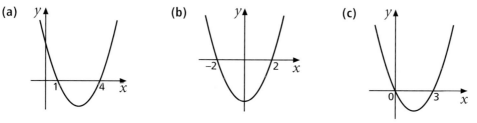

(a)                     (b)                     (c)

**4** A graph has equation $y = x^2 + 4x - 5$.

(a) Work out where the graph crosses the $x$-axis.

(b) Where does the graph cross the $y$-axis?

(c) (i) Write $x^2 + 4x - 5$ in completed-square form.

     (ii) Hence, or otherwise, write down the coordinates of the vertex.

(d) Sketch the graph, showing the points where it crosses the $x$- and $y$-axes
and the vertex.

**5** Draw the graph of each equation below.
Clearly mark the points where each graph crosses the $x$- and $y$-axes and the vertex.

(a) $y = x^2 - 10x + 16$      (b) $y = x^2 + 14x + 40$      (c) $y = x^2 - 7x + 10$

(d) $y = 3x^2 + 18x - 21$     (e) $y = 2x^2 + 6x - 8$       (f) $y = 20 - x - x^2$

**\*6** Each graph below is a parabola.
Find the equation of each one in the form $y = ax^2 + bx + c$.

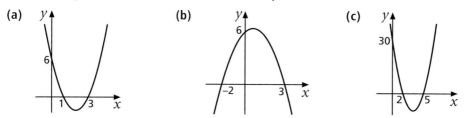

(a)                     (b)                     (c)

## F Solving quadratic equations by completing the square

This is a sketch of the graph with equation $y = x^2 + 2x - 5$.

To find where it cuts the $x$-axis we need to solve the equation $x^2 + 2x - 5 = 0$.

We cannot factorise $x^2 + 2x - 5$ but we can complete the square to try to solve the equation.

$$x^2 + 2x - 5 = (x + 1)^2 - 1 - 5$$
$$= (x + 1)^2 - 6$$

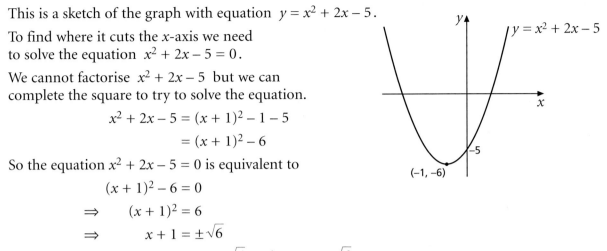

So the equation $x^2 + 2x - 5 = 0$ is equivalent to

$$(x + 1)^2 - 6 = 0$$
$$\Rightarrow \quad (x + 1)^2 = 6$$
$$\Rightarrow \quad x + 1 = \pm\sqrt{6}$$

giving $x = -1 + \sqrt{6}$ and $x = -1 - \sqrt{6}$

These are the exact values in surd form, giving the coordinates $(-1 + \sqrt{6}, 0)$ and $(-1 - \sqrt{6}, 0)$.

If we try to solve the equation $4x^2 - 24x - 7 = 0$, we find that the expression $4x^2 - 24x - 7$ does not factorise.

We can try solving it by completing the square.

$$4x^2 - 24x - 7 = 0 \qquad \textit{We can divide both sides by 4.}$$
$$\Rightarrow \qquad x^2 - 6x - \tfrac{7}{4} = 0$$
$$\Rightarrow \qquad (x - 3)^2 - 9 - \tfrac{7}{4} = 0$$
$$\Rightarrow \qquad (x - 3)^2 - \tfrac{43}{4} = 0 \qquad \textit{$\tfrac{43}{4}$ is easier to deal with than $10\tfrac{3}{4}$.}$$
$$\Rightarrow \qquad (x - 3)^2 = \tfrac{43}{4}$$
$$\Rightarrow \qquad x - 3 = \pm\sqrt{\tfrac{43}{4}} = \pm\frac{\sqrt{43}}{2} = \pm\tfrac{1}{2}\sqrt{43}$$

giving $x = 3 + \tfrac{1}{2}\sqrt{43}$ and $x = 3 - \tfrac{1}{2}\sqrt{43}$

### Exercise F (answers p 173)

**1** Solve each equation and give your answers in surd form.

(a) $(x - 3)^2 = 2$      (b) $(x + 5)^2 - 11 = 0$      (c) $(x - 6)^2 - 6 = 0$

**2** (a) Write $x^2 + 10x + 23$ in completed-square form.

(b) Hence solve $x^2 + 10x + 23 = 0$, giving your solutions exactly in surd form.

**3** Solve each equation by completing the square, giving your solutions exactly in surd form.

   **(a)** $x^2 + 4x + 1 = 0$    **(b)** $x^2 + 2x - 7 = 0$    **(c)** $x^2 - 6x - 2 = 0$

   **(d)** $x^2 - 5x - 1 = 0$    **(e)** $2x^2 + 12x + 6 = 0$    **(f)** $2x^2 - 10x + 5 = 0$

**4** Work out the exact coordinates where the graph of each equation crosses the $x$-axis.

   **(a)** $y = x^2 + 2x - 4$    **(b)** $y = x^2 - 4x + 1$    **(c)** $y = 2x^2 - 14x + 9$

**5 (a)** Write $x^2 + 4x + 10$ in completed-square form.

   **(b)** What happens when you try to solve the equation $x^2 + 4x + 10 = 0$?
   How does this relate to the graph of $y = x^2 + 4x + 10$?

## G Solving quadratic equations by using the formula

Completing the square can be used to establish a general formula for solving quadratic equations.

$$ax^2 + bx + c = 0$$

*Divide by a to make 1 the coefficient of $x^2$.*
$$x^2 + \frac{b}{a}x + \frac{c}{a} = 0$$

*Complete the square.*
$$\left(x + \frac{b}{2a}\right)^2 - \frac{b^2}{4a^2} + \frac{c}{a} = 0$$

*Rearrange the equation.*
$$\left(x + \frac{b}{2a}\right)^2 = \frac{b^2}{4a^2} - \frac{c}{a}$$

$$\frac{c}{a} = \frac{c \times 4a}{a \times 4a} = \frac{4ac}{4a^2}$$
$$\left(x + \frac{b}{2a}\right)^2 = \frac{b^2 - 4ac}{4a^2}$$

*Remember the positive and negative square roots.*
$$x + \frac{b}{2a} = \pm\sqrt{\frac{b^2 - 4ac}{4a^2}}$$

*Simplify the square root.*
$$x = -\frac{b}{2a} \pm \frac{\sqrt{b^2 - 4ac}}{\sqrt{4a^2}}$$

$$\Rightarrow \qquad x = -\frac{b}{2a} \pm \frac{\sqrt{b^2 - 4ac}}{2a}$$

$$\Rightarrow \qquad x = \frac{-b \pm \sqrt{b^2 - 4ac}}{2a}$$

The solutions of the equation are also called the **roots** of the equation.

**Example 14**

Find the roots of $2x^2 + 4x - 1 = 0$.
Give the exact roots in surd form and their decimal values correct to two decimal places.

**Solution**

Using $x = \dfrac{-b \pm \sqrt{b^2 - 4ac}}{2a}$, where $a = 2$, $b = 4$, $c = -1$,

$$x = \frac{-4 \pm \sqrt{4^2 - 4 \times 2 \times (-1)}}{2 \times 2}$$

$$= \frac{-4 \pm \sqrt{24}}{4}$$

$$= \frac{-4 \pm 2\sqrt{6}}{4}$$

giving $x = -1 + \frac{1}{2}\sqrt{6}$ and $x = -1 - \frac{1}{2}\sqrt{6}$     *These are the **exact** solutions.*
or $x = 0.22$ and $x = -2.22$ (correct to 2 d.p.)     *These are **approximate** solutions.*

---

## Exercise G (answers p 173)

1  Use the formula to find the exact solutions to each equation in terms of the simplest possible surds.

   (a)  $3x^2 + 5x + 1 = 0$     (b)  $x^2 - 2x - 2 = 0$     (c)  $2x^2 - 8x + 3 = 0$

2  Use the formula to find the solutions to each equation, correct to three decimal places.

   (a)  $x^2 + 5x - 3 = 0$     (b)  $2x^2 - 6x + 3 = 0$     (c)  $-5x^2 + x + 2 = 0$

3  Work out where the graph of $y = \frac{1}{2}x^2 - 4x + 5$ crosses the $x$-axis.
   Give the coordinates correct to two decimal places.

4  (a)  What happens when you use the formula to solve the equation $x^2 + 2x + 5 = 0$?

   (b)  What does this tell you about the graph of the equation $y = x^2 + 2x + 5$?

5  (a)  What happens when you use the formula to solve the equation $4x^2 - 12x + 9 = 0$?

   (b)  What does this tell you about the graph of the equation $y = 4x^2 - 12x + 9$?

6  The graph of $y = x^2 + 6x + c$ cuts the $x$-axis in two places.
   Work out the range of possible values of $c$.

7  The graph of $y = x^2 + 2x + c$ just touches the $x$-axis.
   Work out the range of possible values of $c$.

*8  The graph of $y = 2x^2 + bx + 8$ does not cut the $x$-axis.
   Work out the range of possible values of $b$.

## H Using the discriminant (answers p 173)

The expression $b^2 - 4ac$ is called the **discriminant** of the equation $ax^2 + bx + c = 0$.

- If the value of the discriminant is less than zero, the equation has no real roots.
- If the value of the discriminant is zero, the equation has one real root, sometimes called a **repeated root**, as both factors of the quadratic give rise to it.

  It is sometimes helpful to think of the equation as having two roots that are the same and call them **equal roots**.

- If the value of the discriminant is greater than zero, the equation has two different (**distinct**) real roots.

**H1** What can you say about the expression $ax^2 + bx + c$ if the value of the discriminant is the square of a whole number or a fraction? What about the equation $ax^2 + bx + c = 0$?

### Exercise H (answers p 173)

**1** What is the value of the discriminant for the equation $x^2 + 8x + 3 = 0$? Hence state if the equation has real roots.

**2** By working out the value of the discriminant, decide which of these equations have two distinct real roots.

A $\quad 2x^2 - 3x + 2 = 0$     B $\quad x^2 + 5x + 3 = 0$     C $\quad 3x^2 + 4x - 2 = 0$

D $\quad x^2 - 12x + 36 = 0$     E $\quad -3x^2 - 7x - 6 = 0$     F $\quad 5 - x - x^2 = 0$

**3** By working out the value of the discriminant, decide which of these equations can be solved by factorising.

A $\quad 5x^2 + 3x - 2 = 0$     B $\quad 6x^2 + 5x - 6 = 0$     C $\quad 4x^2 - 6x + 1 = 0$

**4** Solve these equations, where possible, by any method. Where appropriate, write your solutions in surd form, in terms of the simplest possible surds.

(a) $x^2 - 9x + 14 = 0$     (b) $x^2 - 8x + 14 = 0$     (c) $9x^2 - 6x + 1 = 0$

(d) $9x^2 - 5x + 1 = 0$     (e) $2x^2 - 5x + 2 = 0$     (f) $x^2 + 10x + 3 = 0$

**5** Use the value of the discriminant to decide which of these equations have a graph that

    (i) crosses the $x$-axis at two points

    (ii) just touches the $x$-axis at one point

    (iii) does not cross the $x$-axis

(a) $y = x^2 + 9x + 1$     (b) $y = 25 + 20x + 4x^2$     (c) $y = -3x^2 + 7x - 2$

(d) $y = 6x - 9x^2 - 1$     (e) $y = x^2 + x + 1$     (f) $y = \frac{1}{2}x^2 - 2x + \frac{1}{4}$

**6** For each equation, work out the values of $k$ that give an equation with equal roots.

(a) $4x^2 + kx + 25 = 0$     (b) $kx^2 + kx + 9 = 0$     (c) $x^2 + 2kx + 16 = 0$

**7** Determine the values of $k$ for which the equation $x^2 + kx + (2k - 3) = 0$ has equal roots.

**8 (a)** By completing the square, prove that the roots of $x^2 - 4kx + 9 = 0$ are $2k \pm \sqrt{4k^2 - 9}$.

  **(b)** Show that, for $k = \frac{3}{2}$, the equation $x^2 - 4kx + 9 = 0$ has equal roots.
  State another value of $k$ for which the equation has equal roots.

**9 (a)** By completing the square, find in terms of $k$ the roots of the equation $x^2 + 2kx - 7 = 0$.

  **(b)** Prove that, for all real values of $k$, the roots of $x^2 + 2kx - 7 = 0$ are real and different.

  **(c)** Given that $k = \sqrt{2}$, find the exact roots of the equation.                    Edexcel

**10 (a)** Show that $(2(a - 3))^2$ is equivalent to $4a^2 - 24a + 36$.

  **(b)** Determine the values of $k$ for which the equation $x^2 + 2(k - 3)x + (5k - 1) = 0$ has equal roots.

---

## Key points

- A **quadratic** expression can sometimes be **factorised** into two **linear factors**.
  An example is $x^2 + 4x + 3 = (x + 1)(x + 3)$.                                            (p 33)

- The graph of any quadratic expression in $x$ is a **parabola**.
  The graph of $y - q = k(x - p)^2$ is a **translation** of the graph of $y = kx^2$.

  Using **vector notation**, this translation can be described as $\begin{bmatrix} p \\ q \end{bmatrix}$.

  The equation can also be written as $y = k(x - p)^2 + q$.
  The vertex of the graph is $(p, q)$ and its line of symmetry is $x = p$.                  (pp 36–38)

- A quadratic expression can always be written in **completed-square form**,
  i.e. in the form $k(x + p)^2 + q$, where $k$, $p$ and $q$ are constants.
  An example is $2x^2 + 4x + 5 = 2(x + 1)^2 + 3$.                                            (pp 41–42)

- In the completed-square form of $x^2 + bx + c$, the constant inside the
  brackets is found by halving the coefficient of $x$.
  For example $x^2 - 6x + 5 = (x - 3)^2 - (-3)^2 + 5$
  $$= (x - 3)^2 - 9 + 5$$
  $$= (x - 3)^2 - 4$$                                                                        (p 41)

- A quadratic equation can sometimes be solved by factorising.
  An example is $x^2 - 3x - 4 = 0$
  $$\Rightarrow (x + 1)(x - 4) = 0$$
  $$\Rightarrow x = -1 \text{ and } x = 4$$                                                  (p 45)

- Any quadratic equation with real solutions can be solved by completing the square.
  An example is $x^2 - 4x - 3 = 0$
  $$\Rightarrow \qquad (x - 2)^2 - 7 = 0$$
  $$\Rightarrow \qquad (x - 2)^2 = 7$$
  $$\Rightarrow \qquad x - 2 = \pm\sqrt{7}$$
  $$\Rightarrow x = 2 + \sqrt{7} \text{ and } x = 2 - \sqrt{7}$$                              (p 47)

- Any quadratic equation $ax^2 + bx + c = 0$ with real solutions

  can be solved by using the formula $x = \dfrac{-b \pm \sqrt{b^2 - 4ac}}{2a}$ .

  An example is $x^2 - 4x - 3 = 0$

  $$\Rightarrow \quad x = \frac{-(-4) \pm \sqrt{(-4)^2 - 4 \times 1 \times (-3)}}{2 \times 1}$$

  $$= \frac{4 \pm \sqrt{28}}{2}$$

  $$= \frac{4 \pm 2\sqrt{7}}{2}$$

  $$= 2 \pm \sqrt{7} \qquad \text{(p 48)}$$

- The graph of $y = ax^2 + bx + c$ crosses the $y$-axis when $x = 0$, i.e. when $y = c$.
  It crosses or touches the $x$-axis if the equation $ax^2 + bx + c = 0$ has real solutions.

- The discriminant of $ax^2 + bx + c$ is the expression $b^2 - 4ac$.
  The value of the discriminant tells you the number of real solutions (roots)
  of the equation $ax^2 + bx + c = 0$. \qquad (p 50)

## Test yourself (answers p 174)

None of these questions requires a calculator.

**1** **(a)** Express $x^2 - 14x + 50$ in the form $(x - a)^2 + b$.

    **(b)** Find the least value of $x^2 - 14x + 50$.

**2** **(a)** Express $x^2 + 10x + 20$ in the form $(x + p)^2 + q$.

    **(b)** Sketch the graph of $y = x^2 + 10x + 20$, stating the coordinates of the vertex.

**3** **(a)** Find the constants $a$, $b$ and $c$ such that, for all values of $x$,
$$3x^2 - 6x + 10 = a(x + b)^2 + c$$

    **(b)** Hence write down the equation of the line of symmetry
of the curve $y = 3x^2 - 6x + 10$.

**4** **(a)** Express $x^2 + 5x + 1$ in the form $(x + p)^2 + q$.

    **(b)** Hence give the translation that maps the graph of $y = x^2$ to $y = x^2 + 5x + 1$.

**5** **(a)** Express $x^2 - 8x + 4$ in the form $(x + p)^2 + q$.

    **(b)** Hence, or otherwise, solve the equation $x^2 - 8x + 4 = 0$.
Write your answers in the form $a + b\sqrt{c}$, where $c$ is as small as possible.

**6** Solve the equation $2x^2 + 7x + 4 = 0$, giving your answers in surd form.

**7** Each of these graphs is a translation of $y = x^2$.
Determine the equation of each one in the form $y = ax^2 + bx + c$.

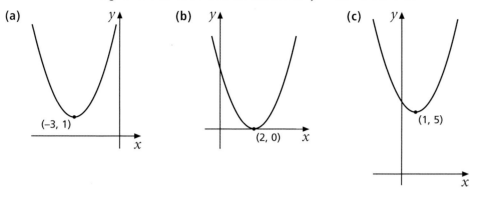

(a)

(−3, 1)

(b)

(2, 0)

(c)

(1, 5)

**8** Solve the equation $2x^2 - 8x - 1 = 0$.
Write your answers in the form $a + b\sqrt{2}$, where $a$ and $b$ are rational numbers.

**9 (a)** Express $\qquad 3x^2 + 24x + 40$
in the form $\qquad 3(x + p)^2 + q$
where $p$ and $q$ are integers.

**(b)** Hence write down the minimum value of $3x^2 + 24x + 40$.

**10 (a)** Express $4x^2 - 32x + 4$ in the form $a(x + b)^2 + c$.

**(b)** Hence find the coordinates of the vertex of the graph of $y = 4x^2 - 32x + 4$.

**(c)** Sketch the graph of $y = 4x^2 - 32x + 4$, giving the $x$-coordinates of the points where the graph meets the $x$-axis.

**11 (a)** Calculate the discriminant of $2x^2 - 3x + 5$.

**(b)** Hence state the number of real roots of the equation $2x^2 - 3x + 5 = 0$.

**12 (a)** When $y = 4 - (x - 5)^2$, write down the maximum value of $y$.

**(b)** Sketch the graph of $y = 4 - (x - 5)^2$, showing the coordinates of the points at which the graph meets the $x$- and $y$-axes.

**13 (a)** Prove, by completing the square, that the roots of the equation $x^2 + 2kx + c = 0$, where $k$ and $c$ are constants, are $-k \pm \sqrt{k^2 - c}$.

The equation $x^2 + 2kx + 81 = 0$ has equal roots.

**(b)** Find the possible values of $k$.

Edexcel

**\*14** A parabola has a vertex with coordinates $(-4, 1)$ and goes through the point with coordinates $(2, -17)$.
Find the equation of the parabola in the form $y = ax^2 + bx + c$.

# 4 Indices

In this chapter you will learn how to
- use the laws of indices to simplify expressions involving indices
- interpret positive, zero, negative and fractional indices
- solve equations that involve indices

## A Positive and negative indices

A number such as $2^5$ is called a power of 2 as it is of the form $2^n$.
The 5 is called the **index**. (The plural is **indices**.)

The following examples demonstrate three basic rules for manipulating powers.

- $x^6 \times x^2 = (x \times x \times x \times x \times x \times x) \times (x \times x) = x^8$

- $x^6 \div x^2 = \dfrac{x \times x \times x \times x \times x \times x}{x \times x} = x^4$

- $(x^6)^2 = x^6 \times x^6 = x^{12}$

K

The rules are
- $x^a \times x^h = x^{u+b}$      When multiplying powers, add the indices.
- $x^a \div x^b = x^{a-b}$      When dividing powers, subtract the indices.
- $(x^a)^b = x^{ab}$      When finding powers of powers, multiply the indices.

Using these rules, we can interpret expressions involving zero or negative indices.

The rule for multiplication gives $x^a \times x^0 = x^{a+0} = x^a$. It follows that

K    $x^0 = 1$

The rule for multiplication gives $x^a \times x^{-a} = x^{a+-a} = x^0 = 1$. It follows that

K    $x^{-a} = \dfrac{1}{x^a}$

---

| **Example 1** | **Solution** |
|---|---|
| Evaluate $(-2)^3$. | $(-2)^3 = -2 \times -2 \times -2 = -8$ |

---

| **Example 2** | **Solution** |
|---|---|
| Write $2^{-3}$ as a fraction. | $2^{-3} = \dfrac{1}{2^3} = \tfrac{1}{8}$ |

---

| **Example 3** | **Solution** |
|---|---|
| Evaluate $\left(\tfrac{2}{5}\right)^{-2}$ as a fraction. | $\left(\tfrac{2}{5}\right)^{-2} = \dfrac{1}{\left(\tfrac{2}{5}\right)^2} = \dfrac{1}{\left(\tfrac{4}{25}\right)} = \tfrac{25}{4}$     *Generally* $\dfrac{1}{\left(\tfrac{a}{b}\right)} = \dfrac{b}{a}$ |

---

**Example 4**

Write $\dfrac{2^4 \times 2}{2^7}$ in the form $2^n$.

**Solution**

$$\dfrac{2^4 \times 2}{2^7} = \dfrac{2^5}{2^7} = 2^{5-7} = 2^{-2}$$

---

**Example 5**

Write $9^4$ as a power of 3.

**Solution**

$$9^4 = (3^2)^4 = 3^{2 \times 4} = 3^8$$

---

**Example 6**

Simplify $\dfrac{\left(a^4\right)^2}{a^3}$.

**Solution**

$$\dfrac{\left(a^4\right)^2}{a^3} = \dfrac{a^{4 \times 2}}{a^3} = \dfrac{a^8}{a^3} = a^{8-3} = a^5$$

---

**Example 7**

Simplify $\dfrac{3n^4 \times 2n^3}{15n^{10}}$.

**Solution**

$$\dfrac{3n^4 \times 2n^3}{15n^{10}}$$

$$= \dfrac{3 \times 2 \times n^4 \times n^3}{15n^{10}}$$

$$= \dfrac{6n^7}{15n^{10}}$$

$$= \dfrac{6}{15} \times \dfrac{n^7}{n^{10}}$$

$$= \tfrac{2}{5} \times n^{7-10} \qquad \textit{Any fractions should be simplified.}$$

$$= \tfrac{2}{5} n^{-3} \qquad \textit{This can also be written as } \dfrac{2}{5n^3}.$$

---

**Example 8**

Write $\dfrac{1-x}{x^3}$ as the sum of powers of $x$.

**Solution**

$$\dfrac{1-x}{x^3} = \dfrac{1}{x^3} - \dfrac{x}{x^3} = x^{-3} - x^{-2}$$

*This is a sum as it could be written as $x^{-3} + -x^{-2}$.*

---

**Example 9**

Solve the equation $3^x = \tfrac{1}{9}$.

**Solution**

$$3^x = \tfrac{1}{9} = \dfrac{1}{3^2}$$

$$\Rightarrow \quad 3^x = 3^{-2}$$

$$\Rightarrow \quad x = -2$$

---

## Exercise A (answers p 175)

**1** Evaluate the following as integers or fractions.

(a) $3^5$  (b) $(-2)^5$  (c) $2^{-5}$  (d) $5^0$  (e) $(-10)^{-1}$

**2** Evaluate the following as decimals.

(a) $\left(\frac{3}{10}\right)^2$     (b) $2^{-2}$     (c) $8^{-1}$     (d) $10^{-4}$     (e) $100^{-3}$

**3** Evaluate the following as fractions.

(a) $\left(\frac{1}{3}\right)^3$     (b) $\left(-\frac{4}{7}\right)^2$     (c) $\left(\frac{2}{3}\right)^{-1}$     (d) $\left(\frac{3}{4}\right)^{-2}$     (e) $\left(\frac{5}{2}\right)^{-3}$

**4** Write each of these as a power of 2.

(a) $32$     (b) $\frac{1}{8}$     (c) $0.5$     (d) $1$     (e) $\frac{1}{64}$

**5** Write each of these in the form $p^n$, where $p$ is a prime number.

(a) $256$     (b) $\frac{1}{125}$     (c) $\frac{1}{16}$     (d) $\frac{1}{81}$     (e) $0.2$

**6** Write each of these as a power of 3.

(a) $\dfrac{3^2 \times 3^5}{3^4}$     (b) $\dfrac{3 \times 3^2}{3^5}$     (c) $\dfrac{1}{3^3 \times 3^4}$     (d) $(3^2)^5$     (e) $\dfrac{\left(3^3\right)^4}{3^2}$

**7** Write each of these as a power of 2.

(a) $4^2$     (b) $8^3$     (c) $2 \times 16^2$     (d) $16^{-1}$     (e) $4 \times 32^{-3}$

**8** (a) Write $\frac{1}{25}$ as a power of 5.

  (b) Hence show that $\left(\frac{1}{25}\right)^{-4}$ is equivalent to $5^8$.

**9** Write each of these as a power of 2.

(a) $\left(\frac{1}{4}\right)^5$     (b) $\left(\frac{1}{8}\right)^2$     (c) $\left(\frac{1}{16}\right)^{-1}$     (d) $\left(\frac{1}{2}\right)^{-3}$     (e) $\left(\frac{1}{32}\right)^{-2}$

**10** Simplify each of these.

(a) $\dfrac{n^2 \times n^6}{n^9}$     (b) $\dfrac{2n^3 \times 6n}{4n^6}$     (c) $n^5 \div n^{-3}$     (d) $5n^3 \div \dfrac{1}{n^3}$     (e) $(n^3)^6 \div \dfrac{1}{n^2}$

(f) $6n^5 \div 3n^{-2}$     (g) $\dfrac{5n^4 \times n^3}{10n^6}$     (h) $3n \div 9n^{-4}$     (i) $\dfrac{4n^2 \times 5n^3}{12n^7}$     (j) $8n^2 \div \dfrac{6}{n^3}$

**11** Write each of these as a sum of powers of 5.

(a) $5^3(5^2 + 5)$     (b) $\dfrac{5^2 + 5^3}{5}$     (c) $\dfrac{5^8 - 5^3}{5^2}$     (d) $\dfrac{5^2 + 5^4}{5^3}$     (e) $\dfrac{5^6 - 5^3 + 5^{-1}}{5^4}$

**12** Write each of these as a sum of powers of $x$.

(a) $x^2(1 + x^3)$     (b) $x^3(x^4 - x^{-2})$     (c) $\dfrac{1 + x^2}{x^4}$     (d) $\dfrac{x^6 + x^2 - x}{x^5}$     (e) $x^2\left(\dfrac{1 - x^5}{x^6}\right)$

**13** Solve each equation.

(a) $2^x = 512$     (b) $5^x = \frac{1}{25}$     (c) $2 \times 4^x = \frac{1}{8}$     (d) $\frac{1}{3}(2^x) = \frac{1}{96}$     (e) $6 \times 3^x = \frac{2}{27}$

**14** Find the positive solution of each equation.

(a) $x^{-2} = \frac{4}{25}$     (b) $x^{-3} = \frac{8}{125}$     (c) $x^{-2} = 0.09$     (d) $4x^{-5} = \frac{1}{8}$     (e) $2x^{-2} = \frac{9}{8}$

# B Roots and fractional indices

Square roots and cube roots occur often in solving area and volume problems.

For example, the cube root of 125 is 5 because $5$ cubed $= 5^3 = 5 \times 5 \times 5 = 125$ and so, if a cube has a volume of $125\,cm^3$, then the length of each edge is the cube root of 125 which is 5.

We can also have fourth roots, fifth roots, sixth roots, and so on.

For example, the fifth root of 32 is 2 because $2^5 = 32$.

> The symbol for the $n$th root of $a$ is $\sqrt[n]{a}$.
> (When $n$ is even, it stands for the **positive** $n$th root.)

For example, although $2^4$ and $(-2)^4$ are both equivalent to 16, we choose the positive value for the fourth root, so $\sqrt[4]{16} = 2$.

We write the square root of $x$ as just $\sqrt{x}$ rather than $\sqrt[2]{x}$.

The rules for manipulating powers enable us to interpret fractional indices.

The rule for multiplication gives $x^{\frac{1}{2}} \times x^{\frac{1}{2}} = x^{\frac{1}{2} + \frac{1}{2}} = x^1 = x$.

It follows that $x^{\frac{1}{2}} = \sqrt{x}$.

Similarly $x^{\frac{1}{3}} \times x^{\frac{1}{3}} \times x^{\frac{1}{3}} = x^{\frac{1}{3} + \frac{1}{3} + \frac{1}{3}} = x^1 = x$.

It follows that $x^{\frac{1}{3}} = \sqrt[3]{x}$.

> In general, $x^{\frac{1}{n}} = \sqrt[n]{x}$ (the $n$th root of $x$).
>
> The rule for finding powers of powers gives
>
> $\bullet\ x^{\frac{m}{n}} = \left(x^{\frac{1}{n}}\right)^m = \left(\sqrt[n]{x}\right)^m$    or
>
> $\bullet\ x^{\frac{m}{n}} = \left(x^m\right)^{\frac{1}{n}} = \sqrt[n]{(x^m)}$

---

**Example 10**

Evaluate $64^{\frac{1}{3}}$.

**Solution**

$64^{\frac{1}{3}} = \sqrt[3]{64} = 4$      $(4^3 = 4 \times 4 \times 4 = 64)$

---

**Example 11**

Evaluate $16^{\frac{3}{2}}$.

**Solution**

$16^{\frac{3}{2}} = \left(16^{\frac{1}{2}}\right)^3 = \left(\sqrt{16}\right)^3 = 4^3 = 64$

---

**Example 12**

Evaluate $32^{-\frac{2}{5}}$.

**Solution**

$32^{-\frac{2}{5}} = \dfrac{1}{32^{\frac{2}{5}}} = \dfrac{1}{\left(\sqrt[5]{32}\right)^2} = \dfrac{1}{2^2} = \dfrac{1}{4}$

---

**Example 13**

Evaluate $\left(\frac{27}{64}\right)^{-\frac{2}{3}}$.

**Solution**

$\left(\frac{27}{64}\right)^{-\frac{2}{3}} = \dfrac{1}{\left(\frac{27}{64}\right)^{\frac{2}{3}}} = \dfrac{1}{\left(\sqrt[3]{\frac{27}{64}}\right)^2} = \dfrac{1}{\left(\frac{3}{4}\right)^2} = \dfrac{1}{\frac{9}{16}} = \dfrac{16}{9}$

---

| **Example 14** | **Solution** |
|---|---|
| Write $8\sqrt{2}$ as a power of 2. | $8\sqrt{2} = 2^3 \times 2^{\frac{1}{2}} = 2^{3+\frac{1}{2}} = 2^{\frac{7}{2}}$ |

| **Example 15** | **Solution** |
|---|---|
| Simplify $\dfrac{a^{\frac{1}{3}} \times a^{\frac{1}{2}}}{a^{\frac{2}{3}}}$. | $\dfrac{a^{\frac{1}{3}} \times a^{\frac{1}{2}}}{a^{\frac{2}{3}}} = \dfrac{a^{\frac{1}{3}+\frac{1}{2}}}{a^{\frac{2}{3}}} = \dfrac{a^{\frac{5}{6}}}{a^{\frac{2}{3}}} = a^{\frac{5}{6}-\frac{2}{3}} = a^{\frac{1}{6}}$ |

| **Example 16** | **Solution** |
|---|---|
| Write $\dfrac{1+x}{\sqrt{x}}$ as the sum of powers of $x$. | $\dfrac{1+x}{\sqrt{x}} = \dfrac{1+x}{x^{\frac{1}{2}}} = \dfrac{1}{x^{\frac{1}{2}}} + \dfrac{x}{x^{\frac{1}{2}}} = x^{-\frac{1}{2}} + x^{\frac{1}{2}}$ |

| **Example 17** | **Solution** |
|---|---|
| Solve $x^{\frac{2}{3}} = 25$. | $x^{\frac{2}{3}} = 25$ |

$$\Rightarrow \quad \left(\sqrt[3]{x}\right)^2 = 25 \qquad or \quad \left(x^{\frac{1}{3}}\right)^2 = 25$$
$$\Rightarrow \quad \sqrt[3]{x} = 5 \qquad\quad or \quad x^{\frac{1}{3}} = 5$$
$$\Rightarrow \quad x = 5^3 = 125$$

**Exercise B** (answers p 175)

**1** Evaluate these.

(a) $36^{\frac{1}{2}}$  (b) $125^{\frac{1}{3}}$  (c) $16^{\frac{1}{4}}$  (d) $32^{\frac{1}{5}}$  (e) $1^{\frac{1}{6}}$

**2** Evaluate these.

(a) $9^{\frac{3}{2}}$  (b) $64^{\frac{2}{3}}$  (c) $81^{\frac{5}{4}}$  (d) $243^{\frac{3}{5}}$  (e) $128^{\frac{2}{7}}$

**3** Show that $125^{-\frac{2}{3}} = \frac{1}{25}$.

**4** Evaluate these as fractions.

(a) $9^{-\frac{1}{2}}$  (b) $64^{-\frac{1}{3}}$  (c) $4^{-\frac{5}{2}}$  (d) $243^{-\frac{2}{5}}$  (e) $16^{-\frac{3}{4}}$

**5** Show that $\left(\frac{1}{9}\right)^{\frac{3}{2}} = \frac{1}{27}$.

**6** Show that $\left(\frac{4}{9}\right)^{-\frac{3}{2}} = \frac{27}{8}$.

**7** Evaluate these as integers or fractions.

(a) $\left(\frac{1}{81}\right)^{\frac{1}{2}}$  (b) $\left(\frac{8}{27}\right)^{-\frac{1}{3}}$  (c) $\left(\frac{1}{4}\right)^{\frac{5}{2}}$  (d) $\left(\frac{8}{125}\right)^{\frac{2}{3}}$  (e) $\left(\frac{1}{8}\right)^{-\frac{4}{3}}$

**8** Write each of these as a power of $a$.

(a) $a^{\frac{1}{2}} \times a^2$  (b) $\dfrac{a^3}{a^{\frac{1}{2}}}$  (c) $a^{\frac{1}{2}} \times a^{\frac{1}{4}}$  (d) $a^{-\frac{1}{2}} \times a^{\frac{3}{2}}$

(e) $\left(a^{\frac{1}{2}}\right)^3$  (f) $\left(a^{10}\right)^{-\frac{1}{5}}$  (g) $\dfrac{\left(a^{\frac{2}{3}}\right)^{\frac{1}{2}}}{a}$  (h) $\dfrac{a^{-\frac{1}{2}} \times a^{\frac{3}{4}}}{a^{\frac{3}{8}}}$

**9** Write each of these as a power of 2.

   (a) $\sqrt{2}$      (b) $\sqrt[5]{2}$      (c) $\dfrac{1}{\sqrt{2}}$      (d) $\dfrac{2}{\sqrt{2}}$      (e) $2\sqrt{2}$

   (f) $16\sqrt{2}$      (g) $\dfrac{4}{\sqrt{2}}$      (h) $\dfrac{\sqrt{2}}{2}$      (i) $\dfrac{\sqrt{2}}{32}$      (j) $\dfrac{\sqrt{2}}{\sqrt[3]{2}}$

   (k) $2\sqrt{2} \times 4\sqrt{2}$   (l) $\sqrt{8}$      (m) $\left(\sqrt{2}\right)^4$      (n) $\left(2\sqrt{2}\right)^2$      (o) $\left(4\sqrt{2}\right)^3$

**10** Write $\left(x\sqrt{x}\right)^3$ as a power of $x$.

**11** Write each of these as a sum of powers of $x$.

   (a) $x^{\frac{1}{2}}\left(x^{\frac{1}{2}} + x^4\right)$   (b) $\dfrac{x^3 - x^5}{x^{\frac{3}{2}}}$    (c) $x\left(x\sqrt{x} - 1\right)$   (d) $\dfrac{1 - x}{\sqrt{x}}$    (e) $x^2\sqrt{x}\left(\sqrt{x} + x^3\right)$

**12** Write each of these in the form $ax^m$, where $a$ and $m$ are constants.

   (a) $\left(2\sqrt{x}\right)^2$   (b) $5\left(\sqrt{x}\right)^3$   (c) $\dfrac{6x}{3\sqrt{x}}$   (d) $\dfrac{4x^2}{8\sqrt{x}}$   (e) $\dfrac{\left(4\sqrt{x}\right)^2}{12\left(\sqrt{x}\right)^3}$

**13** Write each of these in the form $ax^m + bx^n$, where $a$, $b$, $m$ and $n$ are constants.

   (a) $2\sqrt{x}\left(3\sqrt{x} - 4\right)$   (b) $x^2\sqrt{x}\left(5\sqrt{x} + \dfrac{2}{\sqrt{x}}\right)$   (c) $\dfrac{2x^2 + 3x^5}{x\sqrt{x}}$   (d) $\dfrac{x^2\sqrt{x} - 6\sqrt{x}}{9x}$

**14** Solve each equation.

   (a) $\sqrt[3]{x} = 3$   (b) $\sqrt{x} = \frac{1}{7}$   (c) $\sqrt[4]{x} = 1$   (d) $\sqrt[5]{x} = 2$   (e) $\sqrt[3]{x} = \frac{2}{5}$

**15** Find a positive integer or fraction that satisfies each equation.

   (a) $x^{\frac{1}{2}} = 5$   (b) $x^{-\frac{1}{2}} = \frac{1}{4}$   (c) $x^{\frac{1}{3}} = \frac{2}{3}$   (d) $x^{-\frac{1}{4}} = 1$   (e) $x^{\frac{2}{3}} = 9$

   (f) $x^{\frac{4}{5}} = 16$   (g) $x^{-\frac{3}{4}} = \frac{1}{27}$   (h) $x^{-\frac{5}{2}} = \frac{1}{243}$   (i) $x^{\frac{2}{3}} = \frac{1}{9}$   (j) $x^{-\frac{3}{2}} = 8$

## C Further problems

Sometimes there are different ways to solve an equation that involves indices.
Each example below shows just one method of solution but you may be able
to think of others.

---

**Example 18**

Solve $9^x = \frac{1}{27}$.

**Solution**

*Write the expressions $9^x$ and $\frac{1}{27}$ as powers of 3.*      $9^x = (3^2)^x = 3^{2x}$ and

$$\frac{1}{27} = \frac{1}{3^3} = 3^{-3}$$

$$\text{So } 9^x = \tfrac{1}{27} \quad \Rightarrow \quad 3^{2x} = 3^{-3}$$

$$\Rightarrow \quad 2x = -3$$

$$\Rightarrow \quad x = -\tfrac{3}{2}$$

---

## Example 19

Solve $\dfrac{5^x}{\sqrt{5}} = \dfrac{1}{5}$.

**Solution**

*Write the expressions $\dfrac{5^x}{\sqrt{5}}$ and $\dfrac{1}{5}$ as powers of 5.*

$$\dfrac{5^x}{\sqrt{5}} = \dfrac{5^x}{5^{\frac{1}{2}}} = 5^{x - \frac{1}{2}} \text{ and }$$

$$\tfrac{1}{5} = 5^{-1}$$

$$\text{So } \dfrac{5^x}{\sqrt{5}} = \tfrac{1}{5} \quad \Rightarrow \quad 5^{x - \frac{1}{2}} = 5^{-1}$$

$$\Rightarrow \quad x - \tfrac{1}{2} = -1$$

$$\Rightarrow \quad x = -\tfrac{1}{2}$$

## Example 20

Solve $16^x \times 2^{x-1} = 2\sqrt{2}$.

**Solution**

*Work in powers of 2.*

$$16^x \times 2^{x-1} = 2\sqrt{2}$$

$$(2^4)^x \times 2^{x-1} = 2 \times 2^{\frac{1}{2}}$$

$$\Rightarrow \quad 2^{4x} \times 2^{x-1} = 2^1 \times 2^{\frac{1}{2}}$$

$$\Rightarrow \quad 2^{5x-1} = 2^{\frac{3}{2}}$$

$$\Rightarrow \quad 5x - 1 = \tfrac{3}{2}$$

$$\Rightarrow \quad 5x = \tfrac{5}{2}$$

$$\Rightarrow \quad x = \tfrac{1}{2}$$

## Example 21

Solve $3^{2x+1} - 10 \times 3^x + 3 = 0$.

**Solution**

*Write $3^{2x+1}$ in terms of $3^x$.*

$$3^{2x+1} = 3^1 \times 3^{2x} = 3 \times (3^x)^2$$

*Now write the equation $3^{2x+1} - 10 \times 3^x + 3 = 0$ in terms of $3^x$.*

$$3 \times (3^x)^2 - 10 \times 3^x + 3 = 0$$

*Use the substitution $y = 3^x$ to rewrite the equation in terms of $y$.*

$$3y^2 - 10y + 3 = 0$$

*Solve the equation by factorising.*

$$(3y - 1)(y - 3) = 0$$

$$\Rightarrow \quad y = \tfrac{1}{3} \text{ or } y = 3$$

$$y = \tfrac{1}{3} \text{ gives } 3^x = \tfrac{1}{3} \Rightarrow x = -1$$

$$\text{and} \quad y = 3 \text{ gives } 3^x = 3 \Rightarrow x = 1$$

**Exercise C** (answers p 175)

**1** Solve each equation.

(a) $9^{x+1} = 81$    (b) $5^{3x} = 25$    (c) $3^{2x+1} = 1$    (d) $5^{x-3} = \frac{1}{5}$    (e) $2^{3x} = \frac{1}{64}$

**2** Write each of these as a power of 3.

(a) $(3^x)^2$    (b) $3 \times 3^x$    (c) $9 \times 3^{3x}$    (d) $\dfrac{3^x}{3^2}$    (e) $\sqrt{3^x}$

**3** Write each of these as a power of 2.

(a) $4^x$    (b) $8^x$    (c) $\left(\frac{1}{16}\right)^x$    (d) $\dfrac{32^x}{2}$    (e) $\dfrac{2^x}{\sqrt{2}}$

(f) $\dfrac{8^x}{4}$    (g) $\dfrac{4^5}{2^x}$    (h) $\left(\sqrt{2}\right)^x$    (i) $\dfrac{16^x}{2\sqrt{2}}$    (j) $\dfrac{8^x}{4^x}$

**4** Solve each equation.

(a) $9^x = 3$    (b) $16^x = \frac{1}{4}$    (c) $8^x = \frac{1}{2}$    (d) $8^x = 4$    (e) $27^{2x} = 9$

(f) $243^x = \frac{1}{27}$    (g) $8^{2x} = 16$    (h) $25^{2x+1} = \frac{1}{5}$    (i) $125^{\frac{x}{3}} = \frac{1}{25}$    (j) $\left(\frac{1}{16}\right)^x = 8$

**5** Solve each equation.

(a) $4^x \times 8^x = 2$    (b) $3^x \times 9^x = \sqrt{3}$    (c) $\sqrt{5} \times 5^x = 25$    (d) $7^x \times 49 = \sqrt{7}$

(e) $\dfrac{27^x}{9^x} = 9\sqrt{3}$    (f) $\dfrac{7^x}{\sqrt{7}} = \frac{1}{7}$    (g) $4^x \times 2^{3-x} = \frac{1}{8}$    (h) $9^x \times 3^{x-1} = \sqrt{3}$

(i) $8 \times 2^{3x} = 2\sqrt{2}$    (j) $\left(\sqrt{5}\right)^x = \dfrac{1}{\sqrt{125}}$

**6** Solve each equation.

(a) $27^y = 3^{1+y}$    (b) $25^x = 5^{1-x}$    (c) $\left(\sqrt{3}\right)^p = 3^{p-3}$    (d) $\left(\frac{1}{4}\right)^n = 8^{n+1}$

**7** Given that $y = 3^x$, show that $3^{2x} = y^2$.

**8** Given that $u = 2^x$, show that $8^x = u^3$.

**9** Given that $x = 5^n$, show that $5^{n+2} = 25x$.

**10** (a) Using the substitution $y = 2^x$, show that the equation $2^{2x} - 5 \times 2^x + 4 = 0$ can be written in the form $y^2 - 5y + 4 = 0$.

(b) Hence solve the equation $2^{2x} - 5 \times 2^x + 4 = 0$.

**11** (a) Using the substitution $n = 5^x$, show that the equation $25^x - 6 \times 5^x + 5 = 0$ can be written in the form $n^2 - 6n + 5 = 0$.

(b) Hence solve the equation $25^x - 6 \times 5^x + 5 = 0$.

**12** (a) Using the substitution $u = 3^x$, show that the equation $9^x - 4 \times 3^{x+1} + 27 = 0$ can be written in the form $u^2 - 12u + 27 = 0$.

(b) Hence solve the equation $9^x - 4 \times 3^{x+1} + 27 = 0$.

**13 (a)** Using the substitution $y = 9^x$, write the equation $81^x - 4 \times 9^x + 3 = 0$ in terms of $y$.

**(b)** Hence solve the equation $81^x - 4 \times 9^x + 3 = 0$.

**14 (a)** Using the substitution $n = 5^x$, show that the equation $5^{2x+1} - 6 \times 5^x + 1 = 0$ can be written in the form $5n^2 - 6n + 1 = 0$.

**(b)** Hence solve the equation $5^{2x+1} - 6 \times 5^x + 1 = 0$.

**15 (a)** Using the substitution $u = 2^x$, show that the equation $4^{x+1} - 33 \times 2^x + 8 = 0$ can be written in the form $4u^2 - 33u + 8 = 0$.

**(b)** Hence solve the equation $4^{x+1} - 33 \times 2^x + 8 = 0$.

**\*16 (a)** Using the substitution $y = 2^x$, show that the equation $4^{x-1} - 2^x + 1 = 0$ can be written in the form $y^2 - 4y + 4 = 0$.

**(b)** Hence solve the equation $4^{x-1} - 2^x + 1 = 0$.

**\*17 (a)** Using the substitution $u = 4^x$, write the equation $2^{4x-1} - 4^{x+\frac{1}{2}} + 2 = 0$ in terms of $u$.

**(b)** Hence solve the equation $2^{4x-1} - 4^{x+\frac{1}{2}} + 2 = 0$.

---

## Key points

- The rules for manipulating indices are

  $x^a \times x^b = x^{a+b}$

  $x^a \div x^b = x^{a-b}$

  $(x^a)^b = x^{ab}$ (p 54)

- $x^0 = 1$ (p 54)

- $x^{-a} = \dfrac{1}{x^a}$ (p 54)

- $x^{\frac{1}{n}} = \sqrt[n]{x}$ (the $n$th root of $x$) (p 57)

- $x^{\frac{m}{n}} = \left(\sqrt[n]{x}\right)^m$ or $\sqrt[n]{\left(x^m\right)}$ (p 57)

## Test yourself (answers p 176)

None of these questions requires a calculator

**1** Evaluate the following as integers or fractions.

   **(a)** $2^{-4}$      **(b)** $49^{\frac{1}{2}}$      **(c)** $8^{-\frac{1}{3}}$      **(d)** $25^{\frac{3}{2}}$      **(e)** $16^{-\frac{3}{4}}$

**2** Solve each equation.

   **(a)** $3^x = 1$      **(b)** $x^{-3} = \frac{1}{27}$      **(c)** $\left(\frac{1}{2}\right)^x = 4$      **(d)** $x^{\frac{1}{2}} = 5$      **(e)** $27^x = \frac{1}{9}$

**3** Simplify $\dfrac{a^{\frac{1}{2}} \times a^{\frac{3}{4}}}{a^{\frac{1}{4}}}$.

**4** Write $\dfrac{1 + x^2}{\sqrt{x}}$ as a sum of powers of $x$.

**5** Show that $\dfrac{\sqrt{x}\left(5 - 6x^3\sqrt{x}\right)}{10x}$ is equivalent to $\frac{1}{2}x^{-\frac{1}{2}} - \frac{3}{5}x^3$.

**6** Given that $2^x = \dfrac{1}{\sqrt{2}}$ and $2^y = 4\sqrt{2}$

   **(a)** find the exact value of $x$ and the exact value of $y$

   **(b)** calculate the exact value of $2^{y-x}$                                               Edexcel

**7** Given that $3^x = 9^{y-1}$, show that $x = 2y - 2$.                              Edexcel

**8** Solve the equation $16^x = 2^{x+1}$.

**9 (a)** Express $\dfrac{5^{x+1}}{\sqrt{5}}$ as a power of 5.

   **(b)** Solve the equation $\dfrac{5^{x+1}}{\sqrt{5}} = 25$.

**10 (a)** Given that $8 = 2^k$, write down the value of $k$.

   **(b)** Given that $4^x = 8^{2-x}$, find the value of $x$.                        Edexcel

**11** Solve these equations.

   **(a)** $25^x \times 5^{3-x} = \frac{1}{125}$                **(b)** $3^{3x+1} = 9\sqrt{3}$

**12 (a)** Using the substitution $u = 7^x$, show that the equation $7^{2x+1} - 8 \times 7^x + 1 = 0$ can be written in the form $7u^2 - 8u + 1 = 0$.

   **(b)** Hence solve the equation $7^{2x+1} - 8 \times 7^x + 1 = 0$.

# 5 Further equations

In this chapter you will learn how to
- solve equations where rearrangement is involved
- form and solve quadratic equations to solve problems
- solve simultaneous equations where one is linear and one is quadratic
- use the discriminant to find the relationship between two graphs

## A Rearranging to solve equations: revision

Sometimes it is necessary to rearrange an equation to make it easier to solve.

---

**Example 1**

Solve the equation $2(x-1) = x(5-x)$, giving your solutions in surd form.

**Solution**

$$2(x-1) = x(5-x)$$

*Expand the brackets.*                    $2x - 2 = 5x - x^2$

*Add $x^2$ to both sides.*                 $x^2 + 2x - 2 = 5x$

*Subtract $5x$ from both sides.*           $x^2 - 3x - 2 = 0$

*The quadratic expression does not factorise,*   $x = \dfrac{-(-3) \pm \sqrt{(-3)^2 - 4 \times 1 \times (-2)}}{2 \times 1}$
*so use the formula to solve the equation.*

$$= \dfrac{3 \pm \sqrt{17}}{2}$$

*These are the exact solutions in surd form.*   $x = \dfrac{3 - \sqrt{17}}{2}$ or $\dfrac{3 + \sqrt{17}}{2}$

As decimals, these solutions are $-0.562$ and $3.562$ (to 3 d.p.).
You can check these solutions by substituting back into the original equation.

---

**Example 2**

Solve $\dfrac{2}{x} = \dfrac{4}{x+2}$.

**Solution**

$$\dfrac{2}{x} = \dfrac{4}{x+2}$$

*Multiply each side by $x(x+2)$, the 'LCM'*    $\dfrac{2x(x+2)}{x} = \dfrac{4x(x+2)}{x+2}$
*of the denominators.*

*Cancel.*                        $2(x+2) = 4x$

*Multiply out the brackets.*     $2x + 4 = 4x$

*Rearrange.*                     $2x = 4$

$\Rightarrow$                    $x = 2$

---

**Example 3**

Solve $\dfrac{2}{x} = \dfrac{x+2}{4}$ .

**Solution**

$$\frac{2}{x} = \frac{x+2}{4}$$

*Multiply each side by 4x, the 'LCM' of the denominators.*

$$\frac{8x}{x} = \frac{4x(x+2)}{4}$$

*Cancel.*

$$8 = x(x+2)$$

*Multiply out the brackets.*

$$8 = x^2 + 2x$$

*Subtract 8 from both sides.*

$$x^2 + 2x - 8 = 0$$

*The quadratic expression factorises.*

$$(x+4)(x-2) = 0$$

$$\Rightarrow \qquad x = -4 \text{ or } 2$$

---

**Exercise A** (answers p 177)

**1** Solve each equation.
   Give exact solutions, using surd form where appropriate.

   (a) $x^2 = 8x$     (b) $x^2 + 2x = 15$     (c) $x^2 = 4(x+3)$

   (d) $4(x-6) = 3(2-x)$     (e) $x(x-3) = 2(x-3)$     (f) $5x^2 + 12 = 23x$

   (g) $3x^2 + x = 5$     (h) $2x(6x+1) = 5(1-x)$     (i) $2x^2 + x = 6x + 1$

**2** Solve each equation.
   Give exact solutions, using surd form where appropriate.

   (a) $x + 1 = \dfrac{6}{x}$     (b) $\dfrac{x}{5} = \dfrac{1}{x+6}$     (c) $\dfrac{x+8}{3} = \dfrac{3}{x}$

   (d) $\dfrac{x}{5} = \dfrac{3}{2x+7}$     (e) $\dfrac{x}{2+x} = \dfrac{1}{x-3}$     (f) $\dfrac{4x}{x-3} = \dfrac{3}{x+10}$

   (g) $\dfrac{x+5}{6} = \dfrac{x-1}{3}$     (h) $\dfrac{5}{x} = \dfrac{10-x}{5}$     (i) $x = \dfrac{x-7}{x+7}$

   (j) $2x = \dfrac{45}{x} - 1$     (k) $\dfrac{x+2}{x} = \dfrac{3}{4}$     (l) $\dfrac{4x}{x-1} = \dfrac{6}{x-3}$

**3** Solve each equation.
   Give solutions correct to three decimal places.

   (a) $x = \dfrac{3}{x}$     (b) $x(5x+1) = 1 + x(x-3)$

   (c) $3x - 1 = \dfrac{1}{x}$     (d) $(2x+3)^2 + x^2 = 7$

   (e) $\dfrac{4x-1}{5} = \dfrac{x}{6}$     (f) $\dfrac{x}{2} = \dfrac{1}{8+x}$

## B Solving problems

Some problems can be solved by forming an equation, solving it and interpreting the solution.

---

### Example 4

The path round a square lawn is 1 metre wide and made from rectangular slabs.
If the area of the path and the area of the lawn are equal, find the area of the lawn, to 2 d.p.

**Solution**

Let $x$ be the length of the lawn.

*It's often a good idea to draw a diagram.*

*Here the path is shown split into
four equal rectangles, each $x + 1$ by 1.*

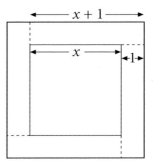

Area of lawn $= x^2$
Area of path $= 4(x + 1)$

*The areas of the path and lawn are the same.*

$$x^2 = 4(x + 1)$$
$$\Rightarrow x^2 - 4x - 4 = 0$$

*The quadratic expression does not factorise,
so use formula to solve the equation.*

$$x = \frac{-(-4) \pm \sqrt{(-4)^2 - 4 \times 1 \times (-4)}}{2 \times 1}$$

$$= \frac{4 \pm \sqrt{32}}{2}$$

$$\Rightarrow x = 4.828\ldots \text{ or } -0.828\ldots$$

*We ignore the negative root as the length is positive.*

Hence the area of the lawn is $(4.828\ldots)^2 = 23.31\,\text{m}^2$ (to 2 d.p.)

---

### Example 5

Find the coordinates of the points of intersection
of the graphs of $y = x + 1$ and $y = x^2 + 3x - 2$.

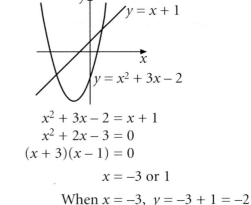

**Solution**

*Where the graphs intersect it is true that*

$$x^2 + 3x - 2 = x + 1$$
$$\Rightarrow \qquad x^2 + 2x - 3 = 0$$

*The quadratic expression factorises.*

$$(x + 3)(x - 1) = 0$$

$$\Rightarrow \qquad x = -3 \text{ or } 1$$

*Substitute into $y = x + 1$ for each value of x.*

When $x = -3$, $y = -3 + 1 = -2$
When $x = 1$, $y = 1 + 1 = 2$

So the points of intersection are $(-3, -2)$ and $(1, 2)$.

---

**Exercise B** (answers p 177)

**1** The path round a square lawn is 2 metres wide.
If the area of the path is equal to the area of the lawn
find the perimeter of the lawn, correct to 3 d.p.

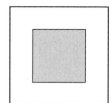

**2** The diagram shows a sketch of the
graphs of $y = \dfrac{x-2}{2}$ and $y = \dfrac{6}{x-3}$.
They intersect at two points.
Find the coordinates of both points of intersection.

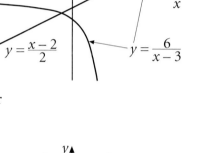

**3** Work out the coordinates of the points of intersection for
the graphs of $y = 2x^2 + x$ and $y = 2(2 - 3x)$.

**4** The sketch shows the graphs of
$y = x^2 - x - 1$ and $y = x + 1$.
They intersect at two points.

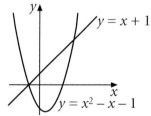

(a) Show that one of the points of intersection is
$(1 - \sqrt{3}, 2 - \sqrt{3})$.

(b) Find the coordinates of the other point of intersection in surd form.

**5** A rectangle has width 1 unit and length $x$ units.
A square is cut off it as shown.

The rectangle left behind is similar to
the original rectangle.

Find the value of $x$ in surd form.

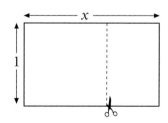

The value of $x$ is called the Golden Ratio.
You may like to find out more about this fascinating number.

**6** A market trader sells radios. She finds that the number of radios she
sells each week depends on the profit she makes per radio.

She uses a formula to estimate the approximate number she will
sell each week. It is

$$N = 60 - 6p$$

where $N$ is the number of radios sold per week and £$p$ is the profit per radio.

(a) Write an expression, in terms of $p$, for the total profit per week from these radios.

(b) One week she wants to make a profit of £80 from her radios.
What profit per radio should she choose?
Show carefully how you decided.

(c) Could she make of profit of £200 per week?
Explain your answer carefully.

## C Solving simultaneous equations by substitution

**Example 6**

The difference between two positive numbers is 2.
Their product is 4.
What are the two numbers?

**Solution**

Let $x$ and $y$ be the two numbers.

*Form a pair of simultaneous equations.*

$$x - y = 2$$
$$xy = 4$$

*Rearrange the first equation.*

$$x = y + 2 \qquad \textit{It could be rearranged as } y = x - 2.$$

*Substitute in the second equation.*

$$(y + 2)y = 4$$
$$\Rightarrow \ y^2 + 2y - 4 = 0$$

*The quadratic expression does not factorise so use completing the square.*

$$(y + 1)^2 - 5 = 0$$
$$\Rightarrow \quad (y + 1)^2 = 5$$
$$\Rightarrow \qquad y + 1 = \pm\sqrt{5}$$
$$\Rightarrow \qquad\qquad y = -1 + \sqrt{5} \ \text{ or } \ -1 - \sqrt{5}$$

*We reject $-1 - \sqrt{5}$ as we know the numbers are positive.*

One number must be $\sqrt{5} - 1$.

*Substitute into $x = y + 2$.*

The other is $\sqrt{5} - 1 + 2 = \sqrt{5} + 1$.
So the two numbers are $\sqrt{5} - 1$ and $\sqrt{5} + 1$.

**Example 7**

Solve the simultaneous equations

$$y - 2x = 7$$
$$x^2 + xy + 2 = 0$$

**Solution**

*Rearrange the first equation.*                     $y = 7 + 2x$

*Substitute in the second equation.*        $x^2 + x(7 + 2x) + 2 = 0$

*Multiply out the brackets and rearrange.*        $3x^2 + 7x + 2 = 0$

*The quadratic expression factorises.*        $(3x + 1)(x + 2) = 0$

$$\Rightarrow \qquad\qquad x = -\tfrac{1}{3} \text{ or } -2$$

*Substitute into $y = 7 + 2x$ to find*
*the corresponding values of $y$.*

When $x = -\tfrac{1}{3}$, $y = 7 + 2 \times -\tfrac{1}{3} = 6\tfrac{1}{3}$
When $x = -2$, $y = 7 + 2 \times -2 = 3$

So the two solutions are

$x = -\tfrac{1}{3}, y = 6\tfrac{1}{3}$ and $x = -2, y = 3$

*Each solution is a **pair** of values so $x = -\tfrac{1}{3}, y = 6\tfrac{1}{3}$ is **one** solution.*

**Exercise C** (answers p 177)

**1** Solve each pair of simultaneous equations.

(a) $y = x^2$
  $6x + y = 7$

(b) $y = x + 1$
  $xy - 4x = 10$

(c) $y = x^2 + 5$
  $x + 4y = 23$

(d) $x = y - 2$
  $x^2 + y^2 = 10$

(e) $y = x - 3$
  $\dfrac{y}{x} = x + 5$

(f) $x = 3 - 2y$
  $2xy - y^2 + 8 = 0$

**2** The graphs of $y = x + 9$ and $xy = 5(x + 1)$ intersect.
Work out the coordinates of both points of intersection.

**3** Two functions are given by $y = \tfrac{1}{2}x^2 - 2x + 1$ and $y = 4 - x$, where $-2 \le x \le 5$.

(a) On graph paper, draw accurate graphs of the functions on the same set of axes.

(b) Use your graphs to estimate to 1 d.p. the coordinates of each point of intersection.

(c) Use algebra to find these coordinates correct to 3 d.p.

**4** Solve each pair of simultaneous equations.

(a) $x + y = 6$
  $x^2 = 16 - 3y$

(b) $y - x = 3$
  $x^2 + xy + y^2 = 21$

(c) $2y + x = 5$
  $3y^2 + 4xy = 0$

**5** Solve each pair of simultaneous equations.
Where appropriate, give your answer using the simplest possible surds.

(a) $y = x + 5$
$y = x^2 - 3x + 1$

(b) $y + 2x = 3$
$x^2 - xy = 9$

(c) $x^2 - 2y = 1$
$\dfrac{y}{x} + 2 = x$

**6** Two positive numbers differ by 2 and have a product of 10.
Find the two numbers exactly.

**7** The perimeter of a rectangle is $20\,\text{cm}$.
The length of one of its diagonals is $3\sqrt{6}\,\text{cm}$.
Work out the dimensions of the rectangle in surd form.

**8** The graphs of $x = y + 4$ and $y = x^2 + (1 - 2\sqrt{5})x - 3$ intersect.
Work out the coordinates of the points of intersection.
Give the coordinates using the simplest possible surds.

**\*9** The graphs of $y = x^2 - 4$ and $x^2 + y^2 = 9$ intersect.
Work out the coordinates of all the points of intersection, correct to 3 d.p.

## D Counting points of intersection

In a plane, two distinct straight lines either intersect at one point or are parallel.

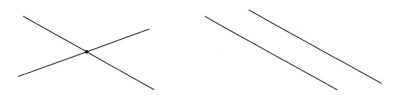

A line and a curve can intersect any number of times depending on the 'wiggliness' of the curve and the position of the line.

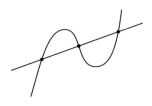

The line meets the curve at three points of intersection.

The line does not meet the curve.

The line meets the curve at four points of intersection.

The line meets the curve at one point. It is a tangent to the curve.

Consider the parabola $y = x^2 + 1$ and the straight line $y = 4x - 3$.

Where they intersect, the $x$-values will satisfy the equation

$$x^2 + 1 = 4x - 3$$

which rearranges to give $\qquad x^2 - 4x + 4 = 0$

$$\Rightarrow \qquad (x - 2)^2 = 0$$

so $x = 2$ is the only solution.

When $x = 2$, $y = 2^2 + 1 = 5$.
So the only point that lies on the curve and the straight line is (2, 5).

This means that the straight line just
touches the curve at one point.
So it is a tangent to the curve.

We can see that the straight line is a tangent to the curve just by looking at
the value of the discriminant of $x^2 - 4x + 4 = 0$.

The value of the discriminant is $(-4)^2 - 4 \times 1 \times 4 = 0$ so the solution is $x = \dfrac{4 \pm \sqrt{0}}{2} = \dfrac{4}{2} = 2$.

Whenever the discriminant is 0, the equation has just one real root.
Hence the straight line meets the curve at just one point and is a tangent to the curve.

Consider the parabola $y = 2x^2 - 4x + 5$ and the straight line $y + x = 3$.

The equation $y + x = 3$ rearranges to give $y = 3 - x$.
So, where the graphs intersect, the $x$-values will satisfy the equation

$$2x^2 - 4x + 5 = 3 - x$$

which rearranges to give $\qquad 2x^2 - 3x + 2 = 0$

The value of the discriminant is $(-3)^2 - 4 \times 2 \times 2 = 9 - 16 = -7$.
The value is negative so we know that the equation has no real roots.

Hence the straight line does not intersect the curve.
This is confirmed by a sketch.

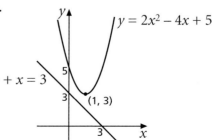

**Exercise D** (answers p 178)

**1** Show that the straight line $y = 3x + 2$ and the curve $y = x^2 + 2x + 4$ do not intersect.

**2** Show that the straight line $y = 1 - 2x$ is a tangent to the curve $y = x^2 - 6x + 5$.

**3 (a)** Show that $y - x = 5$ is a tangent to the curve $y = 2x^2 + 13x + 23$.

   **(b)** Find the coordinates of the point where the straight line meets the curve.

**4** Determine the relationship between the graphs of the following pairs of equations.
Each pair of graphs is a straight line and a parabola.
Do they intersect at two points, meet at one point, or fail to meet at all?

   **(a)** $y + x = 10$            **(b)** $y = 2x - 9$            **(c)** $y = 5 - 4x^2$
   
   $\quad\ y = 3x^2 - 2x - 3$      $\quad\ y = (x - 4)^2$         $\quad\ y + 3x = 6$

**5** Show that the line $x = -1$ does not intersect the curve $y^2 = 4x$.

**6** The graph of $y = 2x + k$ meets the graph of $y = x^2 - 4x + 2$ at only one point.
Find the value of $k$.

**7** The line $y = 3x - 5$ is a tangent to the curve $y = 2x^2 + 9x + k$.
Find the value of $k$.

**8** Show that it is impossible to find two real numbers with a product of 5 and a sum of 4.

**9** The line $y = 1 + kx$ is a tangent to the curve $y = 3x^2 + 5x + 13$.
Find two possible values for $k$.

---

**Key points**

- Some problems can be solved by forming an equation and solving it.
  The solution needs to be interpreted in the context of the original problem.
  For example, a length cannot be negative.                                    (p 66)

- A pair of simultaneous equations can be represented as graphs and the solutions
  interpreted as points of intersection.

- A pair of simultaneous equations can be solved by substituting
  to eliminate one of the unknowns.                                            (pp 68–69)

- If a pair of simultaneous equations leads to a quadratic equation then
  the discriminant tells you the geometrical relationship between
  the graphs of the equations.

  If the value of the discriminant is negative, the graphs do not intersect.

  If the value of the discriminant is positive, the graphs intersect at two points.

  If the value of the discriminant is zero, the graphs meet at just one point.   (pp 70–71)

## Test yourself (answers p 178)

None of these questions requires a calculator.

**1** The area of the rectangle below is 2 square units.

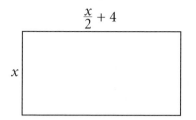

Find the length of each edge in surd form.

**2 (a)** Solve the simultaneous equations

$$y = 2x + 10$$
$$y = 3x^2 - 4x + 1$$

**(b)** Hence write down the coordinates of the points of intersection of the graphs of $y = 2x + 10$ and $y = 3x^2 - 4x + 1$.

**3** Find the values of $x$ and $y$ that satisfy the simultaneous equations

$$y = x - 1$$
$$2x^2 - 3xy + x = 3$$

**4** Solve the simultaneous equations

$$x = 2y - 2$$
$$x^2 = y^2 + 7$$

Edexcel

**5 (a)** Solve the simultaneous equations

$$y = 3x - 5$$
$$y = x^2 - 5x + 11$$

**(b)** Hence describe the geometrical relationship between the straight line with equation $y = 3x - 5$ and the parabola with equation $y = x^2 - 5x + 11$, giving a reason for your answer.

**6** Solve the simultaneous equations

$$x + 2y = 1$$
$$2y^2 + 3xy + 1 = 0$$

**7** Show that the straight line with equation $x + y = 2$ and the curve with equation $y^2 + 7x = 0$ do not intersect.

# 6 Inequalities

In this chapter you will learn how to
• solve linear and quadratic inequalities
• solve problems by forming and solving inequalities

## A  Linear inequalities: revision (answers p 179)

**A1** (a) Decide whether the inequality $3t > t + 6$ is true or false when

(i) $t = 5$　　　(ii) $t = 0$　　　(iii) $t = 4\frac{1}{2}$　　　(iv) $t = -2$　　　(v) $t = 3$

(b) Which of these inequalities describes **all** the values of $t$ for which $3t > t + 6$?

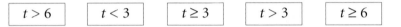

| $t > 6$ | $t < 3$ | $t \geq 3$ | $t > 3$ | $t \geq 6$ |

**A2** The diagram shows sketch graphs of
$y = 2x + 1$ and $y = x + 6$.

(a) Work out the $x$-coordinate of $A$,
the point of intersection.

(b) How can you tell from the graph
that $2x + 1 < x + 6$ when $x = 2$?

(c) Give an inequality that describes the
values of $x$ for which $2x + 1 \geq x + 6$.

(d) Give an inequality that describes the
values of $x$ for which $2x + 1 < x + 6$.

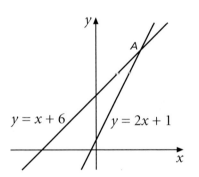

**A3** The diagram shows sketch graphs of
$y = -2x - 1$ and $y = x + 5$.

(a) Work out the $x$-coordinate of $B$,
the point of intersection.

(b) Give an inequality that describes the
values of $x$ for which $-2x - 1 > x + 5$.

(c) Give an inequality that describes the
values of $x$ for which $-2x - 1 < x + 5$.

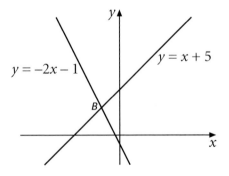

**A4** (a) Decide if the inequality $-p + 3 \geq p - 2$ is satisfied when

(i) $p = 3$　　　(ii) $p = 2$　　　(iii) $p = 0$　　　(iv) $p = 1.4$　　　(v) $p = 2.5$

(b) Which of these inequalities describes **all** the values of $p$ for which $-p + 3 \geq p - 2$?

| $p > 2.5$ | $p < 2.5$ | $p \leq 2.5$ | $p \geq 2.5$ |

The complete set of values that satisfies an equation or inequality is called the **solution set**.

We can see from the diagram that
$2x - 1 > x + 2$ has the solution set $x > 3$.

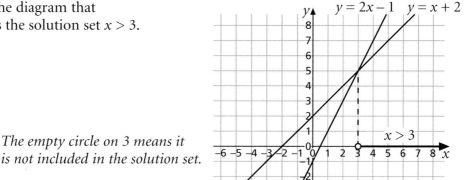

*The empty circle on 3 means it
is not included in the solution set.*

Will the solution set change if we operate on each side of the inequality in the same way?

For example, subtracting 7 from each side gives

$$2x - 1 - 7 > x + 2 - 7$$

which is $\qquad 2x - 8 > x - 5$

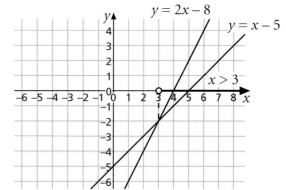

We can see from the diagram that
$2x - 8 > x - 5$ also has the solution set $x > 3$.

So subtracting 7 from both sides of the inequality
has not changed the solution set.

Multiplying each side by $-1$ gives

$$-1(2x - 1) > -1(x + 2)$$

which is $\qquad -2x + 1 > -x - 2$

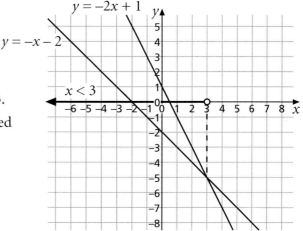

We can see from the diagram that
$-2x + 1 > -x - 2$ has the solution set $x < 3$.

So multiplying both sides by $-1$ has changed
the solution set by **reversing** the direction
of the inequality.

**D**

**A5** What symbol, $>$ or $<$, must be used in the inequality $-2x + 1 \;\square\; -x - 2$ so that
it has the same solution set as $2x - 1 > x + 2$?

**A6** What happens to the solution set if a positive or negative number is added to or
subtracted from both sides of the inequality?
What if you multiply or divide both sides by a positive or negative number?

Finding the solution set of an inequality is called **solving** an inequality.

An inequality such as $2x + 1 \geq x - 7$ is called a **linear inequality** as each expression $2x + 1$ and $x - 7$ is linear.

A linear inequality can be solved like a linear equation except that **multiplying or dividing each side by a negative number reverses the direction of the inequality sign**.

---

**Example 1**

Solve $1 - (x + 4) > 2(2x + 1)$.

**Solution**

$$1 - (x + 4) > 2(2x + 1)$$
$$\Rightarrow \quad 1 - x - 4 > 4x + 2$$
$$\Rightarrow \quad -x - 3 > 4x + 2$$
$$\Rightarrow \quad -3 > 5x + 2$$
$$\Rightarrow \quad -5 > 5x$$
$$\Rightarrow \quad -1 > x$$

that is $\qquad x < -1$ *We usually write the variable on the left.*

---

**Example 2**

Solve $-3x + 10 \leq 4$.

**Solution**

$$-3x + 10 \leq 4$$

*You could add 3x to both sides but here 10 is subtracted from each side.* $\qquad -3x \leq -6$

*Divide each side by $-3$ (remembering to reverse the inequality sign).* $\qquad x \geq 2$

---

**Exercise A** (answers p 179)

**1** Solve the following inequalities.

(a) $5x - 9 \geq 6$      (b) $6y + 1 < 3y + 7$      (c) $3 > 1 + 2z$

(d) $6p - 3 < 10p - 15$      (e) $7 - 2q \leq 1$      (f) $-4a + 5 > 13$

(g) $5b + 3 \geq 2b - 3$      (h) $3 - 2x > 2 - 3x$      (i) $1 - \frac{1}{3}y < 4$

(j) $7z + 1 \leq 4z + 9$      (k) $6 + w < 9 - 5w$      (l) $5 - d \geq 7 + 6d$

**2** Solve the following inequalities.

(a) $2(3x - 1) < 3x + 1$      (b) $3(x + 2) > 11(x - 2)$      (c) $15 - (1 + 2x) \geq 3(3x - 10)$

(d) $4(2y - 1) > 3(y - 2)$      (e) $2y + 1 \leq 7 - 2(y - 3)$      (f) $8 + \frac{1}{2}(y - 6) > y + 9$

**3** Solve the following inequalities.

(a) $\dfrac{x + 6}{5} < 2(x - 3)$      (b) $\dfrac{2(x + 1)}{3} > \dfrac{x - 4}{5}$      (c) $\dfrac{2x + 1}{2} - \dfrac{x - 1}{3} \leq 5$

## B Linear inequalities: solving problems

Some problems can be solved by forming an inequality, solving it and interpreting the solution.

---

**Example 3**

The *Toneway Times* charges a flat rate of £3.25 plus an extra 10p per word to place an advertisement in the 'For Sale' column.

The *Somerlea Gazette* charges 20p per word.

Form and solve an inequality to find when it is cheaper to advertise in the *Toneway Times*.

**Solution**

Let $n$ be the number of words in the advertisement.

Then the cost of the ad (in pence) in the *Toneway Times* is $\qquad$ $325 + 10n$
and the cost of the same ad in the *Somerlea Gazette* is $\qquad$ $20n$

It is less expensive in the *Toneway Times* when $\qquad$ $325 + 10n < 20n$

$$\Rightarrow \qquad 325 < 10n$$

$$\Rightarrow \qquad n > 32.5$$

So it is cheaper to use the *Toneway Times* when the advertisement uses 33 words or more.

---

**Exercise B** (answers p 179)

1 Eve employs a part-time gardener. She pays him a 'retainer' of £11.00 per week plus £8.00 for every hour she asks him to work. A National Insurance contribution must be paid if the total weekly payment is greater than £73.00.

Form and solve an inequality to find the length of time worked beyond which National Insurance must be paid.

2 Cutting Edge hire out tools.
For chain saws, they charge a fixed fee of £10.00 plus £2.00 per day.
A rival company, Helping Hands, charges a fixed fee of £5.00 plus £3.50 per day.

Form and solve an inequality to find when it is less expensive to hire a chain saw from Cutting Edge.

3 A piece of wire is to be bent to make an isosceles triangle.
The base is to be 6 cm longer than each of the other two sides.
Let $l$ cm be the length of the base.

$l$ cm

(a) (i) Show that $l$ must be greater than 12.

(ii) Show that the total length of wire used must be greater than 24 cm.

(b) The maximum length of wire available is 1 metre.
Show that $l$ must satisfy $l \le 37\frac{1}{3}$ cm.

**4** Jamie is fencing off part of his garden. It is to be a rectangular area with a wall along one side and the other three sides fenced as shown in the diagram.

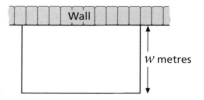

He wants to use 40 metres of fencing.

(a) Explain why the width, $w$, must satisfy the inequality $w < 20$.

(b) Write down the length of the rectangle in terms of $w$.

(c) Jamie wants to plant bushes round the edge of the whole rectangle. He will not have enough bushes if the perimeter is more than 60 m.

   (i) Show that $w$ must satisfy the inequality $80 - 2w \leq 60$.

   (ii) Solve this inequality and hence find the minimum possible value of $w$.

## C Quadratic inequalities (answers p 179)

**C1** (a) Decide whether the inequality $x^2 < 9$ is true or false if

   (i) $x = 5$      (ii) $x = 2.5$      (iii) $x = -2$      (iv) $x = -4$      (v) $x = -3$

   (b) Which of these inequalities describes **all** the values of $t$ for which $x^2 < 9$?

| $x < 3$ | $-3 \leq x \leq 3$ | $x \leq 3$ | $-3 < x < 3$ |
|---|---|---|---|

**C2** The diagram shows a sketch graph of $y = x^2 - 25$.

(a) Work out the coordinates of points $A$ and $B$.

(b) Write down a pair of inequalities that describe the values of $x$ for which $x^2 - 25 \geq 0$.

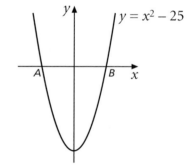

**C3** The diagram shows sketch graphs of $y = x^2 + 2x + 3$ and $y = x + 5$.

(a) Work out the coordinates of the points of intersection, $P$ and $Q$.

(b) Write down an inequality that describes the values of $x$ for which $x^2 + 2x + 3 < x + 5$.

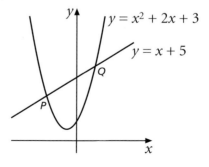

A graphical approach can be used in solving quadratic inequalities.

---

**Example 4**

Solve the inequality $x^2 + x - 6 > 0$.

**Solution**

*Find where the graph of $y = x^2 + x - 6$ cuts the x-axis.*

*The quadratic expression factorises.*

$$x^2 + x - 6 > 0$$
$$x^2 + x - 6 = 0$$
$$(x + 3)(x - 2) = 0$$
$$\Rightarrow \quad x = -3 \text{ or } x = 2$$

*So a sketch graph of $y = x^2 + x - 6$ is*

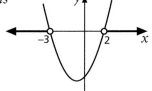

*The heavy lines on the x-axis show where the inequality $x^2 + x - 6 > 0$ is satisfied.*

The solution is the set of values given by $x < -3$ and $x > 2$.

---

**Example 5**

Solve the inequality $x(x + 2) \leq 1$.

**Solution**

*Expand the brackets.*

*Rearrange the inequality to get zero on one side.*

*Find where the graph of $y = x^2 + 2x - 1$ cuts the x-axis.*

*The quadratic does not factorise so use the formula.*

$$x(x + 2) \leq 1$$
$$x^2 + 2x \leq 1$$
$$x^2 + 2x - 1 \leq 0$$
$$x^2 + 2x - 1 = 0$$

$$x = \frac{-2 \pm \sqrt{2^2 - 4 \times (-1)}}{2}$$
$$= \frac{-2 \pm \sqrt{8}}{2}$$
$$= \frac{-2 \pm 2\sqrt{2}}{2}$$
$$= -1 \pm \sqrt{2}$$

*So a sketch graph of $y = x^2 + 2x - 1$ is*

The solution is the set of values given by $-1 - \sqrt{2} \leq x \leq -1 + \sqrt{2}$.

An approach that uses number lines is useful when the quadratic factorises. It involves looking at each factor separately and then looking at the product.

For example, to solve the inequality $2x^2 - 5x - 3 < 0$,
first factorise to give $(2x + 1)(x - 3) < 0$.

So we need to find where the product of $(2x + 1)$ and $(x - 3)$ is negative.

A sign diagram is

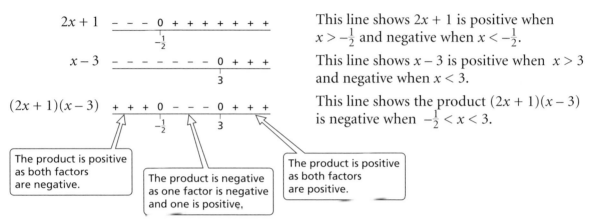

This line shows $2x + 1$ is positive when $x > -\frac{1}{2}$ and negative when $x < -\frac{1}{2}$.

This line shows $x - 3$ is positive when $x > 3$ and negative when $x < 3$.

This line shows the product $(2x + 1)(x - 3)$ is negative when $-\frac{1}{2} < x < 3$.

The product is positive as both factors are negative.

The product is negative as one factor is negative and one is positive,

The product is positive as both factors are positive.

So the solution set is the range of values given by $-\frac{1}{2} < x < 3$.

This method of using number lines has the advantage that you don't have to sketch a graph in order to solve an inequality. This is especially useful in harder examples where a graph might be hard to visualise.

**C4** Use the number line method to solve the inequality $(x + 4)(x - 7) \geq 0$.

**C5** Use the number line method to solve the inequality $(x + 5)(3 - x) \geq 0$. (Be careful with the factor $(3 - x)$.)

**C6** Show that the solution of $x^2 < 5$ is the set of values given by $-\sqrt{5} < x < \sqrt{5}$.

**C7** Show that the solution of $x^2 > 5$ is the set of values given by $x < -\sqrt{5}$ and $x > \sqrt{5}$.

The solution of an inequality of the form $x^2 < k$ is the set of values $-\sqrt{k} < x < \sqrt{k}$.

The solution of an inequality of the form $x^2 > k$ is the set of values $x < -\sqrt{k}$ and $x > \sqrt{k}$.

**Exercise C** (answers p 179)

**1** Solve these inequalities.

(a) $x^2 + 3x - 10 < 0$

(b) $x^2 + 11x + 18 \geq 0$

(c) $x^2 - 9x + 18 > 0$

(d) $x^2 - 5x - 14 \leq 0$

(e) $x^2 - 3x \geq 0$

(f) $x^2 - 4 > 0$

**2** Solve these inequalities.

(a) $2q^2 + 9q - 5 < 0$      (b) $3k^2 - 11k - 4 > 0$      (c) $3y^2 + 12y \geq 0$

(d) $2p^2 + 5p - 3 \leq 0$      (e) $3a^2 - a < 0$      (f) $6t^2 + 5t - 6 \geq 0$

**3** Solve these inequalities, leaving all values in surd form.

(a) $x^2 - 2 < 0$      (b) $x^2 - 2x - 1 \geq 0$      (c) $2x^2 + 4x - 1 < 0$

**4** Solve these inequalities.

(a) $k^2 > 25$      (b) $k^2 - 2k < 3$      (c) $k^2 + 3k \geq 10$

(d) $2k^2 + 8k > k + 4$      (e) $k^2 < 5k$      (f) $3k^2 < 15$

(g) $k^2 > 2k + 2$      (h) $k^2 + 3k > 1 - 3k^2$      (i) $4k^2 < 9$

**5** (a) Show that the inequality $6x - x^2 < 5$ is equivalent to $x^2 - 6x + 5 > 0$.

     (b) Hence solve $6x - x^2 < 5$.

**6** (a) Show that the inequality $5x - x^2 > 6$ is equivalent to $(2 - x)(x - 3) > 0$.

     (b) Hence solve $5x - x^2 > 6$.

**7** Solve these inequalities.

(a) $9 - x^2 > 0$      (b) $-x^2 + 3x + 4 < 0$      (c) $14 - x^2 < 5x$

**8** (a) Show that the inequality $y(y + 2) < 8$ is equivalent to $y^2 + 2y - 8 < 0$.

     (b) Hence solve $y(y + 2) < 8$.

**9** Solve these inequalities.

(a) $x(x - 6) < x - 12$      (b) $(y + 5)(y + 1) < 12$      (c) $2(k^2 - 1) > k(1 - k)$

**10** (a) Write $x^2 + 2x - 15$ in completed square form.

     (b) Hence solve $x^2 + 2x < 15$.

**\*11** Solve each inequality, explaining your answers carefully.

(a) $x^2 + 4x + 5 > 0$      (b) $x^2 + 2x + 1 < 0$

**\*12** Solve the inequality $\dfrac{x - 4}{x - 1} \leq 0$ using the number line method.

**\*13** Solve these inequalities.

(a) $\dfrac{x + 3}{x + 5} > 0$      (b) $(x + 2)(x - 1)(x + 4) \geq 0$      (c) $\dfrac{x^2 + 4x - 5}{x - 6} < 0$

**\*14** Solve these inequalities.

(a) $\dfrac{2x - 5}{x + 1} < 1$      (b) $\dfrac{2x - 7}{x + 5} > 4$

## D Inequalities and the discriminant (answers p 180)

You know that the discriminant of the equation $ax^2 + bx + c = 0$ is the expression $b^2 - 4ac$.

- If the value of the discriminant is less than zero, the equation has no real roots.
- If the value of the discriminant is greater than or equal to zero, the equation has real roots.

**D1** (a) What is the value of the discriminant of the equation $x^2 + 3x + 1 = 0$?

(b) How does this tell you that the equation has real roots?

**D2** (a) What is the value of the discriminant of the equation $x^2 + x + 1 = 0$?

(b) How does this tell you that the equation has no real roots?

**D3** (a) Write down the discriminant of the equation $x^2 + kx + 1 = 0$.

(b) Find the values of $k$ for which the equation has real roots.

**D4** (a) Write down the discriminant of the equation $x^2 + kx + k = 0$.

(b) Find the values of $k$ for which the equation has no real roots.

---

### Example 6

The equation $x^2 + kx + 2k = 0$ has real roots.
Find the set of possible values of $k$.

### Solution

The discriminant is $\qquad\qquad k^2 - 4 \times 2k = k^2 - 8k$

*The discriminant cannot be negative so* $\quad k^2 - 8k \geq 0$

$$k(k - 8) \geq 0$$

A sign diagram is

| | |
|---|---|
| $k$ | – – – 0 + + + + + + + |
| | 0 |
| $k - 8$ | – – – – – – – 0 + + + |
| | 8 |
| $k(k - 8)$ | + + + 0 – – – 0 + + + |
| | 0    8 |

*With practice, you may be able to omit the first two lines.*

*Alternatively, use a graphical approach.*

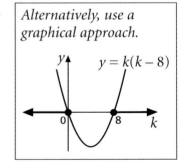

$y = k(k - 8)$

The possible values for $k$ are given by $k \leq 0$ and $k \geq 8$.

---

## Example 7

Find the values of $k$ for which the equation $kx^2 + kx + \frac{1}{2}(k-1) = 0$ has no real roots.

### Solution

The discriminant is
$$k^2 - 4 \times k \times \tfrac{1}{2}(k-1) = k^2 - 2k(k-1)$$
$$= k^2 - 2k^2 + 2k$$
$$= 2k - k^2$$

*The discriminant must be less than zero so*
$$2k - k^2 < 0$$
$$k(2-k) < 0$$

A sign diagram is

$k$  – – – 0 + + + + + + +
           0

*Take care with this factor.*  $2 - k$  + + + + + + + 0 – – –
                   2

$k(2-k)$  – – – 0 + + + 0 – – –
              0       2

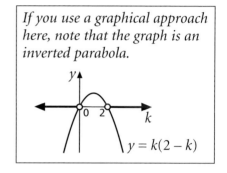

*If you use a graphical approach here, note that the graph is an inverted parabola.*

$y = k(2-k)$

Hence the values for $k$ are given by $k < 0$ and $k > 2$.

## Exercise D (answers p 180)

**1** The equation $x^2 + kx + 16 = 0$, where $k$ is a constant, has real roots.
  **(a)** Show that $k^2 - 64 \geq 0$.
  **(b)** Hence find the set of possible values for $k$.

**2** Work out the values for $k$ for which each equation has real roots.
  **(a)** $5x^2 + kx + 5 = 0$      **(b)** $x^2 + 3kx + k = 0$      **(c)** $x^2 + (k+3)x - k = 0$

**3** The equation $x^2 + 4kx + 5k = 0$, where $k$ is a constant, has **distinct** real roots. Find the set of possible values for $k$.

**4** Work out the values for $k$ for which each equation has distinct real roots.
  **(a)** $x^2 + kx + 4k = 0$      **(b)** $kx^2 - 3x + k = 0$      **(c)** $(2k-3)x^2 + kx + (k-1) = 0$

**5** Show that $x^2 - kx + 2 = 0$ does not have real roots when $-2\sqrt{2} < k < 2\sqrt{2}$.

**6** Work out the values for $k$ for which each equation has no real roots.
  **(a)** $x^2 + 2kx + 3 = 0$      **(b)** $x^2 - kx + 3 - k = 0$      **(c)** $(2k-1)x^2 + (k+1)x + k = 0$

**7** Show that $kx^2 - (k + 4)x + 4 = 0$ has real roots for all possible real values of $k$.

**8** A parabola has equation $y = x^2 + 6x + 2$.
A line has equation $y = 3x + k$, where $k$ is a constant.
Find the possible values for $k$ so that the line intersects the parabola at two points.

**9** A parabola has equation $y = -x^2 + 5x - 5$.
A line has equation $y = kx - 1$, where $k$ is a constant.
Find the possible values for $k$ so that the line does not intersect the parabola.

## E Quadratic inequalities: solving problems

### Example 8

Harry is digging a rectangular flower bed.
The perimeter of the bed is to be $60\,\text{m}$ and the area is to be at least $200\,\text{m}^2$.
Work out the range of possible values for the width of the flower bed.

### Solution

Let $w$ be the width of the rectangle.
A diagram is

$30 - w$

$w$

*The perimeter is $60\,\text{m}$ so the sum of the width and length is $30\,\text{m}$*

*The area is at least $200\,\text{m}^2$ so you have the inequality*

$$w(30 - w) \geq 200$$
$$\Rightarrow \quad 30w - w^2 \geq 200$$

*Rearrange the inequality and get zero on one side.*

$$-w^2 + 30w - 200 \geq 0$$

*Multiplying each side by $-1$ reverses the direction of the inequality.*

$$w^2 - 30w + 200 \leq 0$$

*The quadratic factorises so you can use number lines.*

$$(w - 10)(w - 20) \leq 0$$

A sign diagram is

$w - 10$   $-\ -\ -\ 0\ +\ +\ +\ +\ +\ +\ +$
                    $10$

$w - 20$   $-\ -\ -\ -\ -\ -\ -\ 0\ +\ +\ +$
                                  $20$

$(w - 10)(w - 20)$   $+\ +\ +\ 0\ -\ -\ -\ 0\ +\ +\ +$
                              $10$           $20$

The solution set is the range of values given by $10 \leq w \leq 20$.

So the width of the flower bed can be between $10\,\text{m}$ and $20\,\text{m}$.

## Example 9

The diagrams on the right show the
first four pentagonal numbers   1, 5, 12, 22, ...

The $n$th pentagonal number is $\dfrac{n(3n-1)}{2}$.

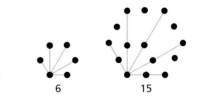

Work out the first pentagonal number that is greater than 100.

### Solution

*You have the inequality*                                        $\dfrac{n(3n-1)}{2} > 100$

*Multiply both sides by 2.*                                     $n(3n-1) > 200$

$\Rightarrow \qquad\qquad\qquad 3n^2 - n > 200$

*Rearrange the inequality to get zero on one side.*     $3n^2 - n - 200 > 0$

*The quadratic factorises so you can use number lines.*   $(3n - 25)(n + 8) > 0$

A sign diagram is

$$3n - 25 \qquad - \; - \; - \; - \; - \; - \; 0 \; + \; + \; + $$
$$8\tfrac{1}{3}$$

$$n + 8 \qquad - \; - \; - \; 0 \; + \; + \; + \; + \; + \; + \; +$$
$$-8$$

$$(3n - 25)(n + 8) \qquad + \; + \; + \; 0 \; - \; - \; - \; 0 \; + \; + \; +$$
$$-8 \qquad\qquad 8\tfrac{1}{3}$$

The solution set is the range of values given by  $n < -8$ and $n > 8\tfrac{1}{3}$.

In this context, $n$ cannot be negative or fractional so the first value of $n$ that
satisfies these inequalities here is 9.

This gives the pentagonal number $\dfrac{9(27-1)}{2} = 117$

---

## Exercise E (answers p 180)

**1** The diagrams on the right show the
first three hexagonal numbers  1, 6, 15, ...

The $n$th hexagonal number is $n(2n - 1)$.

**(a)** By writing an inequality and solving it, find the value of $n$ that gives the first
hexagonal number greater than 465.

**(b)** What is the first hexagonal number that is greater than 465?

**2** Susie is designing a stand for an exhibition.
It is to have display screens round three sides and to be open on the other side.
40 m of screens are available for the stand and the owners want a rectangular
floor space of at least 150 square metres.

What limits must Susie work within for the lengths of the sides of the stand?

**3** The $n$th triangle number is $\dfrac{n(n+1)}{2}$.

   **(a)** By writing an inequality and solving it, find the value of $n$ that gives
       the first triangle number greater than 100.

   **(b)** What is the first triangle number greater than 100?

   **(c)** What value of $n$ gives the first triangle number greater than 1000?

**4** The specification for a new rectangular car park states that its length, $x$ m, is to be
5 m more than its width. The perimeter of the car park is to be greater than 32 m.

   **(a)** Form a linear inequality in $x$.

   The area of the car park is to be less than 104 m$^2$.

   **(b)** Form a quadratic inequality in $x$.

   **(c)** By solving your inequalities, determine the range of possible values of the
       length of the car park.
Edexcel

---

## Key points

- A linear inequality can be solved like a linear equation except that **multiplying or
  dividing each side by a negative number reverses the direction of the inequality sign**.
  For example, multiplying both sides of $4 - \frac{1}{2}x > 5$ by $-2$ gives $-8 + x < -10$.     (p 76)

- A quadratic inequality can be solved using a graphical or an algebraic approach.
  For example, the inequality $x^2 + 4x - 5 < 0$ factorises to give $(x + 5)(x - 1) < 0$.

| Graphical approach | Algebraic approach (using a sign diagram) |
|---|---|
| <br>The curve lies below the $x$-axis<br>for $-5 < x < 1$.   (p 79) | <br>The product is negative for $-5 < x < 1$.  (p 80) |

- If the equation $ax^2 + bx + c = 0$ has real roots, then $b^2 - 4ac \geq 0$.
  If the equation $ax^2 + bx + c = 0$ does not have real roots, then $b^2 - 4ac < 0$.   (p 82)

## Test yourself (answers p 181)

None of these questions requires a calculator.

**1** The *Hambridge Advertiser* charges £5.00 plus an extra 20p per word to publish a Valentine's Day message.

The *Cadzow Times* charges £2.50 plus an extra 50p per word.

Form and solve an inequality to find when it is cheaper to use the *Cadzow Times* for a Valentine's Day message.

**2 (a)** Solve the inequality $3x - 8 > x + 13$.

**(b)** Solve the inequality $x^2 - 5x - 14 > 0$.

Edexcel

**3** Solve these inequalities.

**(a)** $2y + 3 < 1 - 2(y + 2)$          **(b)** $2x^2 + 17x < 9$

**4** Find the set of values for which $(2x + 1)(x - 2) > 2(x + 5)$

Edexcel

**5** Solve $x^2 - 4x + 1 > 0$.

**6** Find the set of values of $x$ for which

**(a)** $6x - 7 < 2x + 3$

**(b)** $2x^2 - 11x + 5 < 0$

**(c)** both $6 - x < 2x + 3$ and $2x^2 - 11x + 5 < 0$.

Edexcel

**7** The equation $x^2 + 5kx + 2k = 0$, where $k$ is a constant, has real roots.

**(a)** Prove that $k(25k - 8) \geq 0$.

**(b)** Hence find the set of possible values of $k$.

Edexcel

**8** The height of a particular ball is given by the formula $h = 12t - 5t^2$, where $h$ is the height above the ground in metres and $t$ is the time in seconds.

Form and solve an inequality to find when the height of the ball above the ground is less than 4 metres.

**9** Jo is designing a rectangular pool.
The perimeter is to be 100 m and the area is to be at least 525 m$^2$.
Work out the possible values for the width of the pool.

**10** A parabola has equation $y = x^2 + 1$.
A line has equation $y = kx - 3$, where $k$ is a constant.
Find the possible values for $k$ so that the line intersects the parabola at two points.

**\*11** A circle has equation $x^2 + y^2 = 20$.
A line has a gradient of 2 and intersects the circle at two points.
Find the possible values for the $y$-intercept of the line.

# 7 Polynomials

In this chapter you will learn how to
- evaluate and manipulate powers of the form $kx^n$, where $n$ is a positive integer ·
- sketch cubic graphs and consider the effect of translations on their equations
- multiply out brackets to give a polynomial expression
- relate the roots of a polynomial to where its graph crosses the $x$-axis
- use function notation

## A Indices: revision

**Example 1**

Evaluate $5x^3$ when $x = 2$.

**Solution**

When $x = 2$, $\quad 5x^3 = 5 \times 2^3$ $\qquad$ *This is not the same as* $(5 \times 2)^3$.
$\qquad\qquad\qquad = 5 \times 8$
$\qquad\qquad\qquad = 40$

**Example 2**

Simplify $2x \times 3x^2$.

**Solution**

$2x \times 3x^2 = 2 \times x \times 3 \times x \times x$
$\qquad\qquad = 2 \times 3 \times x \times x \times x$
$\qquad\qquad = 6x^3$

**Exercise A** (answers p 181)

**1** Evaluate these when $n = 3$.
(a) $n^2 + n^3$ (b) $2n^2$ (c) $(2n)^2$ (d) $(n + 2)^3$ (e) $3(n + 1)^2$
(f) $3n^2 - 5n$ (g) $2n^5 - 3n$ (h) $\frac{1}{3}n^4 + 1$ (i) $2(n^3 - 7)$ (j) $(n - 1)^3 + n^3$

**2** Evaluate these when $x = \frac{1}{2}$.
(a) $6x^2$ (b) $(6x)^2$ (c) $5x(2x - 1)$ (d) $(x - 1)^3$

**3** Evaluate these when $a = -1$.
(a) $10a^4$ (b) $a^9$ (c) $5a^5$ (d) $4(a + 3)^3$

**4** Simplify each of these.
(a) $5x \times x^2$ (b) $4x^2 \times 3x$ (c) $2x^2 \times 5x^3$ (d) $\frac{1}{4}x^3 \times 8x$
(e) $5x^2 \times \frac{1}{3}x$ (f) $(2x)^3$ (g) $(3x^2)^2$ (h) $(\frac{1}{2}x^3)^2$

## B Cubic graphs (answers p 181)

**B1** Use a graph plotter on a computer or graphic calculator to draw some graphs of the form $y = ax^3 + bx^2 + cx + d$, where $a, b, c$ and $d$ are constants.
Include some where the value of $a$ is negative.
What do you notice about the shapes of your graphs?

**B2** Use a graph plotter to draw each graph below.
How many times does each one cross or touch the $x$-axis?

$$y = x^3 + 3x^2 + 4x + 5 \qquad y = x^3 - 2x^2 - x + 2 \qquad y = x^3 - x^2 - x + 1$$

**B3** Use a graph plotter to draw graphs of the three equations below.

$$y = x^3 \qquad\qquad y = x^3 - x \qquad\qquad y = x^3 + x$$

Describe the shape of each graph as fully as you can.
Make sketches that show clearly the shape of each graph for $-1 \le x \le 1$.

**B4** For each equation below

(i)  make a sketch to show what you think the graph will look like

(ii) check by graphing on a graph plotter

**(a)** $y = -x^3$ **(b)** $y = x^3 + 2$ **(c)** $y = -x^3 - 5$

**B5** **(a)** Make a sketch of $y = x^3$.

**(b)** Sketch what you think the graph of $y = (x - 2)^3$ will look like.

**(c)** Check on a graph plotter.

**B6** For each equation below, sketch what you think the graph will look like and then check on a graph plotter.

**(a)** $y = (x + 4)^3$ **(b)** $y = (x - 2)^3 + 5$ **(c)** $y = (x + 6)^3 - 7$

**B7** The graph of $y = x^3$ is translated

by $\begin{bmatrix} 3 \\ -1 \end{bmatrix}$ as shown in the diagram.

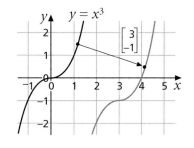

(a) Which do you think is the correct equation for the new graph?

**A** $y = (x - 3)^3 + 1$ **B** $y = (x - 3)^3 - 1$
**C** $y = (x + 3)^3 + 1$ **D** $y = (x + 3)^3 - 1$

(b) Check on a graph plotter.

(c) Work out where the new graph crosses the $y$-axis.

**B8** The graph of $y = x^3$ is translated by $\begin{bmatrix} -2 \\ 4 \end{bmatrix}$.

(a) Write down what you think is the correct equation for the translated graph.

(b) Work out where the translated graph crosses the $y$-axis.

We can work algebraically when translating curves.

In the diagram below, the graph of $y = x^3$ has been translated 3 units to the right and 1 unit up.

Using vector notation this translation is represented by $\begin{bmatrix} 3 \\ 1 \end{bmatrix}$.

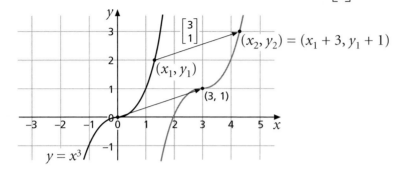

Let $(x_1, y_1)$ be a point on $y = x^3$ and let $(x_2, y_2)$ be its image on the translated curve.

Then $(x_2, y_2) = (x_1 + 3, y_1 + 1)$ giving

$$x_1 = x_2 - 3 \qquad \textit{from rearranging } x_2 = x_1 + 3$$
and $\qquad y_1 = y_2 - 1 \qquad \textit{from rearranging } y_2 = y_1 + 1$

We know that $y_1 = x_1{}^3$, so it must be true that

$$y_2 - 1 = (x_2 - 3)^3$$
and so $\qquad y - 1 = (x - 3)^3 \qquad$ is the equation of the transformed curve.

This can be written as $y = (x - 3)^3 + 1$.

---

So to find the equation of the curve that is the result of translating $y = x^3$ by $\begin{bmatrix} 3 \\ 1 \end{bmatrix}$ replace $x$ by $(x - 3)$ and $y$ by $(y - 1)$.

---

**B9** Which translation will transform the curve $y = x^3$ to $y = (x - 5)^3 + 3$?

**B10** The graph of $y = x^3 + x$ is translated by $\begin{bmatrix} 2 \\ -9 \end{bmatrix}$.

(a) Which do you think is the correct equation for the new graph?

    **A** $y = (x + 2)^3 + (x + 2) + 9$         **B** $y = (x + 2)^3 + (x + 2) - 9$

    **C** $y = (x - 2)^3 + (x - 2) + 9$         **D** $y = (x - 2)^3 + (x - 2) - 9$

(b) Check by graphing on a graph plotter.

(c) Work out where the new graph crosses the $y$-axis.

---

**K** To find the equation of any curve after it has been translated by $\begin{bmatrix} p \\ q \end{bmatrix}$, replace $x$ by $(x - p)$ and replace $y$ by $(y - q)$.

## Example 3

Sketch the graph of $y = (x + 2)^3 + 5$.

### Solution

The equation can be written as $y - 5 = (x + 2)^3$.

This is $y = x^3$ with $x$ replaced by $(x + 2)$ and $y$ replaced by $(y - 5)$.

So the curve $y = x^3$ is translated by $\begin{bmatrix} -2 \\ 5 \end{bmatrix}$.

A sketch is shown on the right.

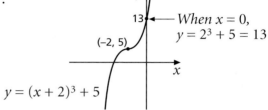

When $x = 0$,
$y = 2^3 + 5 = 13$

$(-2, 5)$

$y = (x + 2)^3 + 5$

---

## Example 4

The graph is a translation of $y = x^3 + x$ by $\begin{bmatrix} 5 \\ 0 \end{bmatrix}$.

Find an equation for the graph.

$(5, 0)$

### Solution

The translation is $\begin{bmatrix} 5 \\ 0 \end{bmatrix}$ so replace $x$ by $(x - 5)$, giving $y = (x - 5)^3 + (x - 5)$.

---

## Exercise B (answers p 182)

**1** Which translation will transform the curve $y = x^3$ to each of these?

    **(a)** $y - 2 = (x - 1)^3$     **(b)** $y + 5 = (x - 3)^3$     **(c)** $y - 1 = (x + 7)^3$

**2** Which translation will transform the curve $y = x^3$ to each of these?

    **(a)** $y = (x - 4)^3 + 5$     **(b)** $y = (x + 2)^3 - 1$     **(c)** $y = (x + 6)^3 + 3$

**3** The curve $y = x^3$ is translated by $\begin{bmatrix} 3 \\ 0 \end{bmatrix}$.

    **(a)** Write an equation for the translated curve.

    **(b)** Sketch the curve, showing where it crosses each axis.

**4** The curve $y = x^3$ is translated by $\begin{bmatrix} 5 \\ -3 \end{bmatrix}$.

    Write the equation of the translated curve in the form $y = (x + a)^3 + b$.

**5** Find the equation of the curve $y = x^3 + x$ after a translation of $\begin{bmatrix} 2 \\ 0 \end{bmatrix}$.

**6** The curve $y = x^3 + x$ is translated by $\begin{bmatrix} 1 \\ 3 \end{bmatrix}$.

(a) Write the equation for the translated curve in the form $y = (x + p)^3 + x + q$.

(b) Work out where the curve crosses the $y$-axis.

**7** The curve $y = x^3 - x$ is translated by $\begin{bmatrix} -3 \\ -2 \end{bmatrix}$.

Write the equation for the translated curve in the form $y = (x + p)^3 - x + q$.

## C Further graphs and manipulation (answers p 183)

A **cubic** expression is one that can be written in the form $ax^3 + bx^2 + cx + d \ (a \neq 0)$, where $a, b, c$ and $d$ are constants.

Graphs of the form $y = ax^3 + bx^2 + cx + d$ have one of these basic shapes:

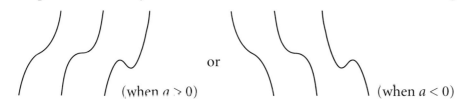

Here is a sketch of $y = (x - 4)^3$.

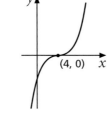

You can multiply out the brackets to write $y = (x - 4)^3$ in the form $y = ax^3 + bx^2 + cx + d$.

$(x - 4)^3 = (x - 4)(x - 4)(x - 4)$

$\qquad = (x - 4)(x^2 - 4x - 4x + 16)$

$\qquad = (x - 4)(x^2 - 8x + 16)$

| × | $x$ | $-4$ |
|---|---|---|
| $x$ | $x^2$ | $-4x$ |
| $-4$ | $-4x$ | $16$ |

$\qquad = x^3 - 8x^2 + 16x - 4x^2 + 32x - 64$

$\qquad = x^3 - 12x^2 + 48x - 64$

| × | $x^2$ | $-8x$ | $16$ |
|---|---|---|---|
| $x$ | $x^3$ | $-8x^2$ | $16x$ |
| $-4$ | $-4x^2$ | $32x$ | $-64$ |

So the equation of the graph can also be written as $y = x^3 - 12x^2 + 48x - 64$.

The constant multipliers in an expression such as $x^3 - 12x^2 + 48x - 64$ are called **coefficients**. In this example, the coefficient of $x^2$ is $-12$.

**C1** Write $y = (x + 3)^3$ in the form $y = ax^3 + bx^2 + cx + d$.

**D** **C2** Each expression below is a product of three different linear expressions. Multiply out the brackets in each one.

(a) $(x + 1)(x + 3)(x + 5)$      (b) $(2x + 1)(x + 2)(x - 3)$

(c) $2x(x - 4)(3x + 1)$      (d) $(5x - 1)(3x - 1)(x + 4)$

**C3** (a) Solve the equation $(x + 3)(x + 2)(x - 1) = 0$.

(b) What does this tell you about the graph of $y = (x + 3)(x + 2)(x - 1)$?

(c) Where will the graph cross the $y$-axis?

(d) Sketch the graph of $y = (x + 3)(x + 2)(x - 1)$.

(e) Write the equation of the graph in the form $y = ax^3 + bx^2 + cx + d$.

**C4** (a) Where will the graph of $y = x(x + 1)(x - 4)$ cross the $x$-axis?

(b) Sketch the graph of $y = x(x + 1)(x - 4)$.

(c) Write the equation of the graph in the form $y = ax^3 + bx^2 + cx + d$.

**C5** (a) (i) Where will the graph of $y = (2x - 1)(x - 3)(x + 1)$ cross the $x$-axis?

     (ii) Where will it cross the $y$-axis?

(b) Sketch the graph of $y = (2x - 1)(x - 3)(x + 1)$.

(c) Write the equation of the graph in the form $y = ax^3 + bx^2 + cx + d$.

**D** **C6** (a) Solve the equation $(x + 3)(x - 1)^2 = 0$.

(b) What does this tell you about the graph of $y = (x + 3)(x - 1)^2$?

(c) Where will the graph cross the $y$-axis?

(d) Sketch the graph of $y = (x + 3)(x - 1)^2$.

(e) Write the equation of the graph in the form $y = ax^3 + bx^2 + cx + d$.

**C7** (a) Show that $(x + 3)^3 + 1$ is equivalent to $x^3 + 9x^2 + 27x + 28$.

(b) Sketch the graph of $y = x^3 + 9x^2 + 27x + 28$.

**D** **C8** (a) Copy and complete the statement $3x^3 - x^2 - 4x = x($      $)$.

(b) Factorise $3x^3 - x^2 - 4x$ completely.

(c) Sketch the graph of $y = 3x^3 - x^2 - 4x$.

**C9** (a) Solve the equation $x^2 - 2x - 4 = 0$.

(b) Hence solve $x^3 - 2x^2 - 4x = 0$ and sketch the graph of $y = x^3 - 2x^2 - 4x$.

**C10** (a) Show that $x(x - 5)(2 - x)$ is equivalent to $-x^3 + 7x^2 - 10x$.

(b) Decide which of the graphs below is a sketch of $y = -x^3 + 7x^2 - 10x$.

**K** The product of three linear expressions can always be written in the form $ax^3 + bx^2 + cx + d$.

### Example 5

Sketch the graph of $y = (2x - 1)(x - 3)(x + 2)$.

### Solution

The expression is the product of three linear factors so the graph is a cubic shape.

The graph cuts the $x$-axis when $(2x - 1)(x - 3)(x + 2) = 0$.

The equation has three solutions:

$2x - 1 = 0$ gives $x = \frac{1}{2}$,

$x - 3 = 0$ gives $x = 3$,

and $x + 2 = 0$ gives $x = -2$.

When $x = 0$, $y = -1 \times -3 \times 2 = 6$.

Hence, a sketch of the graph is

$y = (2x - 1)(x - 3)(x + 2)$

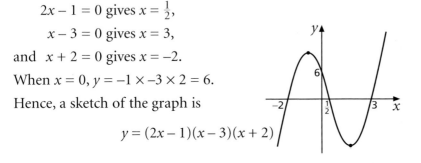

*In Core 2, you will learn how to find the coordinates of the points marked with dots. Concentrate on the x- and y-intercepts for now.*

### Example 6

Write $(2x - 1)(x - 3)(x + 2)$ in the form $ax^3 + bx^2 + cx + d$.

### Solution

$(2x - 1)(x - 3)(x + 2)$

$= (2x - 1)(x^2 + 2x - 3x - 6)$

| $\times$ | $x$ | 2 |
|---|---|---|
| $x$ | $x^2$ | $2x$ |
| $-3$ | $-3x$ | $-6$ |

$= (2x - 1)(x^2 - x - 6)$

$= 2x^3 - 2x^2 - 12x - x^2 + x + 6$

$= 2x^3 - 3x^2 - 11x + 6$

| $\times$ | $x^2$ | $-x$ | $-6$ |
|---|---|---|---|
| $2x$ | $2x^3$ | $-2x^2$ | $-12x$ |
| $-1$ | $-x^2$ | $x$ | 6 |

### Example 7

Solve the equation $2x^3 - 10x^2 + 12x = 0$.

### Solution

$$2x^3 - 10x^2 + 12x = 0$$

*2x is a factor of each term.*

$$2x(x^2 - 5x + 6) = 0$$

*The quadratic factorises.*

$$2x(x - 2)(x - 3) = 0$$

So the solutions are $x = 0$, $x = 2$ and $x = 3$.

**Exercise C** (answers p 184)

**1** For each equation below

    (i) sketch a graph, showing clearly where it crosses the $x$- and $y$-axes

    (ii) write the equation in the form $y = ax^3 + bx^2 + cx + d$

  (a) $y = (x + 1)(x + 3)(x + 4)$        (b) $y = (x + 2)^3$

  (c) $y = (x + 4)(x - 1)(x + 2)$       (d) $y = x(x + 3)(x - 2)$

  (e) $y = (x - 5)^3$                  (f) $y = (2x + 1)(x - 2)(x + 2)$

  (g) $y = \frac{1}{2}x(2x + 3)(x - 2)$        (h) $y = (x + 4)^3 + 1$

**2** (a) Solve the equation $(x + 1)(x - 3)^2 = 0$.

  (b) Sketch the graph of $y = (x + 1)(x - 3)^2$, showing clearly where it meets both axes.

  (c) Write the equation of the graph in the form $y = ax^3 + bx^2 + cx + d$.

**3** (a) Copy and complete the statement $3x^3 - 3x^2 - 18x = 3x($        $)$.

  (b) Factorise $3x^3 - 3x^2 - 18x$ completely.

  (c) Sketch the graph of $y = 3x^3 - 3x^2 - 18x$, showing clearly where it crosses both axes.

**4** (a) Factorise $x^3 + 5x^2 - 6x$ completely.

  (b) Solve the equation $x^3 + 5x^2 - 6x = 0$.

**5** Sketch the graph of $y = 2x^3 + 14x^2 + 24x$, showing clearly where it crosses both axes.

**6** (a) Find the value of $y = (2x - 3)(x + 1)(3 - x)$ when $x = 1$.

  (b) Sketch the graph of $y = (2x - 3)(x + 1)(3 - x)$.

  (c) Write the equation of the graph in the form $y = ax^3 + bx^2 + cx + d$.

**7** Solve the equation $5x^3 - 20x^2 + 20x = 0$.

**8** (a) Solve the equation $x^3 - 10x^2 + 22x = 0$, giving each solution in surd form.

  (b) Sketch the graph of $y = x^3 - 10x^2 + 22x$, showing where it crosses both axes.

**9** Which of the graphs below is a sketch of $y = x^3 - 4x^2 + 5x$?

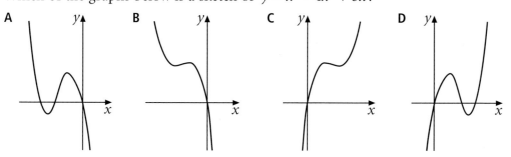

**10** Sketch the graph of $y = (2x + 3)^2(x - 1)$, showing clearly where it meets both axes.

## D Polynomial functions

A **polynomial** is an expression that can be written in the form
$a + bx + cx^2 + dx^3 + ex^4 + fx^5 + \ldots$, where $a, b, c, d, e, f, \ldots$ are constants.

Some examples of polynomials are $7x^4 + x - 10$ and $6 + 5x^2 - x^3 - 5x^7$.

Expressions such as $\sqrt{x} + 3x^2 - 5$ and $\dfrac{1}{x} + 7x$ are not polynomials as they involve terms in $x$ that cannot be written in the form $x^n$ where $n$ is a positive integer ($\sqrt{x}$ and $\dfrac{1}{x}$).

The **degree** of a polynomial is the value of its highest index.
For example, $6 + 5x^2 - x^3 - 5x^7$ is a polynomial of degree 7.

The sum, difference or product of two polynomials is also a polynomial.

For example,  $(x^4 - 5x)(3x^3 + x - 10)$

$= 3x^7 + x^5 - 10x^4 - 15x^4 - 5x^2 + 50x$

$= 3x^7 + x^5 - 25x^4 - 5x^2 + 50x$

| $\times$ | $3x^3$ | $x$ | $-10$ |
|---|---|---|---|
| $x^4$ | $3x^7$ | $x^5$ | $-10x^4$ |
| $-5x$ | $-15x^4$ | $-5x^2$ | $50x$ |

**Function notation** is useful when dealing with polynomials.

For example, if a polynomial function is defined by  $f(x) = x^3 + 4x^2 - 1$,
then $f(3)$ is the value of the polynomial at $x = 3$.

$$\text{So } f(3) = 3^3 + 4 \times 3^2 - 1$$
$$= 27 + 36 - 1$$
$$= 62$$

---

### Example 8

Polynomials are given by  $f(x) = x^4 - 2x^3 + 5$  and  $g(x) = x^3 + 7x^2 - 3$.
Expand and simplify  $2f(x) - g(x)$.

**Solution**

$2f(x) - g(x) = 2(x^4 - 2x^3 + 5) - (x^3 + 7x^2 - 3)$

$\qquad\qquad = 2x^4 - 4x^3 + 10 - x^3 - 7x^2 + 3$

$\qquad\qquad = 2x^4 - 5x^3 - 7x^2 + 13$

---

### Example 9

Polynomials are given by  $p(x) = x^3 - 2$  and  $q(x) = 2x^3 + 3x - 5$.
Expand and simplify  $p(x)q(x)$.

**Solution**

$p(x)q(x) = (x^3 - 2)(2x^3 + 3x - 5)$

$\qquad\quad = 2x^6 + 3x^4 - 5x^3 - 4x^3 - 6x + 10$

$\qquad\quad = 2x^6 + 3x^4 - 9x^3 - 6x + 10$

| $\times$ | $2x^3$ | $3x$ | $-5$ |
|---|---|---|---|
| $x^3$ | $2x^6$ | $3x^4$ | $-5x^3$ |
| $-2$ | $-4x^3$ | $-6x$ | $10$ |

---

**Exercise D** (answers p 185)

**1** Expand and simplify $2(x^3 + 3x - 1) - x(x^2 + x - 5)$.

**2** Work out the value of each polynomial when $x = 2$.

    (a) $x^5 - x^3 + 6$          (b) $4x^3 + 5x^2 - 9$          (c) $2x^5 - 4x^3 - 5x^2 - 7x + 2$

**3** Expand and simplify each of these.

    (a) $(x + 2)(x^4 + 3x + 1)$          (b) $(x^2 + 6)^2$

    (c) $(x^2 + 3x - 1)(2x^3 + x + 5)$          (d) $(1 - x)(x^3 - 1) + 6x$

    (e) $(3x^2 - x)(x^2 + 3) + x^2$          (f) $(x^2 - 1)^3$

    (g) $(x + 1)(x + 4)(x - 2)(x - 3)$      (h) $(1 - 2x)(x + 6)(3x - 2) + x(2x + 1)$

**4** A polynomial is given by $f(x) = 2x^4 - x^3 - 2x + 6$.
  Evaluate each of these.

    (a) $f(1)$          (b) $f(0)$          (c) $f(2)$          (d) $f(-1)$          (e) $f(-2)$

**5** A polynomial is given by $g(x) = x^3 + 2x^2 - 25x - 50$.

    (a) Evaluate $g(5)$, $g(-5)$ and $g(-2)$.

    (b) Hence write down the coordinates of the points where
         the graph of $y = g(x)$ crosses the $x$-axis.

**6** Polynomials are given by $p(x) = x^2 + 1$ and $q(x) = x^5 - 2x^2 - 2$.
  Expand and simplify each of these.

    (a) $2p(x) + q(x)$      (b) $3p(x) - q(x)$      (c) $p(x)q(x)$          (d) $(q(x))^2$

**7** A polynomial is given by $f(x) = -2x^3 - 3x^2 + 3x + 2$.

    (a) Evaluate each of these.

        (i) $f(0)$          (ii) $f(1)$          (iii) $f(2)$          (iv) $f(-\frac{1}{2})$          (v) $f(-2)$

    (b) Sketch the graph of $y = f(x)$.

**8** A function is given by $f(x) = (2x - 3)(x + 4)^2$.

    (a) Write the function in the form $f(x) = ax^3 + bx^2 + cx + d$.

    (b) Sketch the graph of $y = f(x)$.

**9** A function is given by $g(x) = 2x^3 - 7x^2 + 3x$.

    (a) Write $g(x)$ as the product of three linear factors.

    (b) Solve the equation $g(x) = 0$.

**10** A polynomial is given by $p(x) = 2x^4 + 3x + c$.
  If $p(1) = 10$, find the value of $c$.

**11** A polynomial is given by $q(x) = x^4 - x^3 + ax + b$.
  $q(0) = -5$ and $q(2) = 7$.
  Find the values of $a$ and $b$.

## Mixed questions (answers p 185)

**1** The graph of $y = x^3$ is translated by $\begin{bmatrix} 4 \\ 1 \end{bmatrix}$.

(a) Which is the correct equation for the new graph?

   A  $y = (x + 4)^3 + 1$          B  $y = (x + 4)^3 - 1$

   C  $y = (x - 4)^3 + 1$          D  $y = (x - 4)^3 - 1$

(b) Write the correct equation in the form $y = ax^3 + bx^2 + cx + d$.

**2** A polynomial is given by $\mathrm{f}(x) = (2x + 1)(x + 2)(x - 3)$.

(a) Evaluate $\mathrm{f}(0)$.

(b) Sketch the graph of $y = \mathrm{f}(x)$, showing clearly where the graph crosses both axes.

(c) Write the polynomial in the form $\mathrm{f}(x) = ax^3 + bx^2 + cx + d$.

**3** A function is defined as $\mathrm{g}(x) = (x + 3)(x - 2)^2$.

(a) Evaluate $\mathrm{g}(0)$.

(b) Solve the equation $\mathrm{g}(x) = 0$.

(c) Sketch the graph of $y = \mathrm{g}(x)$, showing clearly where the graph meets both axes.

**4** Polynomials are given by $\mathrm{p}(x) = 3x^2 - 2$ and $\mathrm{q}(x) = x^3 - x^2 + 3$.

(a) Evaluate each of these.

   (i) $\mathrm{p}(0)$          (ii) $\mathrm{q}(3)$          (iii) $\mathrm{q}(-2)$

(b) Expand and simplify each of these.

   (i) $2\mathrm{p}(x) - 3\mathrm{q}(x)$     (ii) $\mathrm{p}(x)\mathrm{q}(x)$          (iii) $(\mathrm{p}(x))^2$

**5** A polynomial is given by $\mathrm{p}(x) = 2x^3 - 18x$.

(a) Express $\mathrm{p}(x)$ as a product of linear factors.

(b) Sketch the graph of $y = \mathrm{p}(x)$, showing clearly where the graph crosses both axes.

**\*6** A function is defined as $f(x) = x^3 + 3x^2 + 2x$.

   **(a)** Factorise $f(x)$ completely.

   **(b)** Hence show that the value of $f(a)$ is a multiple of 3 for any integer $a$.

## Test yourself (answers p 186)

None of these questions requires a calculator.

**1** The graph of $y = x^3 + x$ is translated by $\begin{bmatrix} 2 \\ -1 \end{bmatrix}$.

   **(a)** Find the equation of the new graph in the form $y = ax^3 + bx^2 + cx + d$.

   **(b)** Where does this graph cross the $y$-axis?

**2** Match up each equation below with a sketch of its graph.

   **(a)** $y = (3x + 2)(x - 1)(x + 3)$

   **(b)** $y = (1 - 2x)(x - 6)(x + 1)$

   **(c)** $y = x^3 - 6x^2 + 7x$

   **(d)** $y = (x - 2)(x^2 + 3x + 3)$

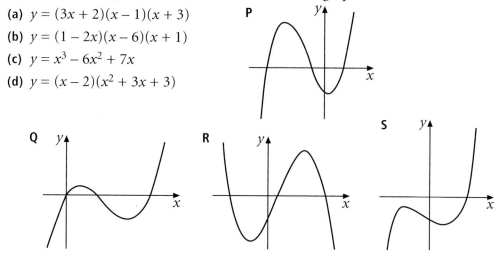

**3** A function is defined as $g(x) = (x + 2)(2x - 1)^2$.

   **(a)** Evaluate $g(0)$ and $g(2)$.

   **(b)** Solve the equation $g(x) = 0$.

   **(c)** Sketch the graph of $y = g(x)$, showing clearly where the graph meets both axes.

   **(d)** Write the function in the form $g(x) = ax^3 + bx^2 + cx + d$.

**4** Polynomials are given by $p(x) = x^2 + 2x$ and $q(x) = x^3 - x^2 - 6x$.

   **(a)** Expand and simplify each of these.

      **(i)** $2p(x) + q(x)$       **(ii)** $p(x)q(x)$

   **(b)** Solve the equation $q(x) = 0$.

   **(c)** Find the values of $x$ for which $p(x) = q(x)$.

**\*5** A function is defined as $f(x) = x^3 + 7x^2 + 6x$.

   **(a)** Factorise $f(x)$ completely.

   **(b)** Hence show that the value of $f(a)$ is even for any integer $a$.

# 8 Graphs and transformations

In this chapter you will learn how to
- sketch a range of graphs including $y = \frac{1}{x}$
- transform graphs by translating, reflecting and stretching, and determine their equations
- transform the graph of $y = f(x)$ to obtain graphs of the form $y = af(x)$, $y = f(ax)$, $y = f(x) + a$ and $y = f(x + a)$

## A Further graphs (answers p 186)

You are already familiar with a range of graphs.
You have sketched linear, quadratic and cubic graphs.

The simplest examples of these are shown below.

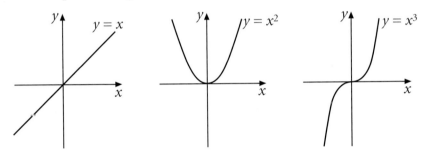

**D**  **A1** (a)  Try to sketch a graph for each equation below.

Considering the following can help you decide on each shape.

- What happens when $x = 0$ or when $y = 0$?
- What happens as $x$ gets very large and positive?
  Try thinking about $x = 100$ and other large positive values of $x$.
- What happens as $x$ gets very large and negative?
  Try thinking about $x = -100$ and other large negative values of $x$.
- Are there any values for which $y$ is not defined?
- Which values of $x$ produce large values of $y$?
- Does the graph have any reflection symmetry?
- Does the graph have any rotation symmetry?

(i)  $y = \dfrac{1}{x}$

(ii)  $y = \dfrac{1}{x - 2}$

(iii)  $y = \sqrt{x}$

(iv)  $y = \sqrt[3]{x}$

(v)  $y = \dfrac{1}{x^2}$

(vi)  $y = \dfrac{1}{x^2 + 1}$

(b)  Check your sketches on a graph plotter.

To draw the graph of an equation such as $y = \dfrac{1}{x}$, you need to consider what happens to $y$ when $x$ is very large or very small.

The graph of $y = \dfrac{1}{x}$ gets closer and closer to the $x$- and $y$-axes but never meets them.

Straight lines that are approached by a graph in this way are called **asymptotes**.

A sketch of the graph is

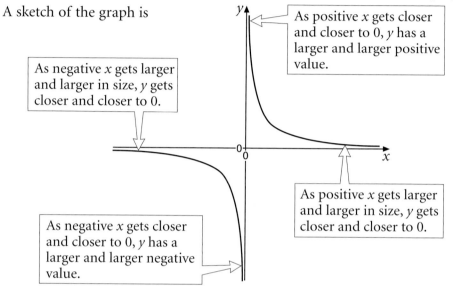

As positive $x$ gets closer and closer to 0, $y$ has a larger and larger positive value.

As negative $x$ gets larger and larger in size, $y$ gets closer and closer to 0.

As negative $x$ gets closer and closer to 0, $y$ has a larger and larger negative value.

As positive $x$ gets larger and larger in size, $y$ gets closer and closer to 0.

**Exercise A** (answers p 186)

**1** Below is a sketch of the graph $y = \dfrac{1}{x-2} + 1$.
The dotted lines are asymptotes.

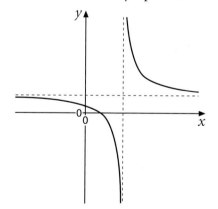

(a) (i) Look at the equation.
What happens to the value of $y$ as positive $x$ gets larger and larger?

(ii) What is the equation of the horizontal asymptote?

(b) What is the equation of the vertical asymptote?

(c) What is the value of the $y$-intercept?

(d) What is the value of the $x$-intercept?

**2** Each equation below belongs to one of the sketch graphs.

Match up the equations and graphs.

(a) $y = \dfrac{2}{x}$

(b) $y = \dfrac{1}{x} + 3$

(c) $y = \dfrac{1}{x+3}$

(d) $y = \dfrac{1}{x} - 1$

(e) $y = \dfrac{1}{x-1}$

(f) $y^2 = x$

(g) $y = \dfrac{1}{x^2} - 1$

(h) $y^2 = x^2 + 1$

(i) $\dfrac{x^2}{9} + y^2 = 1$

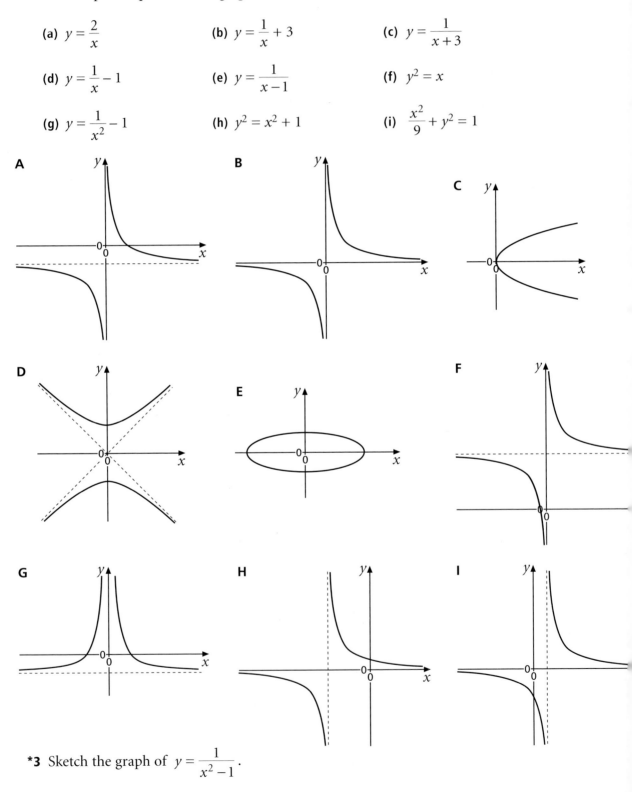

*3 Sketch the graph of $y = \dfrac{1}{x^2 - 1}$.

## B Translating

You have seen from earlier work that to find the equation of a graph after a translation of $\begin{bmatrix} a \\ b \end{bmatrix}$ you can replace $x$ by $(x - a)$ and $y$ by $(y - b)$.

For example, to find the equation of the graph of $y = x^2$ after a translation of $\begin{bmatrix} 3 \\ -2 \end{bmatrix}$, replace $x$ by $(x - 3)$ and $y$ by $(y + 2)$ to give $y + 2 = (x - 3)^2$.

This is usually written as $y = (x - 3)^2 - 2$.

---

### Example 1

Find the equation of the graph of $y = \dfrac{1}{x}$ after a translation of $\begin{bmatrix} -4 \\ 1 \end{bmatrix}$ and sketch the transformed graph.

### Solution

The translation is $\begin{bmatrix} -4 \\ 1 \end{bmatrix}$ so replace $x$ by $x + 4$ and $y$ by $y - 1$ to obtain $y - 1 = \dfrac{1}{x + 4}$.

This is equivalent to $y = \dfrac{1}{x + 4} + 1$.

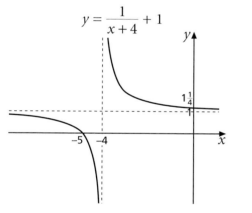

$$y = \frac{1}{x + 4} + 1$$

*The asymptotes are drawn as dotted lines. The x- and y-intercepts of the asymptotes are shown.*

*The x- and y-intercepts of the graph itself are straightforward to calculate so they are shown too.*

*(When $x = 0$, $y = \dfrac{1}{0 + 4} + 1 = 1\frac{1}{4}$.*

*When $y = 0$, $\dfrac{1}{x + 4} + 1 = 0 \Rightarrow x = -5$.)*

---

### Exercise B (answers p 187)

**1** The graph of $y = \dfrac{1}{x}$ is translated by $\begin{bmatrix} 5 \\ -1 \end{bmatrix}$.

    **(a)** Find the equation of the new graph.

    **(b)** Sketch the new graph, showing clearly any x- and y-intercepts.

    **(c)** What are the equations of the asymptotes?

**2** Describe the translation that maps $y = \dfrac{1}{x}$ on to $y = \dfrac{1}{x - 6}$.

**3** Work out the equation of the image of

    **(a)** $y = \sqrt{x}$ after a translation of $\begin{bmatrix} 5 \\ 0 \end{bmatrix}$        **(b)** $y^2 = x + 3$ after a translation of $\begin{bmatrix} 0 \\ 2 \end{bmatrix}$

    **(c)** $y = x^2$ after a translation of $\begin{bmatrix} -1 \\ 0 \end{bmatrix}$       **(d)** $y = \dfrac{2}{x}$ after a translation of $\begin{bmatrix} 0 \\ -3 \end{bmatrix}$

    **(e)** $xy = 3$ after a translation of $\begin{bmatrix} 2 \\ -3 \end{bmatrix}$       **(f)** $x^2 + 3y = 2$ after a translation of $\begin{bmatrix} -7 \\ -5 \end{bmatrix}$

**4** Describe a translation that will transform

    **(a)** the graph of $y = x^2$ to the graph of $y = (x + 5)^2$

    **(b)** the graph of $y = 2\sqrt{x}$ to the graph of $y = 2\sqrt{x - 3}$

    **(c)** the graph of $xy = 1$ to the graph of $x(y + 2) = 1$

**5** The graph of $y = x$ is translated by $\begin{bmatrix} 3 \\ 3 \end{bmatrix}$.

    **(a)** Find the equation of the image and write it in its simplest form.

    **(b)** What do you notice? Can you explain this?

**6 (a)** Work out the equation of the image of $y = x$ after a translation of $\begin{bmatrix} 0 \\ 1 \end{bmatrix}$.
       Write the equation in its simplest form.

    **(b)** Work out the equation of the image of $y = x$ after a translation of $\begin{bmatrix} 3 \\ 4 \end{bmatrix}$.
       Write the equation in its simplest form.

    **(c)** What do you notice? Can you explain this?

## C Reflecting (answers p 187)

**C1 (a)** For each equation below,
- sketch its graph
- sketch its image after a reflection in the *x*-axis
- write down the equation of the reflected graph

      **(i)** $y = x + 1$       **(ii)** $y = x^2 + 1$       **(iii)** $y = x^3 + 1$

    **(b)** What do you notice in each case about the equations of the graph and of its image?

    **(c)** What do you think will be the image of $y = x^4 + 1$ after a reflection in the *x*-axis?
       Check on a graph plotter.

**C2** Repeat question C1 but reflect each graph in the *y*-axis.

**C3 (a)** Sketch the graph of $y = (x - 1)^2$.

    **(b)** What is the equation of this graph after reflection in the *x*-axis?

    **(c)** What is the equation of this graph after reflection in the *y*-axis?

In the diagram below, the graph of $y = x + 2$ has been reflected in the $x$-axis.

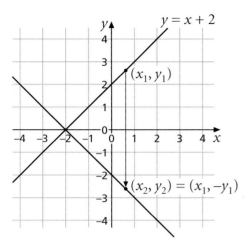

Let $(x_1, y_1)$ be a point on $y = x + 2$ and let $(x_2, y_2)$ be its image on the reflected line.

Then $(x_2, y_2) = (x_1, -y_1)$, giving

$$x_1 = x_2$$

and $\quad y_1 = -y_2 \qquad$ *from rearranging $y_2 = -y_1$.*

We know that $y_1 = x_1 + 2$, so it must be true that

$$-y_2 = x_2 + 2$$

and so $-y = x + 2$ is the equation of the image.

This can be written as $y = -(x + 2)$
$$\text{or } y = -x - 2.$$

A similar argument can be produced for any equation and graph.

So, to find the equation of any graph after reflection in the $x$-axis, replace $y$ by $-y$.

This may seem a complex way to analyse a simple process but it has the advantage that it can be applied to any equation.

For example, the image of $y^2 + x + y = 0$ after reflection in the $x$-axis is $\quad (-y)^2 + x + (-y) = 0$
$$\text{or} \qquad y^2 + x - y = 0.$$

If an equation can be written in the form $y = \ldots\ldots$ where the expression on the right-hand side does not involve $y$, the rule can be applied like this.

The reflected graph will have the equation $\quad -y = \ldots\ldots$
which is equivalent to $\qquad\qquad\qquad\qquad y = -(\ldots\ldots).$

For example, the image of $y = x^2 - 5$ after reflection in the $x$-axis is $\quad y = -(x^2 - 5)$
$$\text{or} \quad y = -x^2 + 5.$$

**C4** (a) What is the equation of the image of $y = x^2 + x$ after reflection in the $x$-axis?

(b) Check by using a graph plotter to draw both graphs.

**D** **C5** Show that the equation of any graph after reflection in the $y$-axis can be found by replacing $x$ by $-x$.

**C6** (a) What is the equation of the image of $y = x^2 + x$ after reflection in the $y$-axis?

(b) Check by using a graph plotter to draw both graphs.

**\*C7** (a) Find a rule that will give you the equation of a graph after reflection in the line $y = x$.

(b) Write down the image of each of the following after reflection in the line $y = x$.

(i) $y = x + 6$         (ii) $x + y = 10$         (iii) $x^2 + (y - 3)^2 = 9$

**K** To find the equation of a graph after reflection in the $x$-axis, replace $y$ by $-y$.

To find the equation of a graph after reflection in the $y$-axis, replace $x$ by $-x$.

**Exercise C** (answers p 188)

**1** Find the image of each of the following after reflection in the $x$-axis.

(a) $y = x - 5$　　　　(b) $y = \dfrac{1}{x} + 3$　　　　(c) $y = x^3 + x$

(d) $x + y = 10$　　　　(e) $xy = 10$　　　　(f) $x^2 + y^2 = 5$

**2** Find the image of each of the following after reflection in the $y$-axis.

(a) $y = x + 2$　　　　(b) $y = \dfrac{1}{x} - 1$　　　　(c) $y = x^2 + 2x$

(d) $y = 2x^2 - 5x$　　　　(e) $x^2 - y^2 = 4$　　　　(f) $y = x^2 - 3x + 5$

**3** Show that the graph of $y = x^4 + x^2 - 9$ has the $y$-axis as a line of symmetry.

**4** $(x + 2)^2 + (y - 3)^2 = 1$ is the equation of a circle.

Show, by using the appropriate rule above, that the equation of its image after a reflection in the $x$-axis can be written as $(x + 2)^2 + (y + 3)^2 = 1$.

## D Stretching (answers p 188)

**K** A stretch from the origin in the $x$-direction by a scale factor $k$ multiplies each $x$-coordinate by $k$.

In this diagram, a stretch by scale factor 3 in the $x$-direction maps the smaller triangle to the larger.

**K** A stretch from the origin in the $y$-direction by a scale factor $k$ multiplies each $y$-coordinate by $k$.

In this diagram, a stretch by scale factor $\frac{1}{2}$ in the $y$-direction maps the larger triangle to the smaller.

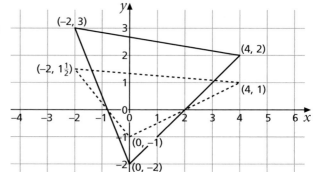

**D1** (a) Plot the points $(2, 0)$, $(-1, -1)$, $(0, 1)$ and $(4, 3)$ and join them to make a quadrilateral.

(b) Draw the image of the quadrilateral after a stretch of scale factor 2 in the $y$-direction.

**D2** (a) Plot and join the points $(8, 2)$, $(0, -1)$, $(-2, 0)$ and $(-4, 4)$ to make a quadrilateral.

(b) Draw the image of the quadrilateral after a stretch by scale factor $\frac{1}{4}$ in the $x$-direction.

**D3** (a) For each equation below,
  - sketch its graph and its image after a stretch by scale factor 2 in the $x$-direction
  - find the equation of the image

  (i) $y = x + 1$     (ii) $y = x^2$     (iii) $y = 2x - 3$

(b) Can you suggest a rule to work out the equation of a graph after a stretch by scale factor 2 in the $x$-direction?

**D4** Repeat question D3 for a stretch by scale factor 3 in the $y$-direction.

In the diagram below, the graph of $y = x^2 + 1$ has been stretched by factor 3 in the $x$-direction.

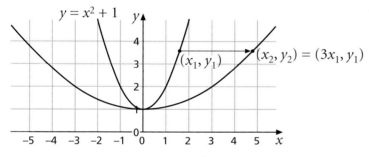

*It is common to use the term 'factor 3' instead of 'scale factor 3'.*

Let $(x_1, y_1)$ be a point on $y = x^2 + 1$ and let $(x_2, y_2)$ be its image on the stretched curve.

Then $(x_2, y_2) = (3x_1, y_1)$, giving

$$x_1 = \tfrac{1}{3}x_2 \qquad \textit{from rearranging } x_2 = 3x_1$$

and $\quad y_1 = y_2$.

We know that $y_1 = x_1^2 + 1$, so it must be true that

$$y_2 = (\tfrac{1}{3}x_2)^2 + 1$$
$$\Rightarrow \qquad y_2 = \tfrac{1}{9}x_2^2 + 1$$

and so $\quad y = \tfrac{1}{9}x^2 + 1 \quad$ is the equation of the image.

A similar argument can be produced for any equation so, to find the equation of a graph after a stretch by factor 3 in the $x$-direction, replace $x$ by $\tfrac{1}{3}x$.

This can be generalised.

**K**    To find the equation of a graph after a stretch by factor $k$ in the $x$-direction, replace $x$ by $\dfrac{1}{k}x$.

**D5** Work out the equation of the image of
(a) $y = x$ after a stretch by factor 3 in the $x$-direction
(b) $y = x^2 - 4$ after a stretch by factor 2 in the $x$-direction
(c) $y^2 + x^2 = 7$ after a stretch by factor 5 in the $x$-direction
(d) $y = x + 6$ after a stretch by factor $\tfrac{1}{3}$ in the $x$-direction
(e) $y = x^2 + 3$ after a stretch by factor $\tfrac{1}{2}$ in the $x$-direction

Using an argument similar to the one on the previous page we can show the following.

**K**  To find the equation of a graph after a stretch by factor $k$ in the $y$-direction, replace $y$ by $\frac{1}{k}y$.

For example, the image of $y^2 + x + y = 0$
after a stretch by factor 2 in the $y$-direction is $\left(\frac{1}{2}y\right)^2 + x + \left(\frac{1}{2}y\right) = 0$

$$\text{or} \quad \tfrac{1}{4}y^2 + x + \tfrac{1}{2}y = 0.$$

If an equation can be written in the form $y = \ldots\ldots$ where the expression on the right-hand side does not involve $y$, the rule can be applied like this.

The stretched graph will have the equation $\quad \frac{1}{k}y = \ldots\ldots$

which is equivalent to $\qquad\qquad\qquad\quad y = k(\ldots\ldots).$

For example, the image of $y = x^2 + 1$
after a stretch of factor 2 in the $y$-direction is $\quad y = 2(x^2 + 1)$
$$\text{or} \quad y = 2x^2 + 2.$$

**D6**  Work out the equation of the image of

(a) $y + x = 4$ after a stretch by factor 3 in the $y$-direction

(b) $y = 4x^2 + 3$ after a stretch by factor $\frac{1}{4}$ in the $y$-direction

**D7**  Describe a stretch that will transform

(a) the graph of $y = x - 4$ to the graph of $y = 3x - 12$

(b) the graph of $y = x - 4$ to the graph of $y = 3x - 4$

(c) the graph of $y = x^2 + 1$ to the graph of $y = 9x^2 + 1$

**Exercise D** (answers p 189)

**1**  Find the image of each of the following after a stretch by factor 2 in the $x$-direction.

(a) $y = x + 3$        (b) $y = 4x - 1$        (c) $y = x^2 - 2$

(d) $y = x^2 + 2x + 1$      (e) $xy = 4$        (f) $x^2 + y^2 = 1$

**2**  Find the image of each of the following after a stretch by factor $\frac{1}{3}$ in the $x$-direction.

(a) $y = x - 1$        (b) $y = x^3 + 5$        (c) $y = \dfrac{1}{x}$

**3**  Find the image of each of the following after a stretch by factor 4 in the $y$-direction.

(a) $y = x + 6$        (b) $y = 3x - 2$        (c) $2y + x = 10$

**4**  Describe a stretch that will transform

(a) the graph of $y = x + 4$ to the graph of $y = 5x + 20$

(b) the graph of $y = x + 4$ to the graph of $y = 5x + 4$

(c) the graph of $y = x^2 - 3$ to the graph of $y = \frac{1}{25}x^2 - 3$

(d) the graph of $y = x^2 + x - 1$ to the graph of $y = 4x^2 + 2x - 1$

(e) the graph of $y = x^2 + x - 1$ to the graph of $y = 4x^2 + 4x - 4$

# E Function notation

If an equation can be written in the form $y = \ldots\ldots$ where the expression on the right-hand side is in terms of $x$, we can use function notation.

For example, we can write $y = x^2$ as $y = f(x)$ where $f(x) = x^2$.

It gives us a useful way of describing transformed graphs.

### Translating

For example, to find the image of a graph after a translation of $\begin{bmatrix} -4 \\ 2 \end{bmatrix}$ we can replace $x$ by $x + 4$ and $y$ by $y - 2$.

So the image of $y = f(x)$ can be written as $y - 2 = f(x + 4)$ or $y = f(x + 4) + 2$.

For $f(x) = x^2$, the image is $y - 2 = (x + 4)^2$, which can be written as $y = (x + 4)^2 + 2$.

In general, to find the image of a graph after a translation of $\begin{bmatrix} a \\ b \end{bmatrix}$ we can replace $x$ by $x - a$ and $y$ by $y - b$.

K    So a translation of $\begin{bmatrix} a \\ b \end{bmatrix}$ transforms the graph of $y = f(x)$ to the graph of

$y - b = f(x - a)$ or $y = f(x - a) + b$.

---

### Example 2

A function f is defined by $f(x) = \dfrac{1}{x}$.

State the geometrical transformation that maps the graph of $y = f(x)$ on to $y = f(x + 3)$ and hence sketch the graph of $y = f(x + 3)$.

### Solution

$x$ has been replaced by $x + 3$ so the transformation is a translation of $\begin{bmatrix} -3 \\ 0 \end{bmatrix}$.

A sketch of the graph of $y = f(x + 3)$ is shown below.

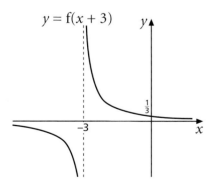

$y = f(x + 3)$

*The vertical asymptote is drawn as a dotted line.*

*When $x = 0$, $y = f(0 + 3) = f(3) = \frac{1}{3}$.*

---

## Reflecting

To find the image of a graph after a reflection in the $x$-axis we can replace $y$ by $-y$.

**K** So a reflection in the $x$-axis transforms the graph of $y = f(x)$ to the graph of $-y = f(x)$ or $y = -f(x)$.

To find the image of a graph after a reflection in the $y$-axis we can replace $x$ by $-x$.

**K** So a reflection in the $y$-axis transforms the graph of $y = f(x)$ to the graph of $y = f(-x)$.

---

**Example 3**

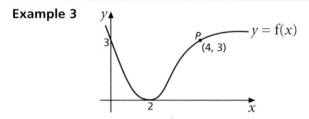

The diagram shows the graph of the curve $y = f(x)$. Point $P$ (4, 3) lies on the curve.

Sketch the graph of $y = f(-x)$ and label clearly the image of point $P$.

### Solution

$x$ has been replaced by $-x$ so the transformation is a reflection in the $y$-axis.

A sketch of the graph of $y = f(-x)$ is shown below.

*Even though you are not given an expression for* f(x) *you can use your knowledge of transformations to draw the graph of y = f(−x).*

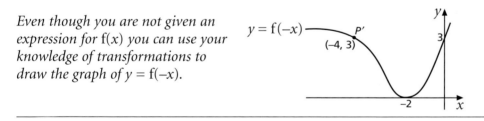

---

## Stretching

To find the image of a graph after a stretch by factor $k$ in the $x$-direction, replace $x$ by $\frac{1}{k}x$.

**K** So a stretch by factor $k$ in the $x$-direction transforms the graph of $y = f(x)$ to the graph of $y = f\left(\frac{1}{k}x\right)$.

To find the image of a graph after a stretch by factor $k$ in the $y$-direction, replace $y$ by $\frac{1}{k}y$.

**K** So a stretch by factor $k$ in the $y$-direction transforms the graph of $y = f(x)$ to the graph of $\frac{1}{k}y = f(x)$ or $y = kf(x)$.

## Example 4

The diagram shows the graph of the curve $y = f(x)$.
Point $P$ (9, 4) lies on the curve.

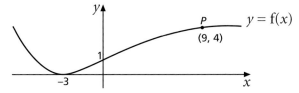

State the geometrical transformation that maps the graph of $y = f(x)$ on to $y = f(3x)$.

Hence sketch the graph of $y = f(3x)$ and label clearly the image of point $P$.

### Solution

$x$ has been replaced by $3x$ so the transformation is a stretch by factor $\frac{1}{3}$ in the $x$-direction.

A sketch of the graph of $y = f(3x)$ is shown below.

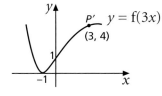

## Example 5

State the geometrical transformation that maps the graph of $y = f(x)$ on to $y = 3f(x)$.

### Solution

The equation $y = 3f(x)$ can be written as $\frac{1}{3}y = f(x)$.
$y$ has been replaced by $\frac{1}{3}y$ so the transformation is a stretch by factor 3 in the $y$-direction.

An alternative method is to note that the equation $y = 3f(x)$ is written in the form $y = kf(x)$ with $k = 3$.
So the transformation is a stretch by factor 3 in the $y$-direction.

## Exercise E (answers p 190)

**1** State the geometrical transformation that maps the graph of $y = f(x)$ on to each of these.

(a) $y = f(x) + 6$      (b) $y = f(x + 6)$      (c) $y = f(x) - 1$      (d) $y = f(x - 1)$

(e) $y = 2f(x)$      (f) $y = f(2x)$      (g) $y = \frac{1}{3}f(x)$      (h) $y = f(\frac{1}{3}x)$

**2** The diagram shows the graph of the curve $y = f(x)$.
$X$ has coordinates $(1, 3)$.

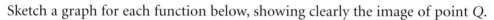

Sketch a graph for each function below, showing clearly the image of point $X$.

(a) $y = f(x) + 2$　　(b) $y = f(x - 3)$　　(c) $y = f(-x)$

(d) $y = -f(x)$　　(e) $y = 3f(x)$　　(f) $y = f(3x)$

**3** The diagram shows the graph of the curve $y = g(x)$.
$Q$ has coordinates $(-2, 3)$.

Sketch a graph for each function below, showing clearly the image of point $Q$.

(a) $y = g(x + 1)$　　(b) $y = g(-x)$　　(c) $y = g(2x)$

(d) $y = g(\frac{1}{2}x)$　　(e) $y = \frac{1}{3}g(x)$　　(f) $y = g(x - 2) + 3$

## Key points

| Transformation | For the equation of the image | Image of $y = f(x)$ | |
|---|---|---|---|
| Translation of $\begin{bmatrix} a \\ b \end{bmatrix}$ | replace $x$ by $(x - a)$ and replace $y$ by $(y - b)$ | $y - b = f(x - a)$ or $\quad y = f(x - a) + b$ | (pp 103, 109) |
| Reflection in the $x$-axis | replace $y$ by $-y$ | $-y = f(x)$ or $\quad y = -f(x)$ | (pp 105, 110) |
| Reflection in the $y$-axis | replace $x$ by $-x$ | $y = f(-x)$ | (pp 105, 110) |
| Stretch by factor $k$ in the $x$-direction | replace $x$ by $\frac{1}{k}x$ | $y = f\left(\frac{1}{k}x\right)$ | (pp 107–108, 110) |
| Stretch by factor $k$ in the $y$-direction | replace $y$ by $\frac{1}{k}y$ | $\frac{1}{k}y = f(x)$ or $\quad y = kf(x)$ | (pp 107–108, 110) |

## Test yourself (answers p 191)

None of these questions requires a calculator.

**1 (a)** Describe the translation that will map $y = \dfrac{1}{x}$ on to $y = \dfrac{1}{x+5}$.

**(b)** Hence sketch the graph of $y = \dfrac{1}{x+5}$.

**(c)** What is the equation of the vertical asymptote?

**2** What is the equation of $y = x^2 + 2x$ after reflection in the $y$-axis?

**3** Describe the transformation that maps the graph of $x + y = 5$ on to the graph of $x - y = 5$.

**4** What is the image of $y = x^3$ after a stretch by factor $\frac{1}{2}$ in the $x$-direction?

**5 (a)** Sketch the graph of $y = 2\sqrt{x}$.

**(b)** The graph of $y = 2\sqrt{x}$ is stretched by a factor of 3 in the $y$-direction. What is the equation of the transformed graph?

**(c)** Describe the transformation that transforms the graph of $y = 2\sqrt{x}$ to the graph of $y = 2\sqrt{x} - 1$.

**6** The diagram shows a sketch of the curve with equation $y = f(x)$.

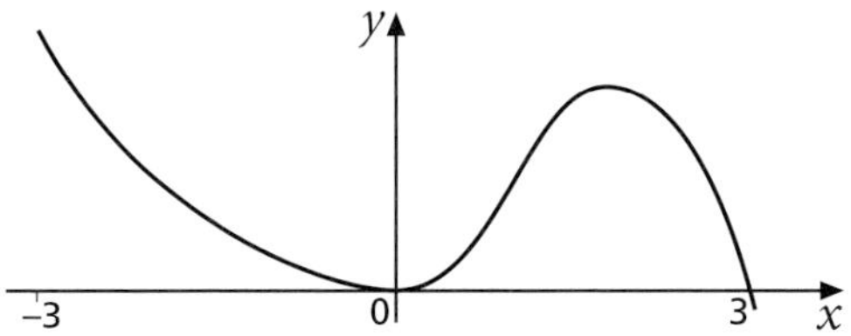

In **separate** diagrams show, for $-3 \le x \le 3$, a sketch of the curve with equation

**(a)** $y = f(-x)$          **(b)** $y = -f(x)$

marking on each sketch the $x$-coordinates of any point, or points, where a curve touches or crosses the $x$-axis.

Edexcel

**7** The diagram shows the graph of $y = f(x)$. It has rotation symmetry about $(0, 0)$. Point $P\ (2, -2)$ lies on the curve.

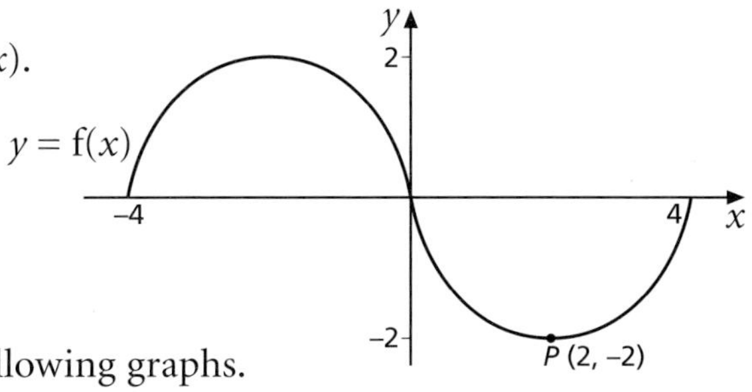

**(a)** Sketch, on separate diagrams, the following graphs. On each graph label the image of point $P$, giving its coordinates.

     **(i)** $y = f(2x)$       **(ii)** $y = 2f(x)$       **(iii)** $f(x + 3)$

**(b)** Describe the transformation that maps the graph of $y = f(x)$ on to the graph of $y = f(2x)$.

**8** Describe the transformation that maps the graph of $x^2 + y^2 = 9$ on to the graph of $x^2 + \frac{1}{4}y^2 = 9$.

# 9 Sequences and series

In this chapter you will
- use subscript notation when working with sequences
- generate a sequence using a rule for the $n$th term
- generate a sequence using an inductive definition (the first term and a rule to get from one term to the next)
- describe the behaviour of sequences, including those that converge to a limit
- learn what is meant by an arithmetic sequence
- find the sum of an arithmetic series
- use sigma notation when working with series

## A Using a rule for the $n$th term (answers p 192)

A sequence is a list of numbers, arranged in a particular order.
The numbers in the list are called the **terms** of the sequence.

Sequences with a first and a last term are **finite**.
For example, the list of numbers

$$6, 7, 9, 8, 6, 8, 6$$

forms a finite sequence that has seven terms.

A sequence can be **infinite**. For example, the list of odd numbers

$$1, 3, 5, 7, 9, 11, \ldots$$

goes on for ever and forms an infinite sequence.

In mathematics, a sequence of numbers often follows a pattern that allows us to describe and understand its behaviour. For example, in the sequence of odd numbers each term is exactly 2 more than the previous one.

### Notation

We usually represent the terms of a sequence by choosing a particular letter and using **subscript** notation (or **suffix** notation).
It is natural to use a subscript of **1** for the 1st term.
Choosing $a$ for the sequence of odd numbers above gives us

$$a_1 = 1, \quad a_2 = 3, \quad a_3 = 5, \quad a_4 = 7, \quad a_5 = 9, \quad a_6 = 11, \ldots$$

We can use $a_n$ to represent the $n$th term of this sequence.

We often define a sequence by giving a rule for the $n$th term.
For example, a sequence defined by the rule $\quad b_n = 2n + 5$

$$\text{gives} \quad b_1 = (2 \times 1) + 5 = 7$$
$$b_2 = (2 \times 2) + 5 = 9$$
$$b_3 = (2 \times 3) + 5 = 11 \ldots$$

**D** **A1** For each of the sequences below,

      **(i)** work out the the first six terms

      **(ii)** work out the 10th, 25th and 100th terms

      **(iii)** describe what happens to the terms of the sequence as $n$ gets larger and larger

**(a)** $a_n = 6n - 1$         **(b)** $b_n = 5 - 3n$         **(c)** $c_n = 2n + 3$

**(d)** $d_n = n^2 + n - 3$     **(e)** $e_n = 5 + \dfrac{1}{10^n}$      **(f)** $f_n = \dfrac{n+3}{n}$

**(g)** $g_n = \dfrac{2n}{n+1}$        **(h)** $h_n = (-2)^n$        **(i)** $i_n = (-0.1)^n$

Sometimes the terms of a sequence get closer and closer to one particular value.

Consider the sequence defined by $u_n = 7 + \dfrac{1}{n}$.

As $n$ gets larger and larger $\dfrac{1}{n}$ gets closer and closer to 0 so $u_n$ gets closer and closer to 7.

We say that $u_n$ **converges to a limit** of 7.

A graph helps to show the behaviour of this sequence: $8, 7\frac{1}{2}, 7\frac{1}{3}, 7\frac{1}{4}, 7\frac{1}{5}, 7\frac{1}{6}, \dots$ getting closer to 7.

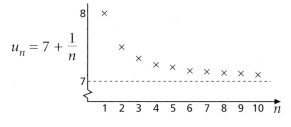

## Exercise A (answers p 192)

**1** A sequence of terms $u_1, u_2, u_3, \dots$ is defined by $u_n = 4n + 1$.

  **(a)** Find the values of $u_1, u_2$ and $u_3$.

  **(b)** What is the value of $u_{100}$?

  **(c)** Find the value of $n$ for which $u_n = 81$.

  **(d)** How many terms in this sequence are smaller than 100?

**2** A sequence of terms $a_1, a_2, a_3, \dots$ has $n$th term $a_n$ where $a_n = 40 - 3n$.

  **(a)** Find the values of $a_1, a_2$ and $a_3$.

  **(b)** What is the value of $a_{16}$?

  **(c)** How many terms in this sequence are positive?

**3** The $n$th term of a sequence is $p_n$ where $p_n = 2 \times 3^n$.

  **(a)** Find the values of $p_1, p_2, p_3$ and $p_{10}$.

  **(b)** What happens to the terms in this sequence as $n$ gets larger and larger?

**4** The $n$th term of a sequence is $h_n$ where $h_n = \dfrac{2}{3^n}$.

  **(a)** Find the value of $h_{30}$ correct to two significant figures.

  **(b)** What happens to the terms in this sequence as $n$ gets larger and larger?

**5** Match each sequence below to a description of its behaviour as $n$ gets larger and larger.

(a) $u_n = 2^n + 5$

(b) $u_n = 50 - 2n$

(c) $u_n = \dfrac{4n-1}{2n+3}$

(d) $u_n = 2 + (0.1)^n$

(e) $u_n = 2 + (-0.1)^n$

**A** The terms decrease at a steady rate.

**B** The terms increase at a faster and faster rate.

**C** The terms go up and down but get closer and closer to a limit of 2.

**D** The terms increase but at a slower and slower rate, converging to a limit of 2.

**E** The terms decrease but converge to a limit of 2.

**6** Match each sequence below to a graph that shows its behaviour.

(a) $u_n = 3n - 2$

(b) $u_n = \dfrac{3n-1}{n+1}$

(c) $u_n = 3 + (-0.7)^n$

**7** Find an expression for $u_n$ that fits each sequence.

(a) $u_1 = 1,\ u_2 = \frac{1}{2},\ u_3 = \frac{1}{3},\ u_4 = \frac{1}{4},\ \dots$

(b) $u_1 = 2,\ u_2 = \frac{3}{2},\ u_3 = \frac{4}{3},\ u_4 = \frac{5}{4},\ \dots$

**8** The $n$th term of a sequence is $u_n = \dfrac{3n+7}{n}$.

(a) Evaluate $u_{1000}$.

(b) Show that $\dfrac{3n+7}{n} = 3 + \dfrac{7}{n}$.

(c) Hence show that, as $n$ gets larger and larger, $u_n$ converges to a limit of 3.

**\*9** Find an expression for the $n$th term of the sequence $\ -6,\ \frac{7}{2},\ -\frac{8}{3},\ \frac{9}{4},\ \dots$

## B. Inductive definition

The sequence defined by $u_n = 3n + 2$ has terms

$$u_1 = 5,\ u_2 = 8,\ u_3 = 11,\ u_4 = 14,\ u_5 = 17,\ u_6 = 20, \dots$$

Each term can be found by adding 3 to the previous term.

So we can write

$$u_2 = u_1 + 3$$
$$u_3 = u_2 + 3$$
$$u_4 = u_3 + 3 \dots$$

This can be summarised as $u_{n+1} = u_n + 3$.

A rule like this that takes you from one term to the next is called a **recurrence relation**.

If we know the first term and a recurrence relation for a sequence, then we can write down the sequence term by term.

For example, a sequence is defined by $u_1 = 5$ and the recurrence relation $u_{n+1} = 2u_n + 3$.

So $u_2 = 2u_1 + 3 = 2 \times 5 + 3 = 13$

$u_3 = 2u_2 + 3 = 2 \times 13 + 3 = 29$

$u_4 = 2u_3 + 3 = 2 \times 29 + 3 = 61 \dots$

A definition of a sequence that states the first term and a recurrence relation is called an **inductive definition**.

---

### Example 1

A sequence is defined by $v_1 = 16\,000$, $v_{n+1} = 0.85v_n$.

Work out enough terms of the sequence to find the smallest value of $n$ for which $v_n < 10\,000$.

### Solution

$v_1 = 16\,000$

$v_2 = 0.85 \times v_1 = 0.85 \times 16\,000 = 13\,600$

$v_3 = 0.85 \times v_2 = 0.85 \times 13\,600 = 11\,560$

$v_4 = 0.85 \times v_3 = 0.85 \times 11\,560 = 9826$ which is the first value that is less than $10\,000$

So the smallest value is $n = 4$.

---

### Example 2

The sequence 5, 14, 36.5, 92.75, ... is defined by a recurrence relation of the form $u_{n+1} = pu_n + q$ where $p$ and $q$ are constants.

Find the values of $p$ and $q$ and hence write down the recurrence relation.

### Solution

$u_2 = pu_1 + q$ *gives the equation* $\qquad\qquad 14 = 5p + q$

$u_3 = pu_2 + q$ *gives the equation* $\qquad\qquad 36.5 = 14p + q$

*Subtract the first equation from the second.* $\qquad\quad 22.5 = 9p$

$\Rightarrow \qquad p = 2.5$

*Substitute $p = 2.5$ in the first equation.* $\qquad\quad 14 = 12.5 + q$

$\Rightarrow \qquad q = 1.5$

So the recurrence relation is $u_{n+1} = 2.5u_n + 1.5$.

---

### Exercise B (answers p 192)

**1** A sequence of terms $u_1, u_2, u_3, \dots$ is defined by $u_1 = 2$, $u_{n+1} = 3u_n - 5$.

Write down the first six terms of this sequence.

**2** Write down the first four terms of each sequence below.

(a) $u_1 = 6$, $u_{n+1} = 0.5u_n + 2$ 　　　　(b) $u_1 = 10$, $u_{n+1} = 1.3u_n - 4$

**3** A sequence is defined by $a_1 = 2$, $a_{n+1} = (a_n)^2$.

Work out enough terms of this sequence to find the smallest value of $n$ for which $a_n$ is larger than a million.

**4** The sequence 2, 4, 7.2, 12.32, ... is defined by a recurrence relation of the form $u_{n+1} = pu_n + q$ where $p$ and $q$ are constants.

(a) Show that $p$ and $q$ satisfy the equations $4 = 2p + q$ and $7.2 = 4p + q$.

(b) Find the values of $p$ and $q$ and hence write down the recurrence relation.

**5** The sequence 4, 3, 1, –3, ... is defined by a recurrence relation of the form $u_{n+1} = au_n + b$ where $a$ and $b$ are constants.

Find the values of $a$ and $b$ and hence write down the recurrence relation.

**6** A sequence is defined by $u_1 = 9$, $u_{n+1} = ku_n + k$ where $k$ is a constant.
In this sequence, $u_2 = 4$.

(a) Find the value of $k$ and hence write down the recurrence relation.

(b) Find the value of $u_4$.

**7** A sequence is defined by $u_1 = 5$, $u_{n+1} = u_n + p$ where $p$ is a constant.
In this sequence, $u_4 = 17$.

Find the value of $p$.

**8** A sequence is defined by $u_1 = 4$, $u_{n+1} = 2u_n + k$ where $k$ is a constant.
In this sequence, $u_3 = 20.5$.

(a) (i) Write an expression for $u_2$ in terms of $k$.

(ii) Hence write an expression for $u_3$ in terms of $k$.

(b) Form and solve an equation to find the value of $k$.

**9** A sequence is defined by $u_1 = 2$, $u_{n+1} = pu_n + 1$ where $p$ is a constant.
In this sequence, $u_3 = 11$.

(a) (i) Write an expression for $u_2$ in terms of $p$.

(ii) Hence write an expression for $u_3$ in terms of $p$.

(b) Form and solve an equation to find the two possible values for $p$.

**10** A sequence is defined by $u_1 = 4$, $u_{n+1} = pu_n + 7$ where $p$ is a constant.
In this sequence, $u_3 = 9$.

(a) Show that one possible values for $p$ is $\frac{1}{4}$ and find the other value of $p$.

(b) For each value of $p$, work out the first four terms of the sequence.

# C Inductive definition and limits (answers p 193)

A spreadsheet is useful for several questions in this section.

**C1** For each sequence below,

    (i) write down the first six terms, giving them to 4 d.p. where appropriate

    (ii) describe what happens to the terms of the sequence as $n$ gets larger and larger

(a) $u_1 = 3$, $u_{n+1} = u_n + 5$          (b) $u_1 = 0$, $u_{n+1} = 4u_n$

(c) $u_1 = -2$, $u_{n+1} = 3u_n$          (d) $u_1 = 3$, $u_{n+1} = \frac{1}{3}u_n$

(e) $u_1 = 5$, $u_{n+1} = 2u_n - 1$          (f) $u_1 = 3$, $u_{n+1} = \frac{u_n}{2} + 1$

(g) $u_1 = 0.9$, $u_{n+1} = \sqrt{u_n}$          (h) $u_1 = 2$, $u_{n+1} = \frac{1}{u_n} + 5$

(i) $u_1 = 3$, $u_{n+1} = 2u_n - 3$          (j) $u_1 = -5$, $u_{n+1} = \frac{u_n}{5} - 4$

The sequence defined by $u_1 = 3$, $u_{n+1} = 2u_n - 3$ has terms 3, 3, 3, 3, 3, ...
As all its terms are the same we call it a **constant sequence**.

**C2** What value for $u_1$, with the relation $u_{n+1} = 2u_n - 1$, gives a constant sequence?

**C3** $u_1 = c$ with the relation $u_{n+1} = 3u_n - 10$ gives a constant sequence.

(a) Explain why $c$ must satisfy the equation $c = 3c - 10$.

(b) Solve the equation to find the value for $c$ that gives a constant sequence.

**C4** $u_1 = c$ with the relation $u_{n+1} = \frac{u_n}{3} + 6$ gives a constant sequence.

(a) Write down an equation that must be satisfied by $c$.

(b) Solve your equation to find the value for $c$ that gives a constant sequence.

**C5** For each of the following recurrence relations, find a value for $u_1$ that will give a constant sequence.

(a) $u_{n+1} = 3u_n - 8$          (b) $u_{n+1} = 4u_n + 9$

(c) $u_{n+1} = \frac{u_n}{2} - 1$          (d) $u_{n+1} = 6 - \frac{u_n}{5}$

**C6** A sequence is defined by $u_1 = a$, $u_{n+1} = \frac{u_n}{3} + 4$.

Investigate the behaviour of this sequence for various values of $a$.
Do the sequences converge to a limit?
Comment on your results.

**C7** A sequence is defined by $u_1 = b$, $u_{n+1} = \frac{u_n}{4} - 1$.

Investigate the behaviour of this sequence for various values of $b$.
Comment on your results.

The starting value $u_1 = 5$ with the recurrence relation $u_{n+1} = \dfrac{u_n}{2} + 1$ gives the sequence
5, 3.5, 2.75, 2.375, 2.1875, 2.09375, …, which appears to converge to a limit of 2.

If the sequence does converge then $u_{n+1}$ and $u_n$ will get closer and closer to each other and must get closer and closer to the solution of the equation

$$c = \frac{c}{2} + 1$$

which is $c = 2$ as we expected.

**K** If a recurrence relation gives a sequence that converges to a limit, then using the limit as a starting value must give a constant sequence.

However, finding a value that gives a constant sequence for a recurrence relation does not ensure that the relation will in fact give any other sequences that converge to it.

For example, $u_{n+1} = 2u_n + 1$ with $u_1 = -1$ gives the constant sequence $-1, -1, -1, \ldots$ but other values for $u_1$ give sequences that do not converge.

---

### Example 3

The sequence defined by $u_1 = 3$, $u_{n+1} = 0.2u_n + 2$ converges to a limit $l$.
Write down and solve an equation to find $l$.

### Solution

$l$ must satisfy the equation 
$$l = 0.2l + 2$$
$$\Rightarrow \quad 0.8l = 2$$
$$\Rightarrow \quad l = 2 \div 0.8$$
$$= 2.5 \qquad \text{\textit{Working out some terms of the sequence confirms}}$$
*this*: 3, 2.6, 2.52, 2.504, 2.5008, 2.50016, …

---

In the following example, a subscript of 0 is used for the first term.
This is often useful where time is involved.

---

### Example 4

The population of slugs in a garden at time $t$ days from the start of a survey is represented by $p_t$.
It is found that the numbers of slugs approximately fits the sequence defined by

$$p_0 = 10, \; p_{t+1} = 0.4p_t + 15$$

(a) Estimate the number of slugs in the garden after 3 days.

(b) The population of slugs converges to a limit. Determine the limit.

### Solution

(a) $p_0 = 10, p_1 = 19, p_2 = 22.6$ and $p_3 = 24.04$ so the population is about 24 after 3 days.

(b) A limit $l$ must satisfy the equation 
$$l = 0.4l + 15$$
$$\Rightarrow \quad 0.6l = 15$$
$$\Rightarrow \quad l = 15 \div 0.6$$
$$= 25$$

---

**Exercise C** (answers p 193)

**1** Each definition below defines a sequence that converges to a limit.
Write down and solve an equation to find each limit, and work out enough
terms to confirm your result.

(a) $u_1 = 6$, $u_{n+1} = \dfrac{u_n}{3} + 5$

(b) $a_1 = -8$, $a_{n+1} = 0.5a_n - 1$

(c) $p_0 = 0.6$, $p_{t+1} = \dfrac{p_t}{8} + 1$

(d) $b_0 = 10$, $b_{t+1} = 0.6b_t + 2$

**2** The population of birds on a cliff face at time $t$ days from the start of a
survey is represented by $p_t$.

It is found that the number of birds approximately fits the sequence defined by

$$p_0 = 15, \quad p_{t+1} = 0.75p_t + 20$$

(a) Estimate the number of birds on the cliff face after 2 days.

(b) The population of birds converges to a limit. Determine the limit.

**\*3** Some sequences are defined by $u_1 = a$, $u_{n+1} = \dfrac{6}{u_n} + 1$.

(a) Show that there are two possible values for $a$ that give a constant sequence.

(b) Consider the sequence where $u_1 = 5$.

(i) Show that $u_2 = 2.2$.

(ii) Work out the values of $u_3$ to $u_{10}$, correct to 4 d.p.

(iii) The sequence converges to a limit. Write down the value of the limit.

(c) Consider the sequence where $u_1 = -1.9$.

(i) Will this sequence converge to a limit? What do you think this limit will be?

(ii) Work out the first 12 terms of this sequence. Were you right about its limit?

**\*4** Investigate sequences that are generated by $x_1 = 0.4$, $x_{n+1} = rx_n(1 - x_n)$
for various values of $r$.

Mathematicians who work on chaos theory investigate recurrence relations
like this one.

# D Arithmetic sequences (answers p 194)

A sequence is defined by $u_1 = 5$, $u_{n+1} = u_n + 4$

giving
$$u_2 = 5 + 4 = 9,$$
$$u_3 = 9 + 4 = 13$$
$$u_4 = 13 + 4 = 17 \ \dots \text{ and so on.}$$

The sequence has a simple structure – each term is found by adding a fixed number to the
previous one. The number added on each time is sometimes called the **common difference**.

Any sequence with a structure like this is called an **arithmetic sequence**.

It has an inductive definition of the form $u_1 = a$, $u_{n+1} = u_n + d$ where $a$ and $d$ are constants.

**D1** An arithmetic sequence is defined by $u_1 = 10$, $u_{n+1} = u_n + 3$.

(a) Write down the first five terms.

(b) Find the values of $u_{10}$, $u_{100}$ and $u_{1000}$.

(c) Find an expression for the $n$th term $u_n$ in terms of $n$.

**D2** An arithmetic sequence is defined by $x_1 = 10$, $x_{n+1} = x_n - 3$.

(a) Find the values of $x_{10}$, $x_{100}$ and $x_{1000}$.

(b) Find an expression for the $n$th term $x_n$ in terms of $n$.

An arithmetic sequence is defined by $u_1 = 3$, $u_{n+1} = u_n + 4$.
The terms follow this pattern:

$$u_2 = 3 + 4 \qquad\qquad = 3 + 1 \times 4$$
$$u_3 = 3 + 4 + 4 \qquad\quad = 3 + 2 \times 4$$
$$u_4 = 3 + 4 + 4 + 4 \quad = 3 + 3 \times 4$$
$$u_5 = 3 + 4 + 4 + 4 + 4 = 3 + 4 \times 4 \dots$$

This gives us the $n$th term $u_n = 3 + (n-1) \times 4$, which simplifies to $u_n = 4n - 1$.

In general the arithmetic sequence with first term $a$ and common difference $d$ can be written
$$a, \ a + d, \ a + 2d, \ a + 3d, \dots$$
and the $n$th term is $a + (n-1)d$.

**D3** An arithmetic sequence is defined by $x_1 = 6$, $x_{n+1} = x_n + 7$.

(a) Find an expression for the $n$th term $x_n$ in terms of $n$.

(b) Work out the value of $x_{100}$.

**D4** The sequence $11, 14, 17, 20, 23, \dots$ is arithmetic.
Find an expression for the $n$th term.

---

## Example 5

How many terms are in the finite arithmetic sequence $-10, -7, -4, -1, \dots 137$?

## Solution

Using $a$ for the first term and $d$ for the common difference we have $a = -10$ and $d = 3$.

So an expression for the $n$th term is $\quad -10 + 3(n - 1) = -10 + 3n - 3$
$$= 3n - 13$$

For the last term 137 we have $\qquad 3n - 13 = 137$
$$\Rightarrow \qquad 3n = 150$$
$$\Rightarrow \qquad n = 50$$

So the sequence has 50 terms.

---

**Example 6**

The 4th term of an arithmetic sequence is –2 and the 20th term of the same sequence is 22. What is the $n$th term of the sequence?

**Solution**

$$\text{From the 4th term} \quad a + 3d = -2$$
$$\text{From the 20th term} \quad a + 19d = 22$$

*Subtract the first equation from the second.*
$$16d = 24$$
$$\Rightarrow \quad d = 1.5$$

*Substitute $d = 1.5$ in the first equation.*
$$a + 4.5 = -2$$
$$\Rightarrow \quad a = -6.5$$

$$\text{So the } n\text{th term is } -6.5 + 1.5(n - 1)$$
$$= -6.5 + 1.5n - 1.5$$
$$= 1.5n - 8$$

---

**Exercise D** (answers p 194)

**1** A sequence is defined by $u_1 = 5$, $u_{n+1} = u_n + 9$.
  **(a)** Write down the first four terms.
  **(b)** Find an expression for $u_n$ in terms of $n$.
  **(c)** Find the value of $u_{50}$.

**2** The sequence 90, 88.5, 87, 85.5, ... is arithmetic.
  **(a)** Find the 20th term.
  **(b)** Find an expression for the $n$th term.
  **(c)** Find the value of $n$ for which the $n$th term in the sequence is 42.

**3** The common difference of an arithmetic sequence is 3 and the 10th term is 35. What is the first term?

**4** Work out how many terms there are in each of these finite arithmetic sequences.
  **(a)** 5, 7, 9, ..., 97
  **(b)** 6, 7.2, 8.4, ..., 27.6
  **(c)** 5, 3.5, 2, ..., –40
  **(d)** $\frac{2}{5}$, $\frac{4}{5}$, $1\frac{1}{5}$, ..., 40

**5** The first term of an arithmetic sequence is 6 and the 10th term is 42. What is the 100th term of this sequence?

**6** The 5th term of an arithmetic sequence is 0 and the 19th term is 7. What is the $n$th term of this sequence?

**7** The 20th term of an arithmetic sequence is –44 and the 3rd term is 7. Find the 50th term of this sequence.

**8** The 7th term of an arithmetic sequence is 22.
The 15th term is six times the first term.
Find the first term and the common difference.

**9** The 12th term of an arithmetic sequence is 35.
The 7th term is four times the 2nd term.
Find the $n$th term of the sequence.

**10** The first term of an arithmetic sequence is six times the 5th term.
The sum of the 2nd and 8th terms is 8.
Find the 20th term of this sequence.

## E Arithmetic series (answers p 194)

**D** **E1** The diagram shows some cans arranged in a pyramid.

(a) How many cans are in this pyramid?

(b) What about a pyramid like this with 100 cans on the bottom row?

The word **series** can be used to mean the sum of the terms of a sequence.
So an **arithmetic series** is the sum of the terms of an arithmetic sequence.

Examples of arithmetic series are

$$4 + 5 + 6 + 7 + \ldots \qquad \text{(an infinite series)}$$
$$19 + 21 + 23 + \ldots + 59 \qquad \text{(a finite series)}$$

Many mathematical problems lead to series.
For example, the pyramid problem in E1 (b) above can be solved by finding the sum

$$1 + 2 + 3 + \ldots + 98 + 99 + 100$$

One way is to consider the sum written out with its 'reverse' below it.

$$1 \ + \ 2 \ + \ 3 \ + \ \ldots \ + \ 98 \ + \ 99 \ + \ 100$$
$$100 \ + \ 99 \ + \ 98 \ + \ \ldots \ + \ 3 \ + \ 2 \ + \ 1$$

This gives 100 pairs of numbers that each add up to 101.
This gives a total of $100 \times 101 = 10\,100$.

However, this is twice the required sum so $1 + 2 + 3 + \ldots + 98 + 99 + 100 = \frac{10\,100}{2} = 5050$.

We can use this method to find the sum of the first $n$ positive integers which can be written

$$1 \ + \ \ 2 \ \ + \ \ 3 \ \ + \ \ldots \ + \ (n-2) \ + \ (n-1) \ + \ n$$

with its reverse $\quad n \ + \ (n-1) \ + \ (n-2) \ + \ \ldots \ + \ \ 3 \ \ + \ \ 2 \ \ + \ 1$

This gives us $n$ pairs of numbers that each add up to $(n + 1)$.

This gives a total of $n(n + 1)$, which is twice the required sum.

**K** So $1 + 2 + 3 + \ldots + n = \frac{1}{2}n(n + 1)$.

**E2** Work out the sum of the first 50 positive integers.

**E3** (a) (i)  Work out the sum  $1 + 2 + 3 + \ldots + 200$.

(ii) Work out the sum  $1 + 2 + 3 + \ldots + 150$.

(b) Hence find the sum of the integers from 151 to 200 inclusive.

**E4** Work out the sum  $60 + 61 + 62 + \ldots + 250$.

**E5** (a) Work out the sum of the first 20 positive integers.

(b) Hence work out the sum of the first 20 multiples of 7.

**D**  **E6** Work out the following sums.

(a)  $4 + 7 + 10 + 13 + 16 + 19 + 22 + 25 + 28 + 31 + 34 + 37 + 40 + 43$

(b)  $4 + 7 + 10 + 13 + \ldots + 301$

Using $l$ for the last term, any arithmetic series and its reverse can be written

$$a \quad + \quad (a + d) \quad + \quad (a + 2d) \quad + \quad \ldots \quad + \quad (l - 2d) \quad + \quad (l - d) \quad + \quad l$$
$$l \quad + \quad (l - d) \quad + \quad (l - 2d) \quad + \quad \ldots \quad + \quad (a + 2d) \quad + \quad (a + d) \quad + \quad a$$

This gives $n$ pairs of numbers that each add up to $(a + l)$.

This gives a total of $n(a + l)$, which is twice the required sum.

**K**  So the sum to $n$ terms of an arithmetic series is  $\frac{1}{2}n(a + l)$
where $a$ is the first term and $l$ is the last term of the arithmetic sequence.

The last term can be written as $(a + (n - 1)d)$ where $n$ is the number of terms.

So $\frac{1}{2}n(a + l) = \frac{1}{2}n(a + a + (n - 1)d) = \frac{1}{2}n(2a + (n - 1)d)$.

**K**  The sum to $n$ terms of an arithmetic series is  $\frac{1}{2}n(2a + (n - 1)d)$
where $a$ is the first term and $d$ is the common difference of the arithmetic sequence.

---

## Example 7

Find the sum of the arithmetic series  $2 + 8 + 14 + \ldots + 284$.

## Solution

$a = 2$  and  $d = 6$  so the last term is  $2 + 6(n - 1)$  where $n$ is the number of terms in the series.

$$\begin{aligned}
\text{Hence} \qquad 2 + 6(n - 1) &= 284 \\
6(n - 1) &= 282 \\
n - 1 &= 47 \\
n &= 48
\end{aligned}$$

$$\begin{aligned}
\text{So the sum is} \qquad \tfrac{1}{2}n(a + l) &= \tfrac{1}{2} \times 48 \times (2 + 284) \\
&= 24 \times 286 \\
&= 6864
\end{aligned}$$

---

**Example 8**

Find the sum of the arithmetic series $3 + 4.5 + 6 + 7.5 + \ldots$ as far as the 50th term.

**Solution**

$a = 3$, $d = 1.5$ and $n = 50$

So the sum is $\frac{1}{2}n(2a + (n-1)d) = \frac{1}{2} \times 50 \times (2 \times 3 + (50-1) \times 1.5)$

$$= 25 \times (6 + 49 \times 1.5)$$
$$= 25 \times 79.5$$
$$= 1987.5$$

**Exercise E** (answers p 194)

**1** Find the sum of the first 200 positive integers.

**2** Find the sum of the integers from 37 to 152 inclusive.

**3** Find the sum of the integers from 200 to 400 inclusive.

**4** Find the sum of all the integers between 1 and 1000 that are divisible by 3.

**5** Find the sum of the first 40 terms of the arithmetic series $9 + 16 + 23 + \ldots$

**6** The first term of an arithmetic series is 10 and the common difference is $\frac{1}{2}$.
Show that the sum of the first 100 terms of the series is 3475.

**7** The first three terms of an arithmetic series are $x$, 22 and $x - 4$ respectively.
(a) Find the value of $x$.
(b) Find the sum of the first 30 terms of the series.

**8** The first term of an arithmetic series is 1 and the 10th term is 7.
Show that the sum of the first 40 terms of the series is 560.

**9** Evaluate the sum of the arithmetic series $2 + 7 + 12 + \ldots + 222$.

**10** The first term of an arithmetic series is 3.
The sum of the first 25 terms is 525.
Find the 2nd term.

**11** The sum of the 5th and 10th terms of an arithmetic series is $11\frac{1}{2}$.
The sum of the first 20 terms is 85.
What is the first term?

**12** A car is accelerating from rest. In the first second it moves 3 m, in the second second it moves 5 m, in the third second it moves 7 m, and so on.
(a) How far will it travel in 15 seconds?
(b) How long will it take to cover a kilometre?

**13** Each year, for 40 years, Anne will pay money into a savings scheme.
In the first year, she pays in £500. Her payments then increase by £50 each year,
so that she pays in £550 in the second year, £600 in the third year, and so on.

(a) Find the amount that Anne will pay in the 40th year.

(b) Find the total amount that Anne will pay in over the 40 years.

Over the same 40 years, Brian will also pay money into the savings scheme.
In the first year he pays in £890 and his payments then increase by £$d$ each year.

Given that Brian and Anne will pay in exactly the same amount over the 40 years,

(c) find the value of $d$. *Edexcel*

**14** Find, in terms of $n$, the sum of the first $n$ odd numbers.

**15** A set of steps for the end of a pier are built of stone.
A sketch of the cross-section of the steps is shown.

Each step has a rise of 0.2 m
and a tread of 0.6 m.

Form a series to calculate
the area of the cross-section.

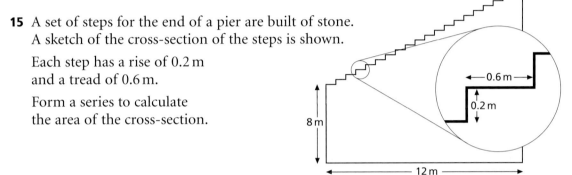

**\*16** The spool for a cassette tape has a circumference of 70 mm.
The thickness of the tape makes each turn is 0.075 mm longer than the previous one.

How many times will the spool turn playing a tape that is 54 metres long?

## F Sigma notation

The sum of the first 20 square numbers can be written as $1^2 + 2^2 + 3^2 + 4^2 + \dots + 20^2$.

We can use shorthand notation to write this sum as

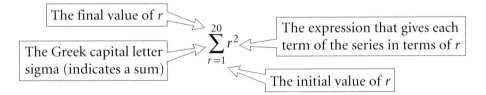

We can use any letter as the variable. For example,

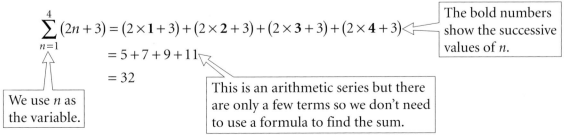

**Example 9**

Evaluate $\displaystyle\sum_{i=0}^{5} i^3$.

**Solution**

$$\sum_{i=0}^{5} i^3 = 0^3 + 1^3 + 2^3 + 3^3 + 4^3 + 5^3$$
$$= 0 + 1 + 8 + 27 + 64 + 125$$
$$= 225$$

---

**Example 10**

Evaluate $\displaystyle\sum_{r=1}^{40} (3r - 5)$.

**Solution**

$$\sum_{r=1}^{40} (3r - 5) = (3 \times 1 - 5) + (3 \times 2 - 5) + (3 \times 3 - 5) + \ldots + (3 \times 40 - 5)$$
$$= -2 + 1 + 4 + \ldots + 115 \qquad\qquad \textit{It's an arithmetic series with 40 terms so use a rule.}$$
$$= \tfrac{1}{2} \times 40 \times (-2 + 115) \qquad\qquad \textit{The rule that the sum is } \tfrac{1}{2}n(a + l) \textit{ is used here.}$$
$$= 2260$$

---

**Example 11**

The $n$th term of an arithmetic sequence is $u_n$ where $u_n = 1 + 2.5n$.

Evaluate $\displaystyle\sum_{n=1}^{100} u_n$.

**Solution**

$$\sum_{n=1}^{100} u_n = u_1 + u_2 + u_3 + \ldots + u_{100}$$
$$= 3.5 + 6 + 8.5 + \ldots + 251$$
$$= \tfrac{1}{2} \times 100 \times (3.5 + 251) \qquad\qquad \textit{The rule that the sum is } \tfrac{1}{2}n(a + l) \textit{ is used here.}$$
$$= 12\,725$$

---

**Exercise F** (answers p 195)

**1** Evaluate each of these.

(a) $\displaystyle\sum_{n=1}^{5} 2n$  (b) $\displaystyle\sum_{i=0}^{7} (i + 1)$  (c) $\displaystyle\sum_{r=1}^{3} r^3$  (d) $\displaystyle\sum_{i=1}^{6} i$

(e) $\displaystyle\sum_{r=3}^{5} (3r - 1)$  (f) $\displaystyle\sum_{n=4}^{7} n^2$  (g) $\displaystyle\sum_{r=2}^{5} r(r + 1)$  (h) $\displaystyle\sum_{i=2}^{4} \frac{1}{i}$

**2** Evaluate each of these by using an appropriate rule.

(a) $\displaystyle\sum_{n=1}^{46} n$  (b) $\displaystyle\sum_{i=1}^{40} 3i$  (c) $\displaystyle\sum_{r=1}^{30} (r + 5)$  (d) $\displaystyle\sum_{i=1}^{60} (2i + 7)$

(e) $\displaystyle\sum_{r=1}^{40} (0.5r - 3)$  (f) $\displaystyle\sum_{n=1}^{25} (8 + 0.5n)$  (g) $\displaystyle\sum_{r=1}^{50} (30 - 3r)$  (h) $\displaystyle\sum_{i=1}^{100} (3 + 1.2i)$

**3 (a)** Evaluate **(i)** $\sum_{i=1}^{50} i$  **(ii)** $\sum_{i=1}^{30} i$  **(b)** Hence evaluate $\sum_{i=31}^{50} i$.

**4 (a)** How many terms are in the sum $\sum_{r=9}^{36} (2r + 5)$?  **(b)** Show that $\sum_{r=9}^{36} (2r + 5) = 1400$.

**5** Evaluate each of these.

**(a)** $\sum_{n=10}^{20} (3n - 2)$  **(b)** $\sum_{i=4}^{40} (1.4i + 5)$  **(c)** $\sum_{r=25}^{70} (28 - 5r)$

**6 (a)** Show that $\sum_{r=1}^{20} (3r - 1) = 610$.  **(b)** Show that $\sum_{r=1}^{n} (3r - 1) = \frac{1}{2}n(3n + 1)$.

---

## Key points

- Subscript notation can be used to label the terms of a sequence.
  For example: $u_1, u_2, u_3, u_4, \ldots$  (p 114)

- A sequence can be defined by a rule for the $n$th term such as $u_n = n^2 + 1$.  (p 114)

- An inductive definition defines a sequence by giving the first term and a rule
  such as $u_{n+1} = 4u_n + 1$ that gives each term in terms of the previous one.  (pp 116–117)

- Some sequences get closer and closer to a value called the limit.
  We say the sequence converges to a limit (or limiting value).

  The limit, $l$, of a converging sequence can be found from the inductive definition
  by replacing $u_{n+1}$ and $u_n$ by $l$ to form an equation in $l$ and then solving it.  (pp 115, 120)

- An arithmetic sequence is one where each term can be found by
  adding a fixed number (the common difference) to the previous one.  (p 121)

- An inductive definition of an arithmetic sequence is $u_1 = a$, $u_{n+1} = u_n + d$
  where $a$ is the first term and $d$ is the common difference.

  The sequence can be written $a, a + d, a + 2d, a + 3d, a + 4d, \ldots$  (pp 121–122)

- The $n$th term of an arithmetic sequence $u_1, u_2, u_3, \ldots$ is $u_n = a + (n - 1)d$.  (p 122)

- When the terms of an arithmetic sequence are added together they form
  an arithmetic series. The sum of the first $n$ terms of an arithmetic series is
  $$\frac{1}{2}n(2a + (n - 1)d)$$
  or  $\frac{1}{2}n(a + l)$  where $l$ is the last term.  (p 125)

- The sum of the first $n$ positive integers is $\frac{1}{2}n(n + 1)$.  (p 124)

- Sigma notation can be used as a shorthand for series.
  For example, the sum of the first 20 multiples of 3 can be written as
  $$\sum_{i=1}^{20} 3i$$
  (p 127)

## Mixed questions (answers p 195)

**1** The 5th term of an arithmetic sequence is $-1$ and the 10th term of the sequence is 1.
Find an expression for the $n$th term of this sequence.

**2** The sequence of terms $u_1, u_2, u_3, \ldots$ is defined by
$$u_1 = 8, \quad u_{n+1} = au_n + 1 \qquad \text{where } a \text{ is a negative constant.}$$
The third term of the sequence is $u_3 = 2.68$.
Find the value of $a$.

**3** The sequence defined by $u_1 = 7, \quad u_{n+1} = 0.2u_n + 4$ converges to a limit $k$.
By forming and solving an equation, find the value of $k$.

**4** Find the sum of the integers from 1 to 150 inclusive.

**5** Find the sum of the 200 integers from 301 to 500 inclusive.

**6** The 10th term of an arithmetic series is 20.
The common difference is 1.8.

(a) Find the first term.

(b) Find the sum of the first thirty terms of the series.

**7** Evaluate $\displaystyle\sum_{n=1}^{200} (2n+5)$.

**8** The first term of an arithmetic series is $-5$ and the 9th term of the series is 1.

(a) Find the common difference and the sum of the first 30 terms of the series.

(b) How many terms of the series are less than 50?

**9** In the first month after opening, a mobile phone shop sold 280 phones.
A model for future trading assumes that sales will increase by $x$ phones per month for the next 35 months, so that $(280 + x)$ phones will be sold in the second month, $(280 + 2x)$ in the third month, and so on.

Using this model with $x = 5$, calculate

(a) (i) the number of phones sold in the 36th month,

  (ii) the total number of phones sold over the 36 months.

The shop sets a sales target of 17 000 phones to be sold over the 36 months.
Using the same model,

(b) find the least value of $x$ required to achieve this target.                     Edexcel

**10** The sum of the first 10 terms of an arithmetic series is 5.
The sum of the second and tenth terms of this series is 4.
Find the first and second terms of this series.

**11** The sum of the first 30 terms of an arithmetic series is 90.
The sum of the next 10 terms is also 90.
Find the first term and the common difference.

## Test yourself (answers p 195)

None of these questions requires a calculator.

**1** The sequence $u_1, u_2, u_3, \ldots u_n$ is defined by the recurrence relation
$$u_{n+1} = pu_n + 5, \quad u_1 = 2, \quad \text{where } p \text{ is a constant.}$$
Given that $u_3 = 8$, show that one possible values for $p$ is $\frac{1}{2}$ and find the other value of $p$.

Edexcel

**2** The sequence defined by $u_1 = 45$, $u_{n+1} = \frac{3}{5}u_n - 2$ converges to a limit $l$.
   **(a)** Find the value of $u_3$.
   **(b)** By forming and solving an equation, find the value of $l$.

**3** An arithmetic sequence $u_1, u_2, u_3, \ldots$ has $n$th term $u_n$, where $u_n = 100 - 4n$.
   **(a)** Write down the values of $u_1$, $u_2$, and $u_3$.
   **(b)** Find the number of positive terms in the sequence.

**4** Find the sum of the integers from 1 to 50 inclusive.

**5** Find the sum of the integers from 21 to 100 inclusive.

**6** Find the sum of the 20 terms of the arithmetic series $1 + 4 + 7 + \ldots + 58$.

**7** The first three terms of an arithmetic series are $k$, 7.5 and $k + 7$ respectively.
   **(a)** Find the value of $k$.
   **(b)** Find the sum of the first 31 terms of this series.

Edexcel

**8** Find the sum of the first 25 terms of the arithmetic series $4 + 4\frac{1}{2} + 5 + \ldots$

**9** The 5th term of an arithmetic series is 42. The common difference is −5.
   **(a)** Find the first term.
   **(b)** Find the sum of the first 20 terms of the series.

**10 (a)** An arithmetic series has first term $a$ and common difference $d$.
   Prove that the sum of the first $n$ terms of the series is $\frac{1}{2}n[2a + (n-1)d]$.

A company made a profit of £54 000 in the year 2001.
A model for future performance assumes that yearly profits will
increase in an arithmetic sequence with common difference £$d$.
This model predicts total profits of £619 200 for the 9 years 2001 to 2009 inclusive.
   **(b)** Find the value of $d$.

Using your value of $d$,
   **(c)** find the predicted profit for the year 2011.

Edexcel

**11 (a)** Find the sum of all the integers between 1 and 1000 which are divisible by 7.
   **(b)** Hence, or otherwise, evaluate $\displaystyle\sum_{r=1}^{142}(7r + 2)$.

Edexcel

# 10 Differentiation

In this chapter you will learn
- that the gradient of a graph gives the rate of change
- how to find the gradient of a curved graph
- what differentiation is
- how to differentiate $x^n$
- how to find the equations of a tangent and a normal to a graph
- about the second order derivative of a function

## A Gradient as rate of change (answers p 196)

The Earth's crust gets hotter as you go deeper.

The graph below shows the relationship between temperature and depth in a mine.
The graph is a straight line, showing that temperature increases at a steady rate with depth.

The **rate of change** of temperature with respect to depth can be measured in °C per metre.

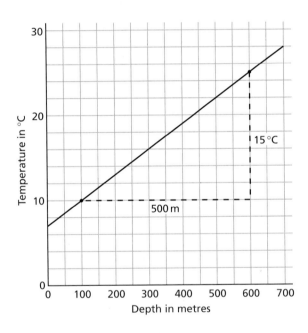

Two points on the graph have been chosen.
The difference in depth between these points is 500 m.
The difference in temperature is 15 °C.

The rate of change of temperature with depth

$$= \frac{\text{difference in temperature}}{\text{difference in depth}}$$

$$= \frac{15\,°C}{500\,m}$$

$$= \textbf{0.03 °C per m}$$

Notice that this is also the **gradient** of the graph.

**A1** (a) Use the value of the rate of change to calculate by how much the temperature increases when the depth increases by 100 m.

    (b) Read from the graph the temperature at the surface.

    (c) Calculate the temperature at a depth of

        (i) 1000 m         (ii) 1300 m         (iii) 2500 m

    (d) At what depth will the temperature be 67 °C?

**A2** This graph shows the relationship between temperature and height on a mountain.

(Note that the scale on the horizontal axis is different from the previous one.)

(a) Find the rate of change of temperature with height in °C per metre. How do you show that it is a rate of **decrease**?

(b) By how much does the temperature decrease for every extra 100 m climbed?

(c) What will the temperature be at a height of 6000 m?

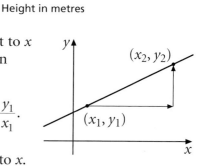

If $y$ is a linear function of $x$, the rate of change of $y$ with respect to $x$ can be found by choosing any two points $(x_1, y_1)$ and $(x_2, y_2)$ on the line and calculating

$$\frac{\text{the difference between the } y\text{-coordinates}}{\text{the difference between the } x\text{-coordinates}}, \text{ which is } \frac{y_2 - y_1}{x_2 - x_1}.$$

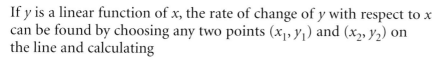

The symbol $\dfrac{dy}{dx}$ is used for the rate of change of $y$ with respect to $x$.
For a linear graph the rate of change is equal to the gradient.

**A3** (a) The sketch on the right shows the graph of $y = 2x + 1$. What is the value of $\dfrac{dy}{dx}$?

(b) What is the value of $\dfrac{dy}{dx}$ for each of these linear functions?

(i) $y = 2x + 3$      (ii) $y = 5x - 1$

(iii) $y = \frac{1}{2}x + 9$      (iv) $y = 6 + 4x$

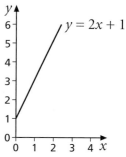

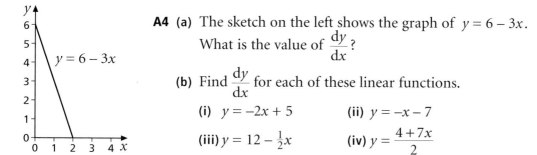

**A4** (a) The sketch on the left shows the graph of $y = 6 - 3x$. What is the value of $\dfrac{dy}{dx}$?

(b) Find $\dfrac{dy}{dx}$ for each of these linear functions.

(i) $y = -2x + 5$      (ii) $y = -x - 7$

(iii) $y = 12 - \frac{1}{2}x$      (iv) $y = \dfrac{4 + 7x}{2}$

**D** **A5** A model vehicle moves along a straight track.
Its position is given by the equation $s = 4t + 5$, where $s$ is its distance in
metres from a fixed point and $t$ is the time in seconds.

(a) Sketch a graph of $s$ against $t$.

(b) What is the value of $\dfrac{ds}{dt}$?

(c) What does $\dfrac{ds}{dt}$ represent in this case?

**A6** You are told that a straight-line graph has gradient given by $\dfrac{dy}{dx} = 3$.

(a) What can you deduce about the equation of the line?

(b) You are given the additional information that the line goes through $(2, 5)$.
What is the equation of the line?

**A7** $y = 5$ is an example of a constant function ($y$ has the value 5 whatever the value of $x$).
Sketch the graph of $y = 5$. What is the value of $\dfrac{dy}{dx}$ for a constant function?

**Exercise A** (answers p 196)

**1** Find the value of $\dfrac{dy}{dx}$ for each of these linear functions.

(a) $y = 3x - 2$    (b) $y = 5 - 7x$    (c) $y = 4 + x$    (d) $y = -2$    (e) $y = \frac{1}{2}(3x - 1)$

**2** The cost of electricity consists of a standing charge of 900p and a charge
of 5p for each unit of electricity used.

(a) Write a formula for the total cost, $C$ pence, in terms of the number of units, $n$.

(b) What is the value of $\dfrac{dC}{dn}$? Explain what it means.

**3** A linear graph has $\dfrac{dy}{dx} = 5$ and passes through the point $(-1, 2)$. Find its equation.

**4** Find the equation of the line through $(3, 2)$ with $\dfrac{dy}{dx} = -2$.

**5** A line passes through the points $(1, 5)$ and $(4, 11)$. Find $\dfrac{dy}{dx}$ and the equation
of the line.

**6** A line passes through $(4, 7)$ and $(10, 4)$. Find $\dfrac{dy}{dx}$ and the equation of the line.

**7** (a) A plumber charges £30 for a call-out plus £20 per hour for labour.

(i) Write a formula for the charge £$C$ in terms of $t$, the number of hours taken.

(ii) What is the value of $\dfrac{dC}{dt}$?

(b) Another plumber charges £70 for a 2-hour job and £145 for a 5-hour job.
Find $\dfrac{dC}{dt}$ in this case and say what it means.

## B Gradient of a curve (answers p 196)

This is the distance–time graph of
a train passing through a station.

The gradient is $\frac{40}{5} = 8$.

This represents the speed of the train in m/s.

The gradient is the same at every point of
the graph.

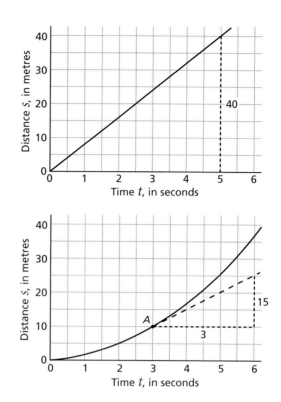

This is the distance–time graph of
a train setting out from a station.

The graph is a curve, getting steeper. This
shows that the train's speed is increasing.

Imagine that the speed stops increasing at
point $A$ and that the train continues at
a constant speed from then on.

The dashed line shows how the graph would
continue. It is the **tangent** at point $A$.

The gradient of the curve at $A$ is defined
as the gradient of the tangent at $A$.

The gradient at $A$ is 5.
So the speed of the train at $A$ is 5 m/s.

**B1** This is the distance–time graph for a
tube train leaving a station.

The tangent to the graph has been drawn
at the point where $t = 3$.

(a) Find the gradient of this tangent.

(b) What does the gradient represent?

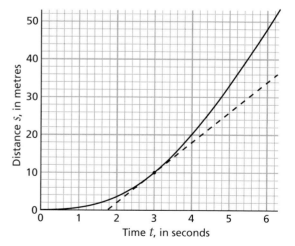

**B2** Use the tangents drawn here to find the gradient of the curve

$$y = -\tfrac{1}{4}x^2 + 2x - 1$$

at the points $(2, 2)$ and $(5, 2.75)$.

**K** The notation $\dfrac{dy}{dx}$ is still used for curved graphs, but now it means the gradient of the tangent to the curve.

**D** **B3** On graph paper, draw accurately the graph of $y = x^2$ for values of $x$ from $-3$ to $3$, using the same scale for both axes.

(a) Draw, as accurately as possible, the tangent at $(1.5, 2.25)$ and hence find the gradient $\dfrac{dy}{dx}$ of the curve at this point.

(b) By repeating this process as necessary, and using the symmetry of the graph, copy and complete this table.

| $x$ | $-2$ | $-1.5$ | $-1$ | $0$ | $1$ | $1.5$ | $2$ |
|---|---|---|---|---|---|---|---|
| $\dfrac{dy}{dx}$ | | | | | | | |

(c) Plot all the points $\left( x, \dfrac{dy}{dx} \right)$ to obtain the gradient graph for $y = x^2$.

(d) What do these points suggest for the equation of the gradient graph?
Write its equation $\dfrac{dy}{dx} = \ldots$

Questions B4 and B5 can be done either by accurate drawing on graph paper or by using a graph plotter.

**B4** Draw the graph of $y = 4x - x^2$ for values of $x$ from $-2$ to $4$, using the same scale for both axes.

(a) Find the gradients of tangents at several points and record your results in a table as in question B3.

(b) Plot the points $\left( x, \dfrac{dy}{dx} \right)$.

(c) Suggest an equation for the gradient graph.

**B5** Draw the graph of $y = 0.1x^3 - x$ for values of $x$ from $-4$ to $5$, using the same scale for both axes.

(a) Find the gradients of tangents at several points and record your results in a table as in question B3.

(b) Plot the points $\left( x, \dfrac{dy}{dx} \right)$.

(c) What type of equation does the gradient graph appear to have?

In questions B3 to B5 you drew a graph of a function ($y$) together with a graph of $\dfrac{dy}{dx}$. The latter graph shows the **gradient function** of the original function.

Here, for example, is a typical curved graph.

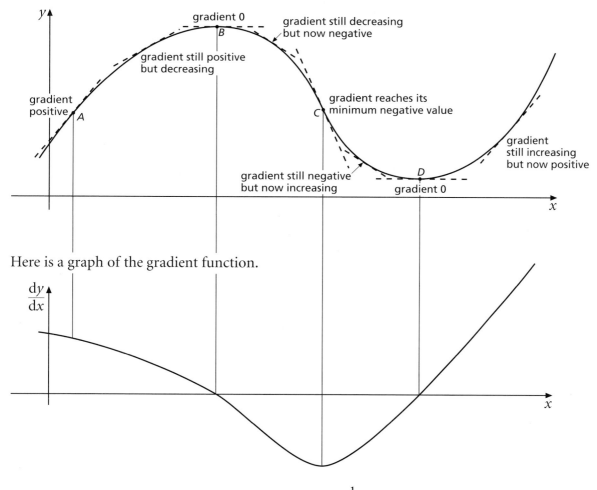

Here is a graph of the gradient function.

At points $B$ and $D$ on the original graph, the value of $\dfrac{dy}{dx}$ is 0.
These are called **stationary points**.

$B$ is called a **local maximum** and $D$ a **local minimum**.

$B$ and $D$ are also called **turning points** because the gradient changes from positive to negative or vice versa.

## Exercise B (answers p 197)

1  Copy this graph.
   Directly beneath it, sketch the graph of its
   gradient function, using the same scale for $x$.

   Mark any points you think are special and
   describe them.

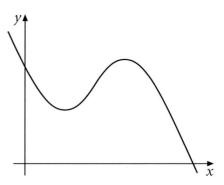

2  Repeat question 1 for each of these graphs.

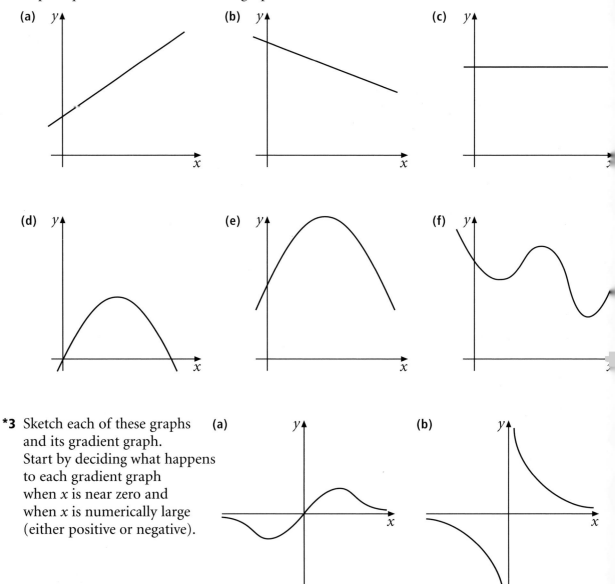

(a)   (b)   (c)

(d)   (e)   (f)

*3  Sketch each of these graphs   (a)   (b)
    and its gradient graph.
    Start by deciding what happens
    to each gradient graph
    when $x$ is near zero and
    when $x$ is numerically large
    (either positive or negative).

## C Calculating the gradient of a curved graph (answers p 197)

The problem of finding the gradient function $\dfrac{dy}{dx}$ for a given function $y$
was crucial for the advance of mechanics, the branch of theoretical physics that
deals with the laws of motion. The problem belongs to a part of mathematics
called 'calculus' which was developed independently by Newton (1642–1727)
in England and Leibniz (1646–1716) in Germany.

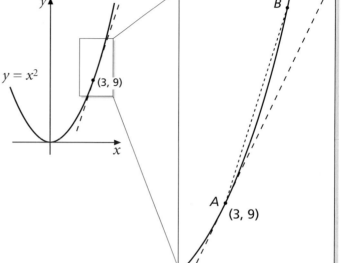

Here we start with a specific example:
how to find the gradient of the graph
of $y = x^2$ at the point $(3, 9)$.

Near the point $(3, 9)$ the graph
itself and the tangent are very
close together. (You can see this by
zooming in on a graph plotter.)

$A$ is the point $(3, 9)$ and $B$ is a
point on the graph very close to $A$.

The gradient of $AB$ will be very
close to the gradient of the tangent.

Also, the gradient of $AB$ gets closer
to the gradient of the tangent as
$B$ gets closer to $A$.

Suppose, for example, that the $x$-coordinate of $B$ is 3.1.
Because $B$ is on the graph $y = x^2$, its $y$-coordinate will be $3.1^2 = 9.61$.

The gradient of $AB$ $\dfrac{\text{difference in } y}{\text{difference in } x} = \dfrac{9.61 - 9}{3.1 - 3} = \dfrac{0.61}{0.1} = 6.1$.

To get a better approximation, move $B$ closer to $A$.

Let the $x$-coordinate of $B$ be 3.01, so that the $y$-coordinate is $3.01^2 = 9.0601$.

Now the gradient of $AB = \dfrac{9.0601 - 9}{3.01 - 3} = \dfrac{0.0601}{0.01} = 6.01$.

**C1** (a) Repeat the calculation when the $x$-coordinate of $B$ is 3.001.

  (b) What do the results, taken together, suggest as the exact value of the
    gradient of the tangent at $(3, 9)$?

**C2** Now let $A$ be the point $(4, 16)$.
  Calculate approximations to the gradient of the tangent at $A$ by letting the
  $x$-coordinate of $B$ be first 4.1, then 4.01 and then 4.001.

  What conclusion do you draw?

The symbol $\delta x$ ('delta $x$') is used for the difference between the $x$-coordinates of two points on the graph. (The $\delta$ is not a number multiplying $x$; $\delta x$ is one complete symbol.)

Similarly, $\delta y$ means the difference between the $y$-coordinates of the two points.

The gradient of the line joining the two points is thus $\dfrac{\delta y}{\delta x}$.

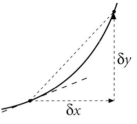

The calculation of $\dfrac{\delta y}{\delta x}$ can be done in a table or spreadsheet.

Here, for example, are the calculations that lead to the gradient of $y = x^2$ at $(5, 25)$.

| $x$-coordinate of A | $y$-coordinate of A | $x$-coordinate of B | $y$-coordinate of B | $\delta x$ | $\delta y$ | $\dfrac{\delta y}{\delta x}$ |
|---|---|---|---|---|---|---|
| 5 | 25 | 5.1 | 26.01 | 0.1 | 1.01 | 10.1 |
| 5 | 25 | 5.01 | 25.1001 | 0.01 | 0.1001 | 10.01 |
| 5 | 25 | 5.001 | 25.010001 | 0.001 | 0.010001 | 10.001 |

It seems clear from this table that as $\delta x$ gets smaller, $\dfrac{\delta y}{\delta x}$ gets closer to 10. So the gradient of the tangent at $(5, 25)$ is 10.

K

$\dfrac{\delta y}{\delta x}$ is the gradient of the line joining two points on the graph.

$\dfrac{dy}{dx}$ is the gradient of the tangent.

As $\delta x$ gets smaller, the value of $\dfrac{\delta y}{\delta x}$ gets closer and closer to $\dfrac{dy}{dx}$.

C3 (a) Find the gradient of $y = x^2$ when $x = 1$, when $x = 2$ and when $x = 6$.
Record all the results so far in a table:

| $x$ | 0 | 1 | 2 | 3 | 4 | 5 | 6 |
|---|---|---|---|---|---|---|---|
| $\dfrac{dy}{dx}$ | | | | | | | |

(b) What is the equation of the gradient function for $y = x^2$?

D  C4 (The work involved in this question can be shared out, with each student calculating the gradient at one of the values of $x$.)

(a) For the function $y = x^2 + 5x + 3$ calculate the gradient at the points where $x = 0, 1, 2, 3, 4$ and $5$.

For example, a table for $x = 3$ starts like this.

| $x$-coordinate of A | $y$-coordinate of A | $x$-coordinate of B | $y$-coordinate of B | $\delta x$ | $\delta y$ | $\dfrac{\delta y}{\delta x}$ |
|---|---|---|---|---|---|---|
| 3 | 27 | 3.1 | 28.11 | 0.1 | 1.11 | 11.1 |

(b) What is the equation of the gradient function for $y = x^2 + 5x + 3$?

The process of finding the gradient function $\dfrac{dy}{dx}$ for a given function $y$ is called **differentiating** the function with respect to $x$.

The gradient function $\dfrac{dy}{dx}$ is called the **derivative** of the original function.

In question C4 you should have found that if $y = x^2 + 5x + 3$, then $\dfrac{dy}{dx} = 2x + 5$.

Note that $x^2 + 5x + 3$ is the sum of $x^2$ and $5x + 3$.
We have already found that the derivative of $x^2$ is $2x$.
We also know that the derivative of the linear function $5x + 3$ is $5$.

This illustrates a general point about derivatives:

**Ⓚ**    The derivative of the sum of two functions is the sum of the separate derivatives.

You could also think of $x^2 + 5x + 3$ as made up of three parts:

$$y \quad = \quad x^2 + 5x + 3$$
$$\frac{dy}{dx} = \quad 2x + 5 + 0 \qquad \text{(because the gradient of a constant function is 0)}$$

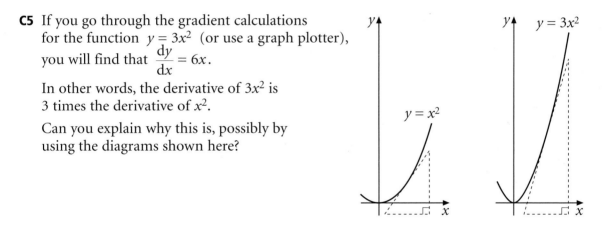

**C5** If you go through the gradient calculations for the function $y = 3x^2$ (or use a graph plotter), you will find that $\dfrac{dy}{dx} = 6x$.

In other words, the derivative of $3x^2$ is 3 times the derivative of $x^2$.

Can you explain why this is, possibly by using the diagrams shown here?

The result in question C5 illustrates another general point about derivatives:

**Ⓚ**    The derivative of $k$ times a function is $k$ times the derivative of the function.

**D**  **C6** (The work in this question can be shared out as in C4.
Or it can be done on a graph plotter if the plotter has the facility for calculating gradients.)

(a) Find the gradient of the function $y = x^3$ when $x = 0, 1, 2, 3, 4, 5$.

(b) From the shape of the graph of $y = x^3$, deduce the gradient at $x = -1, -2, -3, -4, -5$.

(c) Draw the graph of $\dfrac{dy}{dx}$ against $x$. What kind of function does it appear to be?

(d) Find the equation of the graph in (c). This will be the derivative of $y = x^3$.

The derivatives of $y = x^4$, $y = x^5$, and so on, can also be found by the method used so far. The results are:

$$y = x^4 \qquad y = x^5 \qquad y = x^6$$
$$\frac{dy}{dx} = 4x^3 \qquad \frac{dy}{dx} = 5x^4 \qquad \frac{dy}{dx} = 6x^5$$

The general rule for positive integers $n$ is this:

K
If $y = x^n$, then $\dfrac{dy}{dx} = nx^{n-1}$

### Using function notation

If a letter, such as f or g, is used to define a function, the derivative is denoted by f′ or g′.

For example, if $f(x) = x^3 - x^2$, then $f'(x) = 3x^2 - 2x$.

These are all ways of stating essentially the same question:

If $y = x^3 - x^2$, find $\dfrac{dy}{dx}$.

If $f(x) = x^3 - x^2$, find $f'(x)$.

Differentiate $x^3 - x^2$ with respect to x.

If $f(x) = x^3 - x^2$, find the derivative of $f(x)$.

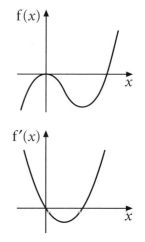

---

### Example 1

If $f(x) = x^4 + 2x^3$, find $f'(x)$.

**Solution**

$f'(x) = 4x^3 + 2(3x^2) = 4x^3 + 6x^2$

---

### Example 2

Find the gradient of the graph of $y = 2x^3 - 5x^2 + 3x + 4$ at the point $P$ where $x = 2$.

**Solution**

*First differentiate.* $\quad \dfrac{dy}{dx} = 2(3x^2) - 5(2x) + 3 + 0 = 6x^2 - 10x + 3$

*Substitute x = 2.* $\quad$ When $x = 2$, $\dfrac{dy}{dx} = 24 - 20 + 3 = 7$

So the gradient at $P$ is 7.

---

### Example 3

If $f(x) = (x^2 + 2)(x^2 - 3)$, find $f'(x)$.

**Solution**

*First multiply out the brackets to get the function in polynomial form.*

$f(x) = x^4 - 3x^2 + 2x^2 - 6 = x^4 - x^2 - 6$. $\qquad$ So $f'(x) = 4x^3 - 2x$.

---

**Exercise C** (answers p 198)

**1** If $y = 2x^3 - 5x + 1$, find $\dfrac{dy}{dx}$.

**2** Find $\dfrac{dy}{dx}$ for each of the following functions.

(a) $y = 4x^2 - x + 9$    (b) $y = 3x^4 - 5x^3 + 1$    (c) $y = 3 + 4x - 6x^2 + 7x^3$

**3** Find the gradient of the graph of $y = x^3 - 6x$ at the point where $x = -1$.

**4** Find the gradient of each of these graphs at the given point.

(a) $y = 4 - 2x^2$ at $(3, -14)$    (b) $y = 2x^3 + 7x$ at $(2, 30)$

**5** (a) Given that $f(x) = 2x^4 - 3x + 1$, find $f'(x)$.

(b) Given that $g(x) = x^5 + 3x^3 - 2x$, find $g'(x)$.

(c) Given that $h(x) = (x^3 + 1)(x - 3)$, find $h'(x)$.

**6** On the same axes, sketch the graphs of $y = x^2$, $y = x^2 + 2$ and $y - x^2 - 3$.
Use the sketch graphs to explain why $\dfrac{dy}{dx}$ is the same for all three functions.

**7** Given that $f(x) = 5x^4 - 6x^3$, find the value of $f'(2)$.

**8** (a) What are the coordinates of the points where the graph of $y = x(x - 2)(x - 3)$ crosses the $x$-axis?

(b) Sketch the graph.

(c) Calculate the gradient of the graph at each point where it crosses the $x$-axis.

**9** The gradient of the graph of $y = 2x^3 + px - 1$, at the point where $x = 1$, is 14.
Find the value of $p$.

**10** The graph of $y = 4x^3 + ax + b$ goes through the point $P(-1, 1)$.
The gradient of the graph at $P$ is 14.
Find the values of $a$ and $b$.

**11** A stone is thrown vertically upwards. While it is in the air, its height $h$ metres above its starting point after $t$ seconds is given by the formula

$$h = 40t - 5t^2$$

(a) For what values of $t$ is $h = 0$?

(b) Sketch the graph of $h$ against $t$.

(c) Find the value of $\dfrac{dh}{dt}$ when $t = 3$. What does this tell you?

(d) Find the value of $\dfrac{dh}{dt}$ when $t = 6$. What does this tell you?

**12** The graph of $y = ax^3 + bx$ has gradient 4 when $x = -1$ and gradient 31 when $x = 2$. Find the values of $a$ and $b$.

# D Differentiating $x^n$, where $n$ is negative or a fraction

If $y = x^n$, where $n$ is a positive integer, then $\dfrac{dy}{dx} = nx^{n-1}$.

This rule also applies when $n$ is negative or a fraction. (The proof of this is beyond the scope of this book.)

---

## Example 4

Given that $y = \dfrac{1}{x^2}$, find $\dfrac{dy}{dx}$.

### Solution

*Write the function as a negative power.*

*Then use the rule for differentiating a power.*

$y = x^{-2}$

$\dfrac{dy}{dx} = -2x^{-2-1} = -2x^{-3} \left( \text{or} -\dfrac{2}{x^3} \right)$

---

## Example 5

Given that $f(x) = 5x^{\frac{2}{3}}$, find $f'(x)$.

### Solution

$f'(x) = 5\left(\frac{2}{3}x^{\frac{2}{3}-1}\right) = \frac{10}{3}x^{-\frac{1}{3}}$

---

## Example 6

Given that $y = x^3\sqrt{x}$, find $\dfrac{dy}{dx}$.

### Solution

*Use the rules of indices to write $x^3\sqrt{x}$ as a single power of x.*   $y = x^3\sqrt{x} = x^3 \times x^{\frac{1}{2}} = x^{\frac{7}{2}}$

$\dfrac{dy}{dx} = \frac{7}{2}x^{\frac{7}{2}-1} = \frac{7}{2}x^{\frac{5}{2}}$

---

## Example 7

Given that $f(x) = \dfrac{1+x}{\sqrt{x}}$, find $f'(x)$.

### Solution

*Write the expression as the sum of two separate fractions.*

$f(x) = \dfrac{1}{\sqrt{x}} + \dfrac{x}{\sqrt{x}} = x^{-\frac{1}{2}} + x^{\frac{1}{2}}$

$f'(x) = -\frac{1}{2}x^{-\frac{3}{2}} + \frac{1}{2}x^{-\frac{1}{2}}$

---

## Exercise D (answers p 198)

**1** Differentiate each of these with respect to $x$.

(a) $x^{-3}$      (b) $\dfrac{1}{x}$      (c) $x^{\frac{1}{3}}$      (d) $\sqrt{x}$      (e) $x^{\frac{3}{4}}$

**2** Find $\dfrac{dy}{dx}$ for each of the following functions.

(a) $y = (\sqrt{x})^3$    (b) $y = x - \dfrac{1}{x}$    (c) $y = \dfrac{3}{x^2}$    (d) $y = \dfrac{1}{4x^3}$    (e) $y = \dfrac{2}{3\sqrt{x}}$

**3 (a)** Write the expression $5x(1 + \sqrt{x})$ without brackets.

**(b)** Given that $f(x) = 5x(1 + \sqrt{x})$, find $f'(x)$.

**4** Find $f'(x)$ for each of the following functions.

**(a)** $\sqrt{x}(3 - x^2)$      **(b)** $x^2(1 + \sqrt{x})$      **(c)** $3x(x - \sqrt{x})$      **(d)** $(x + 3)(\sqrt{x} - 1)$

**5** Find $f'(x)$ for each of the following functions.

**(a)** $f(x) = \dfrac{x+1}{x}$    **(b)** $f(x) = \dfrac{x^2 - 3}{x}$    **(c)** $f(x) = \dfrac{3x + 2}{\sqrt{x}}$    **(d)** $f(x) = \dfrac{1 + \sqrt{x} + x}{x^2}$

**6 (a)** Express $x\sqrt{x}$ in the form $x^p$.

**(b)** Given that $y = x\sqrt{x}$, find the value of $\dfrac{dy}{dx}$ at the point where $x = 9$.

**7 (a)** Expand $\left(\sqrt{x} + \dfrac{1}{\sqrt{x}}\right)^2$.

**(b)** Given that $f(x) = \left(\sqrt{x} + \dfrac{1}{\sqrt{x}}\right)^2$, find $f'(x)$.

## E Tangents and normals

If $A$ is a point on a curve, the line through $A$ perpendicular to the tangent at $A$ is called the **normal** to the curve at $A$.

If the gradient of the tangent is $m$, the gradient of the normal is $-\dfrac{1}{m}$ (because tangent and normal are perpendicular).

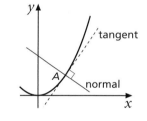

---

**Example 8**

The graph of $y = x^3 - x^2$ passes though the point $P(2, 4)$. Find

**(a)** the gradient of the tangent to the graph at $P$

**(b)** the equation of the tangent to the graph at $P$

**Solution**

**(a)** *First differentiate.*      $\dfrac{dy}{dx} = 3x^2 - 2x$

    *Then substitute $x = 2$.*      When $x = 2$, $\dfrac{dy}{dx} = 12 - 4 = 8$.

         So the gradient of the tangent at $P$ is 8.

**(b)** *The line through $(x_1, y_1)$ with gradient $m$ has equation $y - y_1 = m(x - x_1)$.*

     Equation of tangent at $P$ is $y - 4 = 8(x - 2)$

            $\Rightarrow \quad y = 8x - 12$

---

**Example 9**

The graph of $y = x^2 - 6x + 9$ passes though the point $A$ (4, 1).
Find the equation of the normal to the graph at $A$.

**Solution**

*First find the gradient of the tangent at A.*

$$\frac{dy}{dx} = 2x - 6$$

When $x = 4$, $\dfrac{dy}{dx} = 2$

So the tangent at $A$ has gradient 2.

*Then find the gradient of the normal.*

The normal at $A$ has gradient $-\frac{1}{2}$.

*Use the fact that the normal goes through A.*

Equation of normal at $A$ is $y - 1 = -\frac{1}{2}(x - 4)$

$$\Rightarrow \qquad y = -\tfrac{1}{2}x + 3$$

---

**Exercise E** (answers p 199)

**1** Find the equation of the tangent to $y = x^2$ at the point (3, 9).

**2** Find the equations of the tangent and the normal to $y = x^3$ at the point $(-1, -1)$.

**3** Find the equations of the tangent and the normal to $y = x^3 - 10x + 1$ at the point $P$ where $x = 2$.

**4** Find the equations of the tangent and the normal to $y = x^2(x - 4)$ at (4, 0).

**5** Find the equation of the tangent to $y = x(x^2 - 5)$ at the point where $x = 2$.

**6** Find the equation of the normal to $y = 16 - x^2$ at the point (4, 0).

**7** The graph of $y = (x - 3)(x + 4)$ crosses the $y$-axis at the point $P$.
Find the equation of

(a) the tangent to the graph at $P$     (b) the normal to the graph at $P$

**8** The curve whose equation is $y = 4\sqrt{x}$ passes through the point $A$ (1, 4).

(a) Find the equation of the tangent to the curve at $A$.

(b) Find the equation of the normal to the curve at $A$.

**9** The curve with equation $y = \dfrac{12}{x^2}$ passes through the point $A$ whose $x$-coordinate is 2.

(a) Find the equation of the tangent to the curve at $A$.

(b) Find the equation of the normal to the curve at $A$.

**10** The curve with equation $y = 1 + \dfrac{8}{x}$ passes through the point $A$ whose $x$-coordinate is 4.

   **(a)** Find the equation of the normal to the curve at $A$.

   **(b)** Find the coordinates of the points where this normal crosses the axes.

**11** The curve with equation $y = x + \dfrac{12}{x}$ passes through the points $A\,(4, 7)$ and $B\,(6, 8)$.

   **(a)** Show that the equation of the tangent to the curve at $A$ is $y = \frac{1}{4}x + 6$.

   **(b)** Find the equation of the tangent at $B$.

   **(c)** Find the coordinates of the point where the two tangents intersect.

   **(d)** Show that the equation of the normal to the curve at $A$ is $y = -4x + 23$.

   **(e)** Find the equation of the normal at $B$.

   **(f)** Find the coordinates of the point where the two normals intersect.

## F Second order derivative

Here is the graph of the function
$$y = \tfrac{1}{3}x^3 - 2x^2 + 3x + 1$$

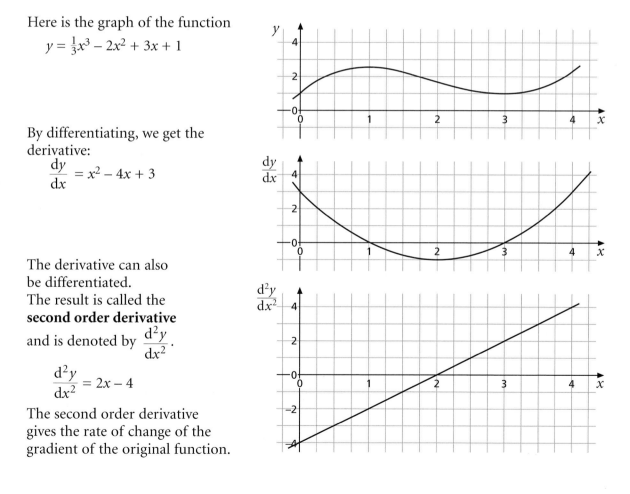

By differentiating, we get the derivative:
$$\frac{\mathrm{d}y}{\mathrm{d}x} = x^2 - 4x + 3$$

The derivative can also be differentiated.
The result is called the **second order derivative** and is denoted by $\dfrac{\mathrm{d}^2 y}{\mathrm{d}x^2}$.

$$\frac{\mathrm{d}^2 y}{\mathrm{d}x^2} = 2x - 4$$

The second order derivative gives the rate of change of the gradient of the original function.

## Example 10

Given that $y = 5x^3 - 2x$, find the value of $\dfrac{d^2y}{dx^2}$ when $x = 2$.

### Solution

$$\frac{dy}{dx} = 15x^2 - 2$$

$$\Rightarrow \quad \frac{d^2y}{dx^2} = 30x. \text{ When } x = 2, \ \frac{d^2y}{dx^2} = 60.$$

**Exercise F** (answers p 199)

**1** Find $\dfrac{d^2y}{dx^2}$ for each of the following functions.

    **(a)** $x^3 - 2x^2 + 5$     **(b)** $x(x^3 - 4)$     **(c)** $(x^2 + 5)(x - 1)$     **(d)** $(x^2 + 1)^2$

**2** Given that $y = \dfrac{12}{x}$ find the value of $\dfrac{d^2y}{dx^2}$ when $x = 2$.

**3** Find $\dfrac{d^2y}{dx^2}$ for each of the following functions.

    **(a)** $y = 4\sqrt{x}$     **(b)** $y = x(x - \sqrt{x})$     **(c)** $y = x^{\frac{2}{3}}$     **(d)** $y = \dfrac{x + \sqrt{x}}{x^2}$

## G Differentiation: algebraic approach

The diagram shows two points on the graph of a function $y = f(x)$.

$A$ is the point $(x, y)$.
$B$ is the point $(x + \delta x, y + \delta y)$.

Both $A$ and $B$ lie on the graph, so

$$y = f(x)$$
$$\text{and } y + \delta y = f(x + \delta x)$$

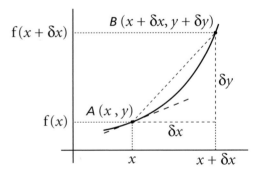

Subtracting, we get

$$\delta y = f(x + \delta x) - f(x)$$

So the gradient of $AB$ is

$$\frac{\delta y}{\delta x} = \frac{f(x + \delta x) - f(x)}{\delta x}$$

To get any further, we need to know the function $f(x)$.
Suppose $f(x) = x^2$.

In this case $\dfrac{\delta y}{\delta x} = \dfrac{(x + \delta x)^2 - x^2}{\delta x} = \dfrac{x^2 + 2x\delta x + (\delta x)^2 - x^2}{\delta x} = \dfrac{\delta x(2x + \delta x)}{\delta x} = 2x + \delta x$

As $B$ gets closer to $A$, $\delta x$ gets closer to 0 and $\dfrac{\delta y}{\delta x}$ gets closer to $2x$.

So $\dfrac{dy}{dx}$, the gradient of the tangent at $A$, is $2x$.

This method can be used to prove that the derivative of $x^3$ is $3x^2$, and so on.

## Key points

- The gradient of a curve at a point is defined as the gradient of the tangent. (p 135)

- If $y$ is given as a function of $x$ (for example $y = x^2 - 3x$), the function that gives the gradient is denoted by $\dfrac{dy}{dx}$ and is called the derivative of the original function. (p 141)

- If a letter is used to denote a function, for example $f(x)$, the derivative is denoted by a dash, $f'(x)$. (p 142)

- The process of finding the derivative of a function is called differentiating the function. (p 141)

- The derivative of $x^n$ is $nx^{n-1}$. (pp 139–142)

- The derivative of a constant function, for example $y = 5$ or $f(x) = 3$, is zero. (p 141)

- The derivative of the sum of functions is the sum of the separate derivatives. The derivative of $k$ times a function is $k$ times the derivative of the function. (p 141)

- The normal to a curve at a point $P$ is the line through $P$ perpendicular to the tangent at $P$. (p 145)

- The second order derivative is the derivative of $\dfrac{dy}{dx}$ and is denoted by $\dfrac{d^2y}{dx^2}$. (p 147)

## Mixed questions (answers p 199)

**1** Given that $f(x) = x^4 - 3x^2 + 5x$, find

    **(a)** $f'(x)$         **(b)** the gradient of the curve $y = f(x)$ at the point where $x = 2$

**2** The distance, $s$ metres, of a model car from its starting point is given by $s = 0.1t^2 + 3t$, where $t$ is the time in seconds from the start.

    **(a)** Find the value of $\dfrac{ds}{dt}$ when $t = 5$.

    **(b)** What does this tell you about the car?

**3** Given that $y = (x^2 + 4)(x - 3)$, find $\dfrac{dy}{dx}$.

**4** The function g is defined by $g(x) = (x + 2)(x^3 - 1)$. Find the value of $g'(-2)$.

**5 (a)** Find the equation of the tangent to the curve $y = 5x^2 - 3x$ at the point $P(1, 2)$.

    **(b)** Find the equation of the normal at $P$.

**6 (a)** Find the equation of the tangent to $y = \frac{1}{4}x^2(x^2 - 6)$ at the point where $x = 2$.

    **(b)** Find the equation of the normal at this point.

**7 (a)** Find the equation of the normal to the graph of $y = 5x - x^2$ at the point $(3, 6)$.

**(b)** This normal intersects the graph again at the point $A$.
Find the coordinates of $A$.

**8** The gradient of the graph of $y = x^5 + kx^2$, at the point where $x = -2$, is 12.
Find the value of $k$.

**9** Find the equation of the tangent to the curve $y = 6x^{-\frac{1}{2}}$ at the point where $x = 4$.

**10** Find the equation of the normal to the curve $y = x - \dfrac{1}{x}$ at the point where $x = 2$.

**11** Given that $y = x^2 - \sqrt{x}$, find the values of $\dfrac{dy}{dx}$ and $\dfrac{d^2y}{dx^2}$ when $x = \frac{1}{4}$.

**12** Given that $y = \dfrac{1 - x^2}{\sqrt{x}}$, find $\dfrac{d^2y}{dx^2}$.

**13** The graph of $y = ax^3 + bx$ goes through $(2, 2)$ and its gradient at this point is 17.
Find the values of $a$ and $b$.

**\*14** Prove that, for all values of $k$,

**(a)** the tangent to $y = x^2$ at the point $(k, k^2)$ crosses the $y$-axis at $(0, -k^2)$

**(b)** the normal to $y = x^2$ at the point $(k, k^2)$ crosses the $y$-axis at $(0, k^2 + \frac{1}{2})$

**\*15** The graph of $y = px^2 + qx + r$ goes through the points $A$ $(-1, 13)$ and $B$ $(1, 7)$.
The gradient of the graph at $A$ is 5. Find the values of $p$, $q$ and $r$.

**\*16** If the algebraic method of differentiation in section G above is applied to
the function $y = x^3$, then
$$\frac{\delta y}{\delta x} = \frac{(x + \delta x)^3 - x^3}{\delta x}$$

**(a)** Expand $(x + \delta x)^3$. You can think of it as $(x + \delta x)(x + \delta x)^2$.

**(b)** Hence show that $\dfrac{\delta y}{\delta x} = 3x^2 + 3x\delta x + (\delta x)^2$.

**(c)** What happens to $\dfrac{\delta y}{\delta x}$ as the value of $\delta x$ gets smaller and smaller?

## Test yourself (answers p 200)

None of these questions requires a calculator.

**1 (a)** Given that $y = (x - 2)(x^2 + 3)$, find $\dfrac{dy}{dx}$.

**(b)** Hence find the equation of the tangent to the curve $y = (x - 2)(x^2 + 3)$
at the point whose $x$-coordinate is 1. Give your answer in the form $y = mx + c$.

**2** Differentiate with respect to $x$

$$2x^3 + \sqrt{x} + \frac{x^2 + 2x}{x^2}$$

Edexcel

**3** Find the equation of the normal to the graph of $y = x^2 - 10x$ at the point where $x = 4$.

**4** Given that $y = (1 + \sqrt{x})^2$, find the value of $\dfrac{d^2 y}{dx^2}$ when $x = 4$.

**5** The curve whose equation is $y = \dfrac{8}{\sqrt{x}} \, (x > 0)$ passes through

the point $A$ whose $x$-coordinate is 4. Find

  **(a)** the equation of the tangent to the curve at $A$, in the form $ax + by + c = 0$

  **(b)** the coordinates of the point where this tangent crosses the $x$-axis

  **(c)** the equation of the normal to the curve at $A$, in the form $ax + by + c = 0$

  **(d)** the coordinates of the point where the normal crosses the $x$-axis

**6** Given that $y = x^{-\frac{3}{4}}$ find the value of $\dfrac{d^2 y}{dx^2}$ when $x = 1$.

**7** A curve $C$ has equation $y = x^3 - 5x^2 + 5x + 2$.

  **(a)** Find $\dfrac{dy}{dx}$ in terms of $x$.

Points $P$ and $Q$ lie on the curve. The gradient at both $P$ and $Q$ is 2. The $x$-coordinate of $P$ is 3.

  **(b)** Find the $x$-coordinate of $Q$.

  **(c)** Find an equation for the tangent to $C$ at $P$, giving your answer in the form $y = mx + c$, where $m$ and $c$ are constants.

This tangent intersects the coordinate axes at points $R$ and $S$.

  **(d)** Find the length of $RS$, giving your answer as a surd.

Edexcel

# 11 Integration

In this chapter you will learn
- what integration is and how it is related to differentiation
- how to integrate functions

## A Thinking backwards (answers p 200)

When a ball rolls down a slope it gets faster and faster. In fact, its speed (in m/s) is proportional to the time $t$ (in seconds) it has been travelling.

In the example shown here, the speed of the ball is equal to $2t$.

Here are a table of values and a graph showing how the speed increases over time.

| $t$ (seconds) | 0 | 1 | 2 | 3 | 4 |
|---|---|---|---|---|---|
| Speed (m/s) | 0 | 2 | 4 | 6 | 8 |

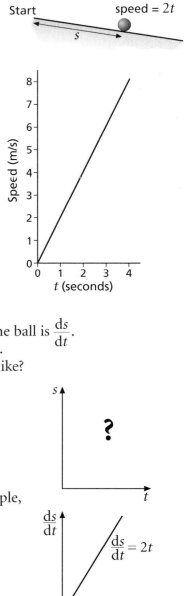

If $s$ is the distance (in m) travelled in time $t$, then the speed of the ball is $\dfrac{\mathrm{d}s}{\mathrm{d}t}$. So the graph above shows the gradient function for the distance. The question arises: what does the distance function itself look like?

This is the reverse problem to finding a gradient function for a given function. We are given the gradient function or derivative and want to find the original function.

**A1** Which function of $t$ has the derivative $2t$?

Once we know the distance function we can work out, for example,
- how far the ball will travel in a given time
- how long it will take to go a given distance

**A2** On a different slope the speed of the ball is $5t$. What is the distance function in this case?

## B Integration as the reverse of differentiation (answers p 200)

If you differentiate $x^2$ the result is the derivative, $2x$.

The reverse process is called **integration**.
Starting with $2x$ you ask: 'What function has derivative $2x$?'

**D** **B1** The obvious answer to the question above is $x^2$, but there is more to it than that.
Differentiate each of these functions: $x^2 + 1$, $x^2 + 5$, $x^2 - 9$, $x^2 + 30$
How would you answer the question: 'What function has $2x$ as its derivative?'

Because the derivative of any constant number, such as 5, is always zero,
any function such as $x^2 + 5$, $x^2 + 7$, $x^2 - 3$, and so on, also has derivative $2x$.

So the function with derivative $2x$ is $x^2 + c$, where $c$ can be any number.
This is illustrated in the graphs on the right.

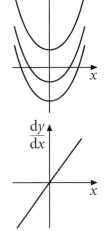

**K** The process of going from $2x$ to $x^2 + c$ is called **integration**.
$x^2 + c$ is called the **indefinite integral** of $2x$
('indefinite' because $c$ can be any number).
$c$ is called the **constant of integration**.

**B2** (a) Write down the derivative of $5x^2$.

(b) Hence write down the indefinite integral of $10x$.

**B3** (a) Write down the derivative of each of these functions of $x$.

(i) $3x^2$     (ii) $4x^2$     (iii) $8x$     (iv) $x^3$     (v) $6x$

(b) Use your answers to (a) to write down the indefinite integral of

(i) $8x$     (ii) $3x^2$     (iii) $6$     (iv) $6x$     (v) $8$

**D** **B4** The derivative of $x^4$ is $4x^3$. Use this fact to find the indefinite integral of $x^3$.

---

### Example 1

Find the indefinite integral of $12x^2$.

### Solution

*You are trying to find the function whose derivative is $12x^2$.*
*You know that the derivative of $x^3$ is $3x^2$.*
*So if you differentiate $4x^3$ you will get $12x^2$.*     The indefinite integral of $12x^2$ is $4x^3 + c$.

---

11 Integration | **153**

**Exercise B** (answers p 200)

**1** Find the indefinite integrals of the following functions.

    **(a)** $4x$         **(b)** $12x$         **(c)** $20x$         **(d)** $x$

**2** Find the indefinite integral of

    **(a)** $6x^2$         **(b)** $15x^2$         **(c)** $x^2$         **(d)** $2x^2$

**3** Find the indefinite integrals of the following functions.
Check each answer by differentiating.

    **(a)** $4x^3$         **(b)** $10x^4$         **(c)** $5x^2$         **(d)** $3x$

**4 (a)** Copy and complete this table of indefinite integrals.

| Function | $x$ | $x^2$ | $x^3$ | $x^4$ |
|---|---|---|---|---|
| Indefinite integral | | | | |

    **(b)** Use your results to help you write down a formula for the indefinite integral of the general function $x^n$, where $n$ is a positive integer.

## C Integrating polynomials (answers p 200)

The notation for 'the indefinite integral of $2x$' is $\int 2x\,dx$ (read as 'integral $2x$ $dx$').
So we write $\int 2x\,dx = x^2 + c$.

The reason for this notation will be explained in Core 2. For now, think of $\int \;\; dx$ as a single symbol with a blank space for the function to be integrated.

**C1** Use the integral notation to write each of these statements.

    **(a)** The indefinite integral of $3x^2$ is $x^3 + c$.

    **(b)** The indefinite integral of $4x$ is $2x^2 + c$.

**C2** Find the indefinite integral of $5x$ and write the statement 'the indefinite integral of $5x$ is …' using the integral notation.

**C3** Repeat C2 for the function $6x^2$.

A rule for integrating a power of $x$ emerged from the questions in exercise B.

$$\int x^n\,dx = \frac{x^{n+1}}{n+1} + c$$

In words, this rule says 'raise the index by 1 and divide by the new index'.
For example, $\int x^5\,dx = \dfrac{x^6}{6} + c$.

## Integrating a sum of functions

To differentiate the function $x^3 + x^2$ you differentiate each term separately and add, getting the derivative $3x^2 + 2x$.

It follows that $\int (3x^2 + 2x)dx = x^3 + x^2 + c$.

So, as with differentiation, you integrate each term separately and add.

## Integrating a multiple of a function

The derivative of $5x^2$ is 5 times the derivative of $x^2$.
The same applies to integration. For example,

$$\int 5x^2 \, dx \; = \; 5\int x^2 \, dx \; = \; 5\left(\frac{x^3}{3}\right) + c \; = \; \tfrac{5}{3}x^3 + c$$

Check that this is correct by differentiating $\tfrac{5}{3}x^3 + c$.

## Integrating a polynomial

Using the rules given above, a polynomial can be integrated term by term. If you are in any doubt about a result, differentiate it and check that you get the original function.

---

### Example 2

If $\dfrac{dy}{dx} = 2x^3 + 9x^2 - x + 3,$ find $y$ in terms of $x$.

### Solution

$y$ is the indefinite integral of $2x^3 + 9x^2 - x + 3$.

$$y = \int \left(2x^3 + 9x^2 - x + 3\right) dx = 2\left(\frac{x^4}{4}\right) + 9\left(\frac{x^3}{3}\right) - \left(\frac{x^2}{2}\right) + 3x + c$$

$$= \tfrac{1}{2}x^4 + 3x^3 - \tfrac{1}{2}x^2 + 3x + c$$

---

### Example 3

Find $\int (x + 3)(x^2 - 5) \, dx$.

### Solution

*Multiply out the brackets to get a polynomial.*

$$\int (x + 3)\left(x^2 - 5\right) dx = \int \left(x^3 + 3x^2 - 5x - 15\right) dx = \left(\frac{x^4}{4}\right) + 3\left(\frac{x^3}{3}\right) - 5\left(\frac{x^2}{2}\right) - 15x + c$$

$$= \tfrac{1}{4}x^4 + x^3 - \tfrac{5}{2}x^2 - 15x + c$$

---

### Exercise C (answers p 201)

**1** Find the following integrals.

(a) $\int x^3 \, dx$ 　　　　(b) $\int 4x^2 \, dx$ 　　　　(c) $\int 6x \, dx$ 　　　　(d) $\int 5x^4 \, dx$

**2** Find $y$ as a function of $x$ for each of these.

(a) $\dfrac{dy}{dx} = x - 4$ 　　(b) $\dfrac{dy}{dx} = 3x^2 + x$ 　　(c) $\dfrac{dy}{dx} = x^2 + x + 1$ 　　(d) $\dfrac{dy}{dx} = 5x^4 + 3$

**3** Given that $f'(x) = 5x + 3x^3$, find an expression for $f(x)$.

**4** Find the following integrals.

(a) $\displaystyle\int (2 - 3x + x^2)\, dx$ 　　　　　　　(b) $\displaystyle\int (5x^3 + 2x^5)\, dx$

**5** Find $y$ as a function of $x$ for each of these.

(a) $\dfrac{dy}{dx} = 2x^3 - 7x + 3$ 　　　　　　(b) $\dfrac{dy}{dx} = (x+1)(x-2)$

**6** Find the indefinite integral of each of the following functions.

(a) $2(3x - 2)$ 　　　　　(b) $3x(x + 4)$ 　　　　　(c) $(2x - 1)^2$

**7** Given that $f'(x) = (x + 2)(x - 1)(x + 4)$, find an expression for $f(x)$.

**8** Find the following integrals.

(a) $\displaystyle\int (x + 2)(x - 5)\, dx$ 　　　　　　(b) $\displaystyle\int x^2(2x + 1)\, dx$

## D Integrating $x^n$, where $n$ is negative or a fraction

The rule for integrating $x^n$ also works when $n$ is negative or a fraction,
except for the case $n = -1$.

$$\int x^n\, dx = \frac{x^{n+1}}{n+1} + c \qquad (n \ne -1)$$

---

**Example 4**

Find $\displaystyle\int \frac{1}{x^4}\, dx$.

**Solution**

$\displaystyle\int \frac{1}{x^4}\, dx = \int x^{-4}\, dx = \frac{x^{-4+1}}{-4+1} + c = \frac{x^{-3}}{-3} + c = -\frac{1}{3x^3} + c$

---

**Example 5**

Find $\displaystyle\int x^{\frac{2}{3}}\, dx$.

**Solution**

$\displaystyle\int x^{\frac{2}{3}}\, dx = \frac{x^{\frac{2}{3}+1}}{\frac{2}{3}+1} + c = \frac{x^{\frac{5}{3}}}{\frac{5}{3}} + c = \frac{3}{5}x^{\frac{5}{3}} + c$

---

**Example 6**

Find $\displaystyle\int \sqrt{x}\left(x + \frac{1}{x}\right) dx$.

**Solution**

$\displaystyle\int \sqrt{x}\left(x + \frac{1}{x}\right) dx = \int\left(x\sqrt{x} + \frac{1}{\sqrt{x}}\right) dx = \int\left(x^{\frac{3}{2}} + x^{-\frac{1}{2}}\right) dx$

$\displaystyle \qquad\qquad = \frac{2}{5}x^{\frac{5}{2}} + 2x^{\frac{1}{2}} + c$

---

**Exercise D** (answers p 201)

**1** Find the following indefinite integrals.

(a) $\int x^{-3}\,dx$  (b) $\int x^{\frac{3}{4}}\,dx$  (c) $\int \sqrt{x}\,dx$  (d) $\int x^{-\frac{3}{4}}\,dx$

**2** (a) (i) Write $x^2\sqrt{x}$ in the form $x^k$, where $k$ is a fraction.

(ii) Hence find $\int x^2\sqrt{x}\,dx$.

(b) Find $\int x^3\sqrt{x}\,dx$.

**3** (a) Multiply out the brackets in the expression $x(x^2 + \sqrt{x})$.

(b) Hence find $\int x(x^2 + \sqrt{x})\,dx$.

**4** (a) Express $\dfrac{x^4 + 1}{x^2}$ in the form $x^p + x^q$, where $p$ and $q$ are integers.

(b) Hence find $\int\left(\dfrac{x^4 + 1}{x^2}\right)dx$.

**5** Find the following indefinite integrals.

(a) $\int x(1 + \sqrt{x})\,dx$  (b) $\int\left(\dfrac{x^2 - 1}{x^2}\right)dx$  (c) $\int\left(\dfrac{1 + \sqrt{x}}{\sqrt{x}}\right)dx$  (d) $\int\left(\dfrac{1 + x}{\sqrt{x}}\right)dx$

(e) $\int\left(\dfrac{1 + x^2}{\sqrt{x}}\right)dx$  (f) $\int(1 + \sqrt{x})^2\,dx$

## E Finding the constant of integration

If you are told that $\dfrac{dy}{dx} = 3x^2 - 2$, then by integration it follows that $y = x^3 - 2x + c$.

The equation $y = x^3 - 2x + c$ represents a family of graphs all having the same derivative, or gradient function.

If you are given the additional information that the graph goes through $(2, 7)$, then you can find the value of $c$:

$$7 = 2^3 - 2\times2 + c$$
$$\Rightarrow c = 3$$

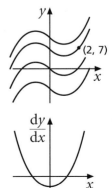

## Example 7

Given that $f'(x) = 8x^3 - 6x$ and that $f(2) = 9$, find $f(x)$ in terms of $x$.

### Solution

*First find the indefinite integral of $8x^3 - 6x$.*  $\qquad f(x) = \int (8x^3 - 6x)\, dx = 2x^4 - 3x^2 + c$

*Now use the fact that $f(2) = 9$ to find $c$.*  $\qquad\qquad 9 = 32 - 12 + c$

$$\Rightarrow \qquad c = -11$$
$$\text{So } f(x) = 2x^4 - 3x^2 - 11$$

## Exercise E (answers p 201)

**1** Given that $f'(x) = 6x^2 + 4$ and that $f(1) = 7$, find an expression for $f(x)$.

**2** Express $y$ as a function of $x$ for each of these.

 (a) $\dfrac{dy}{dx} = 3x^2 + 4x$ and the $(x, y)$ graph passes through $(1, 5)$.

 (b) $\dfrac{dy}{dx} = x^2 + x + 1$ and the $(x, y)$ graph passes through $(0, 3)$.

**3** The curve $C$ passes through the point $P\,(2, 1)$.

 If $\dfrac{dy}{dx} = 2x - \dfrac{6}{x^2}$, find the equation of $C$.

**4** Find an expression for $f(x)$ for each of these.

 (a) $f'(x) = 3x(3x - 2)$ and $f(0) = 2$  (b) $f'(x) = 5 - 3\sqrt{x}$ and $f(4) = 7$

**5** (a) Given that $\dfrac{dy}{dx} = (x + 1)(2x - 3)$, find $y$ as a function of $x$.

 (b) If $y = 1$ when $x = 0$, find the value of $y$ when $x = 3$.

**6** The curve $y = f(x)$ passes through the points $(1, 5)$ and $(2, k)$.

 Given that $\dfrac{dy}{dx} = 6x + \dfrac{4}{x^2}$, find the value of $k$.

**7** The rate of growth of a population of micro-organisms is modelled by the equation

 $$\dfrac{dP}{dt} = 3t^2 + 6t$$

 where $P$ is the population size at time $t$ hours.
 Given that $P = 100$ when $t = 1$, find $P$ in terms of $t$.

**8** The equation of a curve is $y = f(x)$. The curve goes through the points $(1, 3)$ and $(3, 7)$. Given that $f'(x) = 4x + p$, where $p$ is a number, find

 (a) the value of $p$

 (b) the equation of the curve

**9** $\dfrac{dy}{dx} = 5 + \dfrac{1}{x^2}$

    **(a)** Use integration to find $y$ in terms of $x$.

    **(b)** Given that $y = 7$ at $x = 1$, find the value of $y$ at $x = 2$.              Edexcel

**\*10** The curve with equation $y = f(x)$ goes through the points $(0, 5)$, $(1, 11)$ and $(2, 37)$.
Given that $f'(x) = ax^2 + bx$, find

    **(a)** the values of $a$, $b$ and $c$ (the constant of integration)

    **(b)** the equation of the curve

---

**Key points**

- Integration is the reverse of differentiation.          (p 153)

- The indefinite integral of a function includes a constant term.          (p 153)

- The indefinite integral of a function $f(x)$ is denoted by $\int f(x)\, dx$.          (p 154)

- $\int x^n\, dx = \dfrac{x^{n+1}}{n+1} + c$ for all values of $n$ except $-1$          (pp 154, 156)

- The indefinite integral of a sum of functions is the sum of
  the separate indefinite integrals.
  The indefinite integral of $k$ times a function is $k$ times
  the indefinite integral of the function.          (p 155)

- Given $\dfrac{dy}{dx}$ (or $f'(x)$) and the value of $y$ (or $f(x)$) for a given value of $x$,
  the value of the constant of integration can be found.          (p 157)

---

## Mixed questions (answers p 201)

**1** Find

    **(a)** $\int (2x^2 + 3x - 1)\, dx$     **(b)** $\int x(5x^4 + 2)\, dx$     **(c)** $\int (2x^2 + 3)(x - 4)\, dx$

**2** Given that $f'(x) = x^3 + 12x^2 - 2$ and $f(2) = 0$, find $f(x)$ in terms of $x$.

**3** The curve $C$ goes through the point $(3, 5)$.
The gradient $\dfrac{dy}{dx}$ at the point $(x, y)$ on $C$ is given by the equation $\dfrac{dy}{dx} = \frac{1}{2}x^2 - 3x$.
Find the equation of $C$.

**4** Given that $\dfrac{ds}{dt} = (t + 3)(t - 1)$ and that $s = 10$ when $t = 3$, find $s$ in terms of $t$.

**5** Given that $f'(x) = 3x^2 + ax$, $f(-2) = 8$ and $f(1) = 2$, find

  **(a)** the value of $a$         **(b)** an expression for $f(x)$ in terms of $x$

**6** The rate of growth of a bird population is modelled by the equation $\dfrac{dP}{dt} = a + bt$ where $P$ is the population at time $t$, and $a$ and $b$ are constants.

  Given that $P = 100$ when $t = 0$, $P = 172$ when $t = 4$, and $P = 202$ when $t = 6$,

  **(a)** find the formula for $P$ in terms of $t$

  **(b)** find the values of $t$ for which $P = 250$

**7** Given that $f'(x) = x + \sqrt{x}$ and $f(1) = 1$, find $f(x)$.

**8** The curve $C$ has the equation $y = f(x)$, $x > 0$. Given that $f'(x) = 6\sqrt{x} + \dfrac{4}{x^2}$ and that $f(1) = 5$,

  **(a)** find the equation of $C$

  **(b)** find the equation of the tangent to $C$ at the point where $x = 1$

**9** The curve $C$ passes through the point $(4, 5)$.

  The gradient $\dfrac{dy}{dx}$ at the point $(x, y)$ on $C$ is given by the equation $\dfrac{dy}{dx} = 3 - \dfrac{1}{\sqrt{x}}$.

  **(a)** Find the equation of $C$.

  **(b)** Find the coordinates of the stationary point of $C$.

In the next question '$x \in \mathbb{R}$' means '$x$ is a real number (i.e. rational or irrational)'.

**10** The function f, defined for $x \in \mathbb{R}$, $x > 0$, is such that
$$f'(x) = x^2 - 2 + \frac{1}{x^2}$$

  **(a)** Find the value of $f''(x)$ at $x = 4$.

  **(b)** Given that $f(3) = 0$, find $f(x)$.

  **(c)** Prove that f is an increasing function.            Edexcel

**\*11** The rate of spread of an illness affecting animals in a colony is modelled by the equation
$$\frac{dN}{dt} = 5 - \tfrac{4}{9}t - \tfrac{1}{9}t^2$$
where $N$ is the number of animals affected and $t$ is the time in weeks since recording began.

  When recording began, 36 animals were affected.

  **(a)** Find a formula for $N$ in terms of $t$.

  **(b)** How many affected animals are there after 3 weeks?

  **(c)** After how many weeks does the number of affected animals reach a maximum?

  **(d)** Show that, according to the model, the number of affected animals decreases after reaching a maximum and is zero when $t = 12$.

## Test yourself (answers p 202)

None of these questions requires a calculator.

**1** Find

(a) $\int (x^3 + 2x^2 - x)\,dx$      (b) $\int (x^4 + 7x - 1)\,dx$      (c) $\int (x^8 + 5x^6)\,dx$

**2** Find

(a) $\int 3x^2(x - 2)\,dx$      (b) $\int (4x + 1)(3x^2 - 1)\,dx$      (c) $\int (3x - 2)^2\,dx$

**3** The gradient function of a curve is given by $\dfrac{dy}{dx} = 6x^2 - 1$.

The curve goes through the point $(-1, 4)$. Find the equation of the curve.

**4** Given that $\dfrac{dy}{dx} = (6x + 5)(x - 1)$ and that $y = 0$ when $x = 1$, find $y$ in terms of $x$.

**5** Given that $f'(x) = 10x^4 - 12x^3 - 4$ and $f(2) = 10$, find

(a) $f(x)$ in terms of $x$                  (b) $f(-2)$

**6** Given that $f'(x) = (x + 1)(3x - 5)$ and $f(3) = 6$, find $f(x)$ in terms of $x$.

**7** The curve $C$ goes through the point $(-2, 2)$.

The gradient function of $C$ is given by $\dfrac{dy}{dx} = (3x - 1)^2$.

Find the equation of $C$.

**8** The curve $C$ has equation $y = f(x)$. Given that

$$\frac{dy}{dx} = 3x^2 - 20x + 29$$

and that $C$ passes through the point $P\,(2, 6)$,

(a) find $y$ in terms of $x$.

(b) Verify that $C$ passes through the point $(4, 0)$.

(c) Find the equation of the tangent to $C$ at $P$.

The tangent to $C$ at the point $Q$ is parallel to the tangent to $C$ at $P$.

(d) Calculate the exact $x$-coordinate of $Q$.

                                                                            Edexcel

# Answers

## 1 Linear graphs and equations

### A Linear graphs (p 6)

**A1** A $\frac{5}{2}$     B $-1$     C $-\frac{1}{3}$     D $\frac{5}{2}$

A and D are parallel.

**A2** (a)    (b)    (c)    (d)

**A3** (a) $4y - 24 = 0 \Rightarrow y = 6$
so the graph goes through $(0, 6)$.

(b) $3x - 24 = 0 \Rightarrow x = 8$
so the graph goes through $(8, 0)$.

**A4** Sketches of straight lines going through these labelled points

(a) $(0, 4)$ and $(10, 0)$    (b) $(0, 7)$ and $(4, 0)$

(c) $(0, 2)$ and $(-4, 0)$    (d) $(0, -4)$ and $(3, 0)$

(e) $(0, -6)$ and $(-5, 0)$    (f) $(0, -1)$ and $(-5, 0)$

**A5** Sketches of straight lines going through these labelled points

(a) $(0, 3)$ and $(7, 0)$    (b) $(0, -5)$ and $(-1, 0)$

(c) $(0, 4.5)$ and $(-4.5, 0)$

**A6** $4x + 3y = 24$ (or an equivalent equation)

**A7** (a) $y = -3x + 2$    (b) $y = \frac{1}{2}x + 3$    (c) $y = -\frac{3}{5}x + \frac{?}{?}$

**A8** With gradient 3
$3x - y - 4 = 0$    $y = 3x + \frac{1}{2}$    $y = -\frac{1}{2} + 3x$

With gradient $-\frac{1}{2}$
$y = -\frac{1}{2}x + 2$    $y = 7 - \frac{1}{2}x$

With gradient $-3$
$y = -3x + 4$    $3x + y - 7 = 0$    $y = -2 - 3x$

**A9** (a) A (gradient 1) and B (gradient $-1$)
C $(-\frac{3}{4})$ and D $(\frac{4}{3})$
E $(3)$ and F $(-\frac{1}{3})$
G $(-2)$ and H $(\frac{1}{2})$
An explanation such as:
Multiplying the two gradients together gives $-1$.
or:
One gradient is the negative reciprocal of the other gradient.

(b) $-\frac{3}{2}$    (c) $\frac{1}{4}$    (d) $-1$

**A10** B and C are perpendicular.

**A11** A and C, B and D, F and G

**A12** Where one line is vertical and the other is horizontal.

### Exercise A (p 9)

**1** $\dfrac{x}{6} + \dfrac{y}{5} = 1$ and $y = -\frac{5}{6}x + 4$

**2** (a)    (b)    (c)

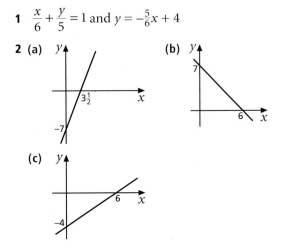

**3** A, C and G with gradient $-\frac{1}{7}$
B and E with gradient $-\frac{2}{7}$
D, F and H with gradient $\frac{7}{2}$

**4** (a) (i) $y = -3x - 7$    (ii) $-3$    (iii) $-7$

(b) (i) $y = -\frac{1}{2}x + 4$    (ii) $-\frac{1}{2}$    (iii) $4$

(c) (i) $y = -\frac{4}{5}x - \frac{1}{5}$    (ii) $-\frac{4}{5}$    (iii) $-\frac{1}{5}$

**(d) (i)** $y = \frac{3}{2}x - 3$  **(ii)** $\frac{3}{2}$  **(iii)** $-3$

**(e) (i)** $y = \frac{7}{2}x - \frac{3}{2}$  **(ii)** $\frac{7}{2}$  **(iii)** $-\frac{3}{2}$

**(f) (i)** $y = -\frac{2}{3}x + \frac{3}{2}$  **(ii)** $-\frac{2}{3}$  **(iii)** $\frac{3}{2}$

**5** $-\dfrac{a}{b}$

**6** $y = 4x + 8$ and $-8x + 2y - 7 = 0$

**7** $4x + 6y + 3 = 0$ and $y = -\frac{2}{3}x$

**8** $y = -\frac{1}{3}x + 2$ and $x + 3y = 1$

**9** $-3x - 5y + 1 = 0$ and $y = 6 - \frac{3}{5}x$

**10** $AB\ -5$, $BC\ \frac{1}{5}$, $CA\ -\frac{3}{11}$
It has a right angle at $B$.

**11** $AB$ and $DC\ -\frac{2}{3}$, $AD\ \frac{3}{2}$, $BC\ \frac{1}{5}$
It is a trapezium with right angles at $A$ and $D$.

## B Finding the equation of a linear graph (p 10)

**B1** Any three points with coordinates conforming to
$y = 3x - 1$

**B2** $y = 3x - 1$

**B3 (a)** $y = 4x - 10$  **(b)** $y = -x + 6$  **(c)** $y = 3x + 1$
**(d)** $y = \frac{1}{4}x + \frac{5}{2}$  **(e)** $y = -\frac{1}{2}x + \frac{1}{2}$

### Exercise B (p 12)

**1 (a)** $y = 3x - 19$  **(b)** $y = \frac{1}{2}x - \frac{3}{2}$  **(c)** $y = 2x + 1$
**(d)** $y = -\frac{3}{2}x + 1$

**2 (a)** $y = \frac{1}{3}x + 2$  **(b)** $y = -x + 3$

**3 (a)** $(4, 4)$  **(b)** $(1, 2)$  **(c)** $(\frac{1}{2}, -3)$

**4 (a)** $y = \frac{1}{2}x$  **(b)** $y = \frac{4}{3}x - 6$  **(c)** $y = -\frac{2}{5}x - \frac{12}{5}$

**5 (a) (i)** $(5, 7)$  **(ii)** $y = 3x - 8$
**(iii)** $\sqrt{40}$ or $2\sqrt{10}$

**(b) (i)** $(6, 1)$  **(ii)** $y = \frac{3}{2}x - 8$
**(iii)** $\sqrt{52}$ or $2\sqrt{13}$

**(c) (i)** $(-2.5, 3.5)$  **(ii)** $y = -x + 1$
**(iii)** $\sqrt{18}$ or $3\sqrt{2}$

**6 (a)** $y = \frac{2}{3}x - \frac{1}{3}$  **(b)** $a = 8$

**7** $(-4, 4.5)$

**8** $y = -\frac{5}{2}x + \frac{47}{4}$ or $y = -2.5x + 11.75$

## C Problem solving with linear graphs (p 12)

**C1 (a)** $C = 0.09E$

**(b)** (and C2 (a))

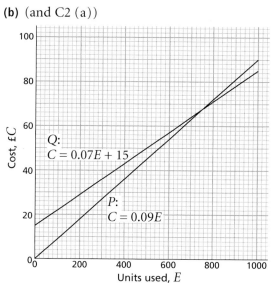

**C2 (b)** $C = 0.07E + 15$

**(c)** £15 standing charge (or service charge) plus
£0.07 (or 7p) for every unit of electricity used

**C3 (a)** $P$, charging £27

**(b)** There is nothing to choose between them; they
would both charge £67.50.

**(c)** $Q$, charging £78

### Exercise C (p 13)

**1 (a)**

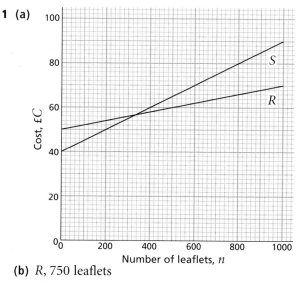

**(b)** $R$, 750 leaflets

**2 (a)** 6 litres per second

**(b)** $V = 220 - 6t$
$0 = 220 - 6t \Rightarrow t = 36.7$ (to 1 d.p.)

**(c)** Linear graph from $(0, 220)$ to $(36.7, 0)$

**(d)** $V = 250 - 8t$

When the tank is empty,
$0 = 250 - 8t \Rightarrow t = 31.3$ (to 1 d.p)
Linear graph from $(0, 250)$ to $(31.3, 0)$

**(e)** 15 seconds from the start they will both hold 130 litres.

**3 (a)** $H = 0.3t$

**(b)** $H = 320 - 0.2t$

**(c)**
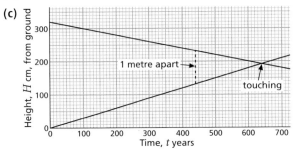

**(d)** About 440 years from the start

**(e)** They will touch after about 640 years at a point about 192 cm above the ground.

**4 (a)** Company X:
From the points $(20, 110)$, $(100, 190)$
gradient $= \frac{80}{80} = 1$
Using $y - y_1 = m(x - x_1)$ and $(20, 110)$
$C - 110 = n - 20$
$\Rightarrow C = n + 90$

Company Y:
gradient $= 2$ (because £2 per additional copy)
Using $y - y_1 = m(x - x_1)$ and $(10, 50)$
$C - 50 = 2(n - 10)$
$\Rightarrow C - 50 = 2n - 20$
$\Rightarrow C = 2n + 30$

**(b) (i)** Y (£130 instead of £140)

**(ii)** X (£170 instead of £190)

## D Solving simultaneous linear equations

### Exercise D (p 16)

**1 (a)** $p = 6, q = 1$     **(b)** $a = 2.5, b = -1.5$

**(c)** $h = -4, j = 3$

**2 (a)** $x = 3, y = 6$     **(b)** $x = -2, y = -3$

**(c)** $p = 1, q = -4$

**3 (a)** $x = \frac{1}{2}, y = \frac{5}{2}$     **(b)** $x = -4, y = 3$

**(c)** $x = 3, y = -5$

**4 (a)** $x = \frac{3}{2}, y = \frac{3}{2}$     **(b)** $x = \frac{3}{2}, y = 1$

**(c)** $t = \frac{8}{3}, s = \frac{7}{3}$

**5 (a)** $x = 5, y = -4$     **(b)** $x = -\frac{1}{2}, y = \frac{5}{2}$

**(c)** $x = -3, y = -2$

**6 (a)** $(6, 5)$    **(b)** $(\frac{5}{2}, \frac{7}{2})$    **(c)** $(2, 5)$

**7 (a)** You get a nonsense statement like $2 = 6$; the two linear graphs that correspond to the equations are parallel, so do not intersect.

**(b)** You get a trivially true statement like $-\frac{5}{3}x - 5 = -\frac{5}{3}x - 5$; the equations are equivalent (either equation can be rearranged into the other) so both correspond to the same linear graph. This intersects itself at every point on itself.

**(c)** You get a nonsense statement like $-4 = 5$; the corresponding linear graphs are parallel, so do not intersect.

**8** $(10\frac{1}{2}, 25)$, $(4, -1)$, $(-\frac{7}{8}, 2\frac{1}{4})$

**9 (a)** Plumber A: $C = 40t + 40$
Plumber B: $C = 44t + 29$

**(b)** $2\frac{3}{4}$ hours

**(c)** Plumber A

**10** 15 seconds from the start they will both hold 130 litres.

**11** They will touch 640 years from the start, at a point 192 cm from the ground.

### Mixed questions (p 19)

**1** A rectangle

**2 (a)** A trapezium

**(b)** $(5, 0)$, $(10, 0)$, $(0, 6)$, $(0, 3)$

**3 (a)**
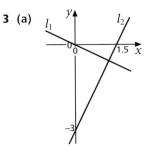

**(b)** $\left(\frac{4}{3}, -\frac{1}{3}\right)$    **(c)** $12x - 3y - 17 = 0$

**4 (a)** $\left(\frac{19}{6}, -\frac{3}{2}\right)$    **(b)** $2x + 3y = 1$    **(c)** $\left(\frac{14}{13}, -\frac{5}{13}\right)$

**5 (a)** $y = 2x - 1$

**(b)** $y = 6\frac{1}{2} - \frac{1}{2}x$; $(3, 5)$

**(c)** $y = 14 - \frac{1}{2}x$; $(6, 11)$

**(d)** By Pythagoras, $PQ = \sqrt{3^2 + 6^2}$
$= \sqrt{45} = \sqrt{9} \times \sqrt{5} = 3\sqrt{5}$
Similarly, $AC = \sqrt{6^2 + 12^2}$
$= \sqrt{180} = \sqrt{36} \times \sqrt{5} = 6\sqrt{5}$
So $PQ$ is half the length of $AC$.

**6 (a)** $AC$: $y = \frac{3}{2}x - 2$
$BD$: $y = -\frac{1}{4}x + 5$
They intersect at $(4, 4)$.

**(b)** $(3, 6)$, $(1, 3)$, $(7, 1\frac{1}{2})$, $(9, 4\frac{1}{2})$

**(c)** Two opposite sides have gradient $\frac{3}{2}$.
The other two opposite sides have gradient $-\frac{1}{4}$.

**(d)** Opposite sides are parallel, so this is a parallelogram.

**7** The equation of the perpendicular through the origin is $y = \frac{3}{4}x$. The point of intersection is $(4, 3)$. By Pythagoras, the perpendicular distance of $8x + 6y - 50 = 0$ from the origin is 5 units.

**8** The points are not on the same straight line. This can be shown by finding the equation of the straight line between two of the points and showing that the third point does not satisfy it; or by calculating the gradient of the line between a pair of points and showing that it differs from the gradient of the line between a different pair.

**9 (a)** $i = 2, j = 3$

**(b)** From its equation, the gradient of $PQ$ is 2. From the coordinates of $R$ and $P$, the gradient of $RP$ is $-\frac{1}{2}$.
Since $2 \times \frac{1}{2} = -1$, $PQ$ and $RP$ are perpendicular, so the triangle $PQR$ has a right angle at $P$.

**(c)** $12\sqrt{5}$

**10 (a)** Through $A$ and $(5, 7)$: $y = -x + 12$
Through $B$ and $(6, 3)$: $y = 2x - 9$
Through $C$ and $(10, 5)$: $y = 5$

**(b)** Any two of the above solved simultaneously to give the point of intersection $(7, 5)$; a check that these values of $x$ and $y$ satisfy the equation of the third line

**11 (a)** $(5, 5)$

**(b)** $y = \frac{3}{4}x + \frac{5}{4}$

**(c)** $p = 2, q = 13$

**(d)** Gradient of $AD = \frac{7}{1} = 7$
Gradient of $DC = \frac{-1}{7} = -\frac{1}{7}$
$7 \times -\frac{1}{7} = -1$, so $AD$ and $DC$ are perpendicular, so $\angle ADC$ is a right angle.

**(e)** 75 square units

## Test yourself (p 21)

**1 (a)** $y = -5x + 4$    **(b)** $y = \frac{1}{2}x + 3$

**(c)** $y = -\frac{1}{2}x + \frac{3}{2}$    **(d)** $y = 2x + 14$

**2 (a)** Neither    **(b)** Perpendicular

**(c)** Parallel    **(d)** Perpendicular

**3 (a)** $-\frac{1}{4}$    **(b)** $y = -\frac{1}{4}x + \frac{7}{2}$

**4** $y = \frac{5}{2}x$ or $5x - 2y = 0$

**5** $\sqrt{13}$

**6 (a)** $y = 6x - 6$    **(b)** $y = -\frac{1}{6}x - \frac{1}{2}$

**7 (a)** $x = -1, y = 2$    **(b)** $x = -\frac{3}{10}, y = \frac{7}{10}$

**(c)** $x = \frac{3}{2}, y = \frac{3}{2}$    **(d)** $x = -1, y = 3$

**(e)** $x = \frac{15}{2}, y = \frac{3}{2}$    **(f)** $x = -6, y = -5$

**8 (a)** $3x + 4y - 10 = 0$

**(b)** From the coordinates of $A$ and $B$, the gradient of $AB$ is $-\frac{3}{4}$.
The coordinates of $D$ are $(2, 1)$.
From the coordinates of $C$ and $D$, the gradient of $CD$ is $\frac{4}{3}$.
Since $-\frac{3}{4} \times \frac{4}{3} = -1$, $AB$ and $CD$ are perpendicular.

**9 (a)** $x + 2y - 16 = 0$    **(b)** $y = -4x$

**(c)** $\left(\frac{6}{7}, 7\frac{4}{7}\right)$

# 2 Surds

## A Understanding surds

### Exercise A (p 22)

**1** (a) 7    (b) −9    (c) $\frac{1}{3}$    (d) 18

(e) 40    (f) 20    (g) $\frac{5}{2}$    (h) $\frac{5}{4}$

(i) 10    (j) 4    (k) 0.4    (l) 7

(m) 9    (n) 12    (o) 0.6    (p) 0.001

**2** $\sqrt{109}$ cm

**3** (a) $2\sqrt{3}$    (b) $4\sqrt{3}$    (c) $3\sqrt{3}$

(d) $9\sqrt{3}$    (e) $288\sqrt{3}$

**4** A proof such as:
By Pythagoras, the length of a sloping edge is $\sqrt{2^2+5^2} = \sqrt{29}$. The perimeter is the length of the base $+ 2 \times$ the length of the sloping edge, i.e. $4+2\sqrt{29}$.

**5** Use any two adjacent points to show that the length of one edge is $\sqrt{5}$. For example, the length of the line joining (2, 1) to (4, 2) is
$\sqrt{(4-2)^2+(2-1)^2} = \sqrt{5}$.

**6** $\dfrac{4}{\sqrt{17}}$

**7** $8\sqrt{3}$

## B Simplifying surds (p 23)

**B1** The true statements are A, B, D and F.

**B2** (a) A proof such as:
$\sqrt{p^2} = p$ and $\sqrt{q^2} = q$
so $\sqrt{p^2} \times \sqrt{q^2} = pq$. Now $p^2 \times q^2 = (pq)^2$
so $\sqrt{p^2 \times q^2} = pq$.
Hence $\sqrt{p^2} \times \sqrt{q^2} = \sqrt{p^2 \times q^2}$ as required.

(b) A proof such as:
$\sqrt{p^2} = p$ and $\sqrt{q^2} = q$
so $\dfrac{\sqrt{p^2}}{\sqrt{q^2}} = \dfrac{p}{q}$. Now $\dfrac{p^2}{q^2} = \left(\dfrac{p}{q}\right)^2$ so $\sqrt{\dfrac{p^2}{q^2}} = \dfrac{p}{q}$.
Hence $\dfrac{\sqrt{p^2}}{\sqrt{q^2}} = \sqrt{\dfrac{p^2}{q^2}}$ as required.

**B3** (a) One way is to use the result of the proof in B2(a) with $p = \sqrt{a}$ and $q = \sqrt{b}$
to give $\sqrt{\left(\sqrt{a}\right)^2} \times \sqrt{\left(\sqrt{b}\right)^2} = \sqrt{\left(\sqrt{a}\right)^2 \times \left(\sqrt{b}\right)^2}$,
i.e $\sqrt{a} \times \sqrt{b} = \sqrt{ab}$

(b) One way is to use the result of the proof in B2(b) with $p = \sqrt{a}$ and $q = \sqrt{b}$
to give $\dfrac{\sqrt{\left(\sqrt{a}\right)^2}}{\sqrt{\left(\sqrt{b}\right)^2}} = \sqrt{\dfrac{\left(\sqrt{a}\right)^2}{\left(\sqrt{b}\right)^2}}$,
i.e $\dfrac{\sqrt{a}}{\sqrt{b}} = \sqrt{\dfrac{a}{b}}$

**B4** The easiest way is to give a counter-example such as $a = 9$ and $b = 4$, then $\sqrt{a} = 3, \sqrt{b} = 2$ and $\sqrt{a} + \sqrt{b} = 5$ which is not equivalent to $\sqrt{a+b} = \sqrt{13}$.

### Exercise B (p 25)

**1** (a) $\sqrt{10}$    (b) 4    (c) $2\sqrt{21}$    (d) $10\sqrt{6}$

**2** (a) $2\sqrt{2}$    (b) $3\sqrt{6}$    (c) $4\sqrt{2}$    (d) $5\sqrt{2}$

(e) $10\sqrt{6}$    (f) $15\sqrt{11}$    (g) $30\sqrt{2}$    (h) $16\sqrt{2}$

**3** (a) $\sqrt{2}$    (b) 3    (c) $3\sqrt{7}$    (d) 6

**4** (a) $\dfrac{2}{\sqrt{7}}$   (b) $\dfrac{\sqrt{3}}{5}$   (c) $\dfrac{12}{\sqrt{5}}$   (d) $2\sqrt{7}$   (e) $\dfrac{\sqrt{11}}{3}$

**5** (a) (i) $2\sqrt{3}$      (ii) $5\sqrt{3}$

(b) $3\sqrt{3}$

**6** (a) $6\sqrt{3}$    (b) $\sqrt{5}$    (c) $13\sqrt{2}$    (d) $2\sqrt{2}$

(e) 2    (f) $16\sqrt{3}$    (g) 4

**7** A proof such as:
The diagonals intersect at right angles so each edge is the hypotenuse of a right-angled triangle whose shorter sides measure 7 cm and 1 cm. Hence the length of one edge is
$\sqrt{7^2+1^2} = \sqrt{50} = 5\sqrt{2}$ cm.

**8** (a) $3+3\sqrt{15}$       (b) $10\sqrt{3} - 2\sqrt{5}$

**9** (a) $26\sqrt{2} - 3$       (b) $\sqrt{10} - 2 + \sqrt{15} - \sqrt{6}$

(c) $9-14\sqrt{5}$       (d) $52+14\sqrt{3}$

**10** (a) 14    (b) 13    (c) −2    (d) 19

**11** (a) $a - b^2$    (b) $x^2 - y$    (c) $p - q$

**12** Expanding the brackets gives $a^2b - c^2d$ which is a rational number for rational $a$, $b$, $c$ and $d$.

## C Rationalising the denominator

**1** (a) $\dfrac{7\sqrt{6}}{6}$      (b) $4\sqrt{3}$

  (c) $\dfrac{\sqrt{5}}{5}$      (d) $\dfrac{\sqrt{2}-\sqrt{10}}{2}$

  (e) $\dfrac{4\sqrt{6}-\sqrt{2}}{3}$

**2** (a) (i) $2\sqrt{7}$      (ii) $3\sqrt{7}$

  (b) $5\sqrt{7}$

**3** (a) $\dfrac{\sqrt{3}-1}{2}$      (b) $\sqrt{6}+1$

  (c) $\dfrac{5\sqrt{2}+1}{7}$      (d) $\sqrt{10}-\sqrt{5}+4\sqrt{2}-4$

  (e) $2(\sqrt{5}-\sqrt{2})$      (f) $\dfrac{\sqrt{5}-\sqrt{3}}{2}$

  (g) $\dfrac{\sqrt{39}-3\sqrt{3}}{4}$      (h) $21\sqrt{2}-28$

  (i) $2\sqrt{2}+\sqrt{5}$      (j) $21-2\sqrt{110}$

**4** $\dfrac{\sqrt{3}+5}{3-\sqrt{3}} = \dfrac{(\sqrt{3}+5)(3+\sqrt{3})}{(3-\sqrt{3})(3+\sqrt{3})}$

            $= \dfrac{8\sqrt{3}+18}{6}$

            $= \dfrac{8\sqrt{3}}{6}+\dfrac{18}{6}$

            $= \tfrac{4}{3}\sqrt{3}+3$

**5** $p=\tfrac{5}{3}, q=\tfrac{4}{3}$

**6** $a=-4, b=3$

**7** $\dfrac{1}{3\sqrt{2}-4} = \tfrac{3}{2}\sqrt{2}+2 > 2$

**8** (a) (i) $4\sqrt{3}-\sqrt{33}$      (ii) $2\sqrt{33}-2\sqrt{11}$

  (b) $4\sqrt{3}-2\sqrt{11}+\sqrt{33}$

**9** (a) $\sqrt{14}+4\sqrt{7}+9\sqrt{2}$      (b) $\sqrt{15}+2\sqrt{5}+\sqrt{3}$

  (c) $2\sqrt{2}-\sqrt{3}$

**10** $5\sqrt{7}-10$

**11** $\sqrt{2}+\tfrac{1}{3}\sqrt{3}$ or $\sqrt{2}+\dfrac{1}{\sqrt{3}}$

**12** $\dfrac{2\sqrt{3}+3\sqrt{2}-\sqrt{30}}{12}$ or $\tfrac{1}{6}\sqrt{3}+\tfrac{1}{4}\sqrt{2}-\tfrac{1}{12}\sqrt{30}$

## D Further problems

**1** $4\sqrt{5}$

**2** $26$

**3** $63\pi$

**4** A proof such as:

$XY^2 + XZ^2 = (2\sqrt{3})^2 + (\sqrt{13})^2 = 12 + 13 = 25$

Also $YZ^2 = 5^2 = 25$

Hence $XY^2 + XZ^2 = YZ^2$ and so triangle $XYZ$ is right-angled.

**5** $2\sqrt{7}\,\pi$

**6** $(\sqrt{2}-1, 11-\sqrt{2})$

**7** A proof such as:

Let $r$ be the radius of the whole circle.

The area of the quarter-circle is $\dfrac{\pi r^2}{4} = 6\pi$

so $\dfrac{r^2}{4} = 6$. Hence $r^2 = 24$, giving $r = \sqrt{24} = 2\sqrt{6}$.

Then the perimeter of the whole circle is

$r + r + \dfrac{2\pi r}{4} = 2r + \dfrac{\pi r}{2}$

$= 2 \times 2\sqrt{6} + \dfrac{\pi \times 2\sqrt{6}}{2} = 4\sqrt{6} + \pi\sqrt{6}$

$= \sqrt{6}(4 + \pi)$, as required.

**8** A proof such as:

Let $r$ be the radius of the whole circle.

The area of the circle is $\pi r^2 = 50$ so

$r^2 = \dfrac{50}{\pi}$. Hence $r = \sqrt{\dfrac{50}{\pi}} = \dfrac{5\sqrt{2}}{\sqrt{\pi}} = 5\sqrt{\dfrac{2}{\pi}}$,

as required.

The circumference of the circle is

$2\pi r = 2\pi \times 5\sqrt{\dfrac{2}{\pi}} = 10\pi \times \dfrac{\sqrt{2}}{\sqrt{\pi}} = 10\sqrt{\pi}\sqrt{2} = 10\sqrt{2\pi}$,

as required.

**9** (a) $\sqrt{5}(2 + \pi)\,\text{cm}$      (b) $(\tfrac{5}{2}\pi - 4)\,\text{cm}^2$

**10** A proof such as:

Let $r$ be the radius of the whole circle.

By Pythagoras, $r^2 + r^2 = 100$ so $r^2 = 50$ and $r = \sqrt{50} = 5\sqrt{2}$.

Then the perimeter of the quarter-circle is

$r + r + \tfrac{1}{4}(2\pi r) = 2r + \tfrac{1}{2}\pi r$

$= 2 \times 5\sqrt{2} + \tfrac{1}{2}(\pi \times 5\sqrt{2}) = 5\sqrt{2}(2 + \tfrac{1}{2}\pi)$ as required.

**Test yourself** (p 31)

**1** By Pythagoras,
$AB^2 = (4--2)^2 + (1--1)^2 = 6^2 + 2^2 = 40.$
So $AB = \sqrt{40} = 2\sqrt{10}$, which is in the form $p\sqrt{10}$
with $p = 2$.

**2 (a) (i)** $3\sqrt{2}$      **(ii)** $5\sqrt{2}$
   **(b)** $8\sqrt{2}$

**3** $5\sqrt{7}$

**4** A proof such as:
$$\frac{8}{\sqrt{3}} \times \frac{\sqrt{15}}{\sqrt{20}} = \frac{8}{\sqrt{3}} \times \sqrt{\frac{15}{20}} = \frac{8}{\sqrt{3}} \times \sqrt{\frac{3}{4}}$$
$$= \frac{8}{\sqrt{3}} \times \frac{\sqrt{3}}{\sqrt{4}} = \frac{8}{2} = 4,$$ which is an integer.

**5 (a) (i)** $AB = \sqrt{8}, BC = \sqrt{72}, AC = \sqrt{80}$
     **(ii)** $AB^2 + BC^2 = 8 + 72 = 80$
       Also $AC^2 = 80$
       Hence $AB^2 + BC^2 = AC^2$ and so triangle
       $ABC$ is right-angled.

   **(b)** 12

**6 (a)** $a = 1, b = 2$      **(b)** $c = \frac{1}{9}, d = \frac{2}{9}$

**7** $-\sqrt{6} + 2\sqrt{3} + \sqrt{2}$
giving $p = -1, q = 2, r = 1$

**8** A proof such as:
Let $X$ be the mid-point of $BC$.
Triangle $ABC$ is equilateral so $\angle AXB = 90°$ and, by
Pythagoras, $AX^2 = 8^2 - 4^2 = 64 - 16 = 48.$
So $AX = \sqrt{48} = 4\sqrt{3}$ cm and the area of triangle
$ABC$ is $4 \times 4\sqrt{3} = 16\sqrt{3}$ cm$^2$.
As triangle $ABC$ is equilateral, $\angle BAC = 60°$ and
the area of the sector is $\frac{1}{6}\pi \times 8^2 = \frac{64}{6}\pi = \frac{32}{3}\pi$ cm$^2$.
So the shaded area is
$\frac{32}{3}\pi - 16\sqrt{3} = 16\left(\frac{2}{3}\pi - \sqrt{3}\right)$ cm$^2$, as required.

# 3 Quadratic graphs and equations

## A Expanding brackets: revision

### Exercise A (p 32)

**1 (a)** $12x - 21$      **(b)** $2x^2 + 10x$
   **(c)** $-3x^2 + x$

**2 (a)** $x^2 + 11x + 30$      **(b)** $x^2 + 2x - 15$
   **(c)** $2x^2 - 7x + 5$      **(d)** $-3x^2 + 20x + 7$
   **(e)** $x^2 - 8x + 12$      **(f)** $3x^2 + 9x - 120$
   **(g)** $-12x^2 + 64x - 84$      **(h)** $x^2 - 4$
   **(i)** $16x^2 - 9$      **(j)** $x^2 + 6x + 9$
   **(k)** $2x^2 + 44x + 242$      **(l)** $x^2 - 12x + 36$

**3 (a)** $x^2 + ax + bx + ab$      **(b)** $x^2 + 2ax + a^2$
   **(c)** $kx^2 + 2akx + ka^2$      **(d)** $x^2 - a^2$
   **(e)** $a^2x^2 + 2abx + b^2$      **(f)** $a^2x^2 - b^2$

## B Factorising quadratic expressions: revision

### Exercise B (p 34)

**1 (a)** $x(5 + x)$      **(b)** $x(x - 10)$
   **(c)** $3x(x - 2)$      **(d)** $2x(2x + 5)$
   **(e)** $6x(2 + 3x)$      **(f)** $x(9 - x)$
   **(g)** $3x(5 - 3x)$      **(h)** $x(-x + 7)$

**2 (a)** $(x + 1)(x + 5)$      **(b)** $(x - 1)(x - 5)$
   **(c)** $(x + 3)^2$      **(d)** $(x + 1)(x + 9)$
   **(e)** $(x - 3)(x - 6)$      **(f)** $(x - 3)(x + 7)$
   **(g)** $(x + 3)(x - 4)$      **(h)** $(x + 1)(x - 15)$
   **(i)** $(x - 5)^2$

**3 (a)** $(2x + 3)(x + 1)$      **(b)** $(3x + 1)(x + 5)$
   **(c)** $(5x - 3)(x - 1)$      **(d)** $(3x + 1)(x - 7)$
   **(e)** $3(2x - 1)(x + 5)$      **(f)** $(3x + 2)(x + 3)$
   **(g)** $(3x + 1)(x + 6)$      **(h)** $2(2x - 3)(x - 4)$
   **(i)** $(3x + 2)(x - 8)$      **(j)** $(2x - 1)^2$
   **(k)** $(6x + 1)(x - 5)$      **(l)** $(5x - 12)(2x - 1)$

**4 (a)** $(x + 3)(x - 3)$      **(b)** $(x + 10)(x - 10)$
   **(c)** $(x + 1)(x - 1)$      **(d)** $(2x + 5)(2x - 5)$
   **(e)** $(3x + 1)(3x - 1)$      **(f)** $2(4 + 5x)(4 - 5x)$

**5 (a)** $(2x + 3)(x - 3)$

**(b)** Not possible

**(c)** $2(x + 5)(x - 6)$

**(d)** Not possible

**(e)** $3(2x + 5)(x - 1)$

**(f)** $(4x + 1)(4x - 3)$

**(g)** $(-x - 5)(x - 3)$  or  $-(x + 5)(x - 3)$  or
$(x + 5)(3 - x)$

**(h)** $(6x + 5)(6x - 5)$

**(i)** $(-2x - 9)(x - 5)$  or  $-(2x + 9)(x - 5)$  or
$(2x + 9)(5 - x)$

**6 (a)** Yes, the value is $144 = 12^2$.

**(b)** $x^2 + 10x + 25 = (x + 5)^2$, which is always a
square number

**7 (a) (i)** 56          **(ii)** $56 = 7 \times 8$

**(b)** $x^2 + 3x + 2 = (x + 1)(x + 2)$.
As $(x + 1) + 1 = (x + 2)$, this is the product of
two consecutive numbers.

**8 (a)** Yes, the value is $121 = 11^2$ and 121 is an odd
number.

**(b)** $16x^2 - 8x + 1 = (4x - 1)^2$ is a square number.
$4x$ is always even so $(4x - 1)$ is odd. Any odd
number squared will be an odd number itself.
So the expression will give an odd square
number.

**9 (a) (i)** 99          **(ii)** $99 = 9 \times 11$

**(b)** $4x^2 - 1 = (2x - 1)(2x + 1)$.
$2x$ is always even so $(2x - 1)$ and $(2x + 1)$ are
odd. Also $(2x - 1) + 2 = 2x + 1$ so the numbers
are consecutive odd numbers.

## C **Parabolas** (p 35)

**C1** Comments such as:
Every graph is basically the same shape though,
when $x$ is negative, the graphs are 'upside down'.
The shape is an open curve which has a vertical
line of symmetry. The coefficient of $x^2$ affects how
shallow or steep the curve shape is. The coefficient
of $x$ affects where the curve is positioned on the
coordinate grid. The constant gives the $y$-intercept.

**C2 (a)** Each parabola shares the point $(0, 0)$.
The graph of $y = 2x^2$ can be obtained from
$y = x^2$ by a stretch of scale factor 2 in the
direction of the $y$-axis.
The graph of $y = \frac{1}{3}x^2$ can be obtained from
$y = x^2$ by a stretch of scale factor $\frac{1}{3}$ in the
direction of the $y$-axis.

**(b)** Each parabola shares the point $(0, 0)$.
The graph of $y = kx^2$ can be obtained from
$y = x^2$ by a stretch of scale factor $k$ in the
direction of the $y$-axis.
When $k$ is negative this has the effect of
reflecting the graph in the $x$-axis as well as
stretching it.

**C3** The graph of $y = x^2 + q$ can be obtained from
$y = x^2$ by a vertical translation of $q$ units (up if $q$ is
positive and down when $q$ is negative).

**C4** The graph of $y = (x + p)^2$ can be obtained from
$y = x^2$ by a horizontal translation of $-p$ units
(left if $p$ is positive and right when $p$ is negative).

**C5 (a)** $(-5, 2)$

**(b)** $x = -5$

**(c) (i)** $(x + 5)^2 + 2 = x^2 + 10x + 25 + 2$
$\qquad\qquad\quad = x^2 + 10x + 27$ as required

**(ii)** $(0, 27)$

**C6** The graph of $y = (x + p)^2 + q$ can be obtained
from $y = x^2$ by a horizontal translation of $-p$ units
followed by a vertical translation of $q$ units,
i.e. by $\begin{bmatrix} -p \\ q \end{bmatrix}$.

**C7** $(6, 9)$

**C8** $x = -4$

**C9** The graph of $y = 2(x + p)^2 + q$ can be obtained
from $y = 2x^2$ by a horizontal translation of $-p$
units followed by a vertical translation of $q$ units,
i.e. by $\begin{bmatrix} -p \\ q \end{bmatrix}$.

**C10** The graph of $y = k(x + p)^2 + q$ can be obtained
from $y = kx^2$ by a horizontal translation of $-p$
units followed by a vertical translation of $q$ units,
i.e. by $\begin{bmatrix} -p \\ q \end{bmatrix}$.

**C11 (a) (i)** $(2, -5)$ **(ii)** $x = 2$

**(b) (i)** $3(x - 2)^2 - 5$
$$= 3(x^2 - 4x + 4) - 5$$
$$= 3x^2 - 12x + 12 - 5$$
$$= 3x^2 - 12x + 7$$

**(ii)** $(0, 7)$

**C12** $y = (x - 6)^2 + 5$  or  $y = x^2 - 12x + 41$

**C13** $y = 2(x + 3)^2 + 2$  or  $y = 2x^2 + 12x + 20$

**C14** 9 units to the right and 7 units up, i.e. $\begin{bmatrix} 9 \\ 7 \end{bmatrix}$

**C15** 1 unit to the left and 6 units down, i.e. $\begin{bmatrix} -1 \\ -6 \end{bmatrix}$

### Exercise C (p 38)

All translations are given as column vectors.

**1** $\begin{bmatrix} 4 \\ -5 \end{bmatrix}$

**2** $\begin{bmatrix} -8 \\ 1 \end{bmatrix}$

**3** $(5, 7)$

**4** $x = -2$

**5 (a) (i)** $y = x^2 + 14x + 44$

**(ii)** 44

**(b)** Sketch of a parabola with a vertex of $(-7, -5)$ and a $y$-intercept of 44

**6 (a)** Sketch of a parabola with a vertex of $(2, 5)$ and a $y$-intercept of 9

**(b)** Sketch of a parabola with a vertex of $(4, 0)$ and a $y$-intercept of 16

**(c)** Sketch of a parabola with a vertex of $(-6, -20)$ and a $y$-intercept of 16

**7** The graph is a parabola that is open at the top with a vertex of $(-3, 1)$, which is above the $x$-axis. Hence the whole graph is above the $x$-axis and does not cross it.

**8 (a)** $y = (x - 3)^2 + 1$  or  $y = x^2 - 6x + 10$

**(b)** $y = (x + 4)^2 + 2$  or  $y = x^2 + 8x + 18$

**(c)** $y = (x - 3)^2 - 2$  or  $y = x^2 - 6x + 7$

**9 (a) (i)** $\begin{bmatrix} -1 \\ -3 \end{bmatrix}$ **(ii)** $(-1, -3)$

**(b)** $y = 2x^2 + 4x - 1$

**(c)** Sketch of a parabola with a vertex of $(-1, -3)$, a $y$-intercept of $-1$ and the axis of symmetry $x = -1$

**10 (a)** Sketch of a parabola with a vertex of $(-4, 1)$ and a $y$-intercept of 33

**(b)** Sketch of a parabola with a vertex of $(2, -7)$ and a $y$-intercept of 5

**(c)** Sketch of a parabola with a vertex of $(-1, -3)$ and a $y$-intercept of 1

**11 (a) (i)** $\begin{bmatrix} -2 \\ 5 \end{bmatrix}$ **(ii)** $(-2, 5)$

**(b)**

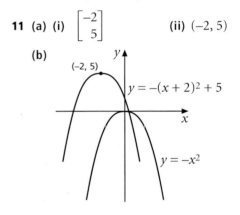

**(c)** 1

**12 (a)** $-2(x - 3)^2 + 11$
$$= -2(x^2 - 6x + 9) + 11$$
$$= -2x^2 + 12x - 18 + 11$$
$$= -2x^2 + 12x - 7$$

**(b)** Sketch of a parabola with a vertex of $(3, 11)$ and a $y$-intercept of $-7$

**13** $y = 3(x - 8)^2 + 1$  or  $y = 3x^2 - 48x + 193$

**14** $y = -4(x + 5)^2 - 3$  or  $y = -4x^2 - 40x - 103$

**15 (a)** $y = 2(x - 1)^2 + 5$  or  $y = 2x^2 - 4x + 3$

**(b)** $y = \frac{1}{2}(x + 4)^2 - 1$  or  $y = \frac{1}{2}x^2 + 4x + 7$

**(c)** $y = -3(x - 1)^2 - 5$  or  $y = -3x^2 + 6x - 8$

### D Completing the square (p 40)

**D1 (a)** $x^2 + 8x + 16$ **(b)** $x^2 - 18x + 81$

**(c)** $x^2 + 40x + 400$ **(d)** $x^2 - 2x + 1$

**(e)** $x^2 + \frac{1}{2}x + \frac{1}{16}$ **(f)** $x^2 - \frac{2}{3}x + \frac{1}{9}$

**D2** A $(x + 5)^2$, C $(x - 8)^2$, F $(x - 6)^2$, G $(x + \frac{1}{2})^2$

**D3** (a) 49  (b) 22  (c) 16

**D4** (a) $x^2 + 10x$  (b) $x^2 + 6x$
(c) $x^2 - 6x$  (d) $x^2 - 14x$

**D5** (a) $(x + 3)^2$
(b) $(x + 3)^2 - 9$
(c) $(x + 3)^2 - 4$
(d) Sketch of a parabola with a vertex of $(-3, -4)$ and a $y$-intercept of 5

**D6** (a) $(x - 7)^2 - 49$
(b) $(x - 7)^2 + 1$
(c) Sketch of a parabola with a vertex of $(7, 1)$ and a $y$-intercept of 50

**D7** (a) $(x + 7)^2 - 47$  (b) $(x - 3)^2 + 3$
(c) $(x + 4)^2 - 19$

**D8** (a) $(x + 1)^2 - 5$
(b) Sketch of a parabola with a vertex of $(-1, -5)$ and a $y$-intercept of $-4$

**D9** (a) $(x + 9)^2 + 1$
(b) $(x + 9)^2 \geq 0$ for all values of $x$ so $(x + 9)^2 + 1 > 0$

**D10** (a) $(x + 2)^2 + 7$
(b) (i) $(x + 2)^2 \geq 0$ for all values of $x$ so $(x + 2)^2 + 7 \geq 7$ so 7 is the minimum value.
(ii) $x = -2$

**D11** (a) $x^2 - x + \frac{1}{4}$  (b) $(x - \frac{1}{2})^2 - \frac{1}{4}$
(c) $(x - \frac{1}{2})^2 - 5\frac{1}{4}$  or  $(x - \frac{1}{2})^2 - \frac{21}{4}$

**D12** (a) $(x + 1\frac{1}{2})^2 - 1\frac{1}{4}$  or  $(x + \frac{3}{2})^2 - \frac{5}{4}$
(b) $(x + 2\frac{1}{2})^2 + 3\frac{3}{4}$  or  $(x + \frac{5}{2})^2 + \frac{15}{4}$
(c) $(x - 4\frac{1}{2})^2 - 23\frac{1}{4}$  or  $(x - \frac{9}{2})^2 - \frac{93}{4}$

**D13** (a) $(x - \frac{1}{2})^2 + 1\frac{1}{2}$
(b) $(x - \frac{1}{2})^2 \geq 0$ for all values of $x$ so $(x - \frac{1}{2})^2 + 1\frac{1}{2} \geq 1\frac{1}{2}$ so $1\frac{1}{2}$ is the minimum value

**D14** (a) $3(x - 2)^2 - 16$
(b) Sketch of a parabola with a vertex of $(2, -16)$ and a $y$-intercept of $-4$

**D15** (a) $2(x + 4)^2 + 8$  (b) $3(x - 3)^2 - 28$
(c) $2(x + \frac{5}{2})^2 - 20\frac{1}{2}$  or  $2(x + \frac{5}{2})^2 - \frac{41}{2}$

**Exercise D** (p 42)

**1** (a) $(x + 3)^2 + 1$  (b) $(x - 5)^2 - 22$
(c) $(x + 9)^2 - 83$  (d) $(x - 2)^2 + 9$
(e) $(x + 1\frac{1}{2})^2 - 3\frac{1}{4}$  or  $(x + \frac{3}{2})^2 - \frac{13}{4}$
(f) $(x - 2\frac{1}{2})^2 + 2\frac{3}{4}$  or  $(x - \frac{5}{2})^2 + \frac{11}{4}$

**2** (a) One way is to multiply out the brackets to give $(x - 6)^2 + 5 = x^2 - 12x + 36 + 5 = x^2 - 12x + 41$.
(b) $(6, 5)$
(c) When $x = 0$, $y = 0^2 - 12 \times 0 + 41 = 41$ so the graph crosses the $y$-axis at $(0, 41)$.

**3** (a) (i) $(x + 3)^2 + 6$
(ii) Sketch of a parabola with a vertex of $(-3, 6)$ and a $y$-intercept of 15
(b) (i) $(x + 4)^2 - 18$
(ii) Sketch of a parabola with a vertex of $(-4, -18)$ and a $y$-intercept of $-2$
(c) (i) $(x - 1)^2 + 4$
(ii) Sketch of a parabola with a vertex of $(1, 4)$ and a $y$-intercept of 5
(d) (i) $(x - 2)^2 - 7$
(ii) Sketch of a parabola with a vertex of $(2, -7)$ and a $y$-intercept of $-3$
(e) (i) $(x + \frac{3}{2})^2 + \frac{19}{4}$
(ii) Sketch of a parabola with a vertex of $(-\frac{3}{2}, \frac{19}{4})$ and a $y$-intercept of 7
(f) (i) $(x - \frac{7}{2})^2 - \frac{57}{4}$
(ii) Sketch of a parabola with a vertex of $(\frac{7}{2}, -\frac{57}{4})$ and a $y$-intercept of $-2$

**4** In completed-square form, the equation is $y = (x - 3)^2 + 4$, so the vertex is $(3, 4)$ and the minimum value for $y$ is 4. Hence the graph is completely above the $x$-axis and does not cross it.

**5** (a) $(x + 1)^2 + 4$
(b) (i) $(x + 1)^2 \geq 0$ for all $x$, so $(x + 1)^2 + 4 \geq 4$ and so the minimum value is 4.
(ii) $x = -1$

**6** In completed-square form, the equation is $y = (x + 2)^2 - 3$ so the vertex is $(-2, -3)$. Hence the graph is partially below the $x$-axis and so crosses it twice.

**7 (a)** $(x + 5)^2 - 24$ which is the form $(x + p)^2 + q$ with $p = 5$ and $q = -24$

**(b)** $-24$

**8** In completed-square form, the equation is $y = (x + 2)^2$, so the vertex is $(-2, 0)$ which is on the $x$-axis. Hence the graph just touches the $x$-axis.

**9 (a)** $2(x + 1)^2 - 3$     **(b)** $3(x - 2)^2 + 1$

**(c)** $5(x - 1)^2 - 6$     **(d)** $2(x + 4)^2$

**(e)** $3(x + \frac{1}{2})^2 + \frac{17}{4}$     **(f)** $4(x - \frac{3}{2})^2 - 14$

**10 (a)** $3(x + 2)^2 - 19$
$= 3(x^2 + 4x + 4) - 19$
$= 3x^2 + 12x + 12 - 19$
$= 3x^2 + 12x - 7$

**(b)** $(-2, -19)$

**(c)** When $x = 0$, $y = 3 \times 0^2 + 12 \times 0 - 7 = -7$ so the graph crosses the $y$-axis at $(0, -7)$.

**(d)** $x = -2$

**11 (a) (i)** $y = 2(x - 3)^2 + 3$

    **(ii)** Sketch of a parabola with a vertex of $(3, 3)$ and a $y$-intercept of 21

**(b) (i)** $y = 3(x + 1)^2$

    **(ii)** Sketch of a parabola with a vertex of $(-1, 0)$ and a $y$-intercept of 3

**(c) (i)** $y = 4(x + \frac{1}{2})^2 + 2$

    **(ii)** Sketch of a parabola with a vertex of $(-\frac{1}{2}, 2)$ and a $y$-intercept of 3

**12** $5x^2 - 20x + 24 = 5(x - 2)^2 + 4$, so the minimum value of $y$ is 4. So the graph does not cross the $x$-axis.

**13 (a) (i)** $3(x + 3)^2 - 2$   **(ii)** $-2$   **(iii)** $x = -3$

**(b) (i)** $2(x - 1)^2 + 3$   **(ii)** 3   **(iii)** $x = 1$

**(c) (i)** $2(x + \frac{7}{2})^2 - \frac{47}{2}$  **(ii)** $-\frac{47}{2}$  **(iii)** $x = -\frac{7}{2}$

**14 (a)** $2(x + 4)^2 - 29$   **(b)** $-29$

**15 (a)** $d = (t - 4)^2 + 3$ **(b)** $3\,\text{km}$ **(c)** 4 hours

**16 (a)** $2(x + \frac{3}{4})^2 - \frac{1}{8}$   **(b)** $3(x - \frac{1}{2})^2 - \frac{11}{4}$

**(c)** $4(x - \frac{3}{8})^2 - \frac{25}{16}$

**17 (a)** $-2(x + 1)^2 + 5 = -2(x^2 + 2x + 1) + 5$
$= -2x^2 - 4x - 2 + 5 = -2x^2 - 4x + 3$

**(b)** $(-1, 5)$     **(c)** 3

**(d)** Sketch of a parabola with a vertex of $(-1, 5)$ and a $y$-intercept of 3

**18 (a) (i)** $y = -(x + 3)^2 + 10$

    **(ii)** Sketch of a parabola with a vertex of $(-3, 10)$ and a $y$-intercept of 1

**(b) (i)** $y = -(x - 4)^2 + 19$

    **(ii)** Sketch of a parabola with a vertex of $(4, 19)$ and a $y$-intercept of 3

**(c) (i)** $y = -2(x + 3)^2 - 7$

    **(ii)** Sketch of a parabola with a vertex of $(-3, -7)$ and a $y$-intercept of $-25$

**19 (a)** 1         **(b)** 5

**20 (a)** $h = -5(t - 3)^2 + 45$ **(b)** 45 metres

**(c)** 3 seconds

## E Zeros of quadratics

**Exercise E** (p 46)

**1 (a)** $x = 0, 4$   **(b)** $x = 0, -2$   **(c)** $x = -1, -6$

**(d)** $x = 3$     **(e)** $x = -2, 8$   **(f)** $x = 3, 6$

**(g)** $x = \frac{1}{2}, -3$  **(h)** $x = -\frac{2}{3}, 1$  **(i)** $x = \frac{3}{2}, -7$

**(j)** $x = \frac{6}{5}, 2$  **(k)** $x = \frac{1}{3}, -12$  **(l)** $x = \frac{5}{2}$

**2 (a)** $(-4, 0), (3, 0)$   **(b)** $(1, 0), (8, 0)$

**(c)** $(-6, 0), (-\frac{1}{2}, 0)$  **(d)** $(-7, 0), (\frac{2}{3}, 0)$

**(e)** $(0, 0), (7, 0)$   **(f)** $(-3, 0), (3, 0)$

**(g)** $(1, 0), (3, 0)$   **(h)** $(-5, 0)$

**(i)** $(-2, 0), (4, 0)$

**3 (a)** $y = x^2 - 5x + 4$   **(b)** $y = x^2 - 4$

**(c)** $y = x^2 - 3x$

**4 (a)** $(-5, 0), (1, 0)$   **(b)** $(0, -5)$

**(c) (i)** $(x + 2)^2 - 9$   **(ii)** $(-2, -9)$

**(d)** Sketch of a parabola with a vertex of $(-2, -9)$ that cuts the axes at $(-5, 0), (1, 0)$ and $(0, -5)$

**5 (a)** Sketch of a parabola with a vertex of $(5, -9)$ that cuts the axes at $(2, 0)$, $(8, 0)$ and $(0, 16)$

**(b)** Sketch of a parabola with a vertex of $(-7, -9)$ that cuts the axes at $(-10, 0)$, $(-4, 0)$ and $(0, 40)$

**(c)** Sketch of a parabola with a vertex of $(\frac{7}{2}, -\frac{9}{4})$ that cuts the axes at $(2, 0)$, $(5, 0)$ and $(0, 10)$

**(d)** Sketch of a parabola with a vertex of $(-3, -48)$ that cuts the axes at $(-7, 0)$, $(1, 0)$ and $(0, -21)$

**(e)** Sketch of a parabola with a vertex of $(-\frac{3}{2}, -\frac{25}{2})$ that cuts the axes at $(-4, 0)$, $(1, 0)$ and $(0, -8)$

**(f)** Sketch of a parabola with a vertex of $(-\frac{1}{2}, \frac{81}{4})$ that cuts the axes at $(-5, 0)$, $(4, 0)$ and $(0, 20)$

**6 (a)** $y = 2x^2 - 8x + 6$  **(b)** $y = -x^2 + x + 6$
**(c)** $y = 3x^2 - 21x + 30$

## F Solving quadratic equations by completing the square

**Exercise F** (p 47)

**1 (a)** $x = 3 - \sqrt{2},\ 3 + \sqrt{2}$
**(b)** $x = -5 - \sqrt{11},\ -5 + \sqrt{11}$
**(c)** $x = 6 - \sqrt{6},\ 6 + \sqrt{6}$

**2 (a)** $(x + 5)^2 - 2$  **(b)** $x = -5 - \sqrt{2},\ -5 + \sqrt{2}$

**3 (a)** $x = -2 - \sqrt{3},\ -2 + \sqrt{3}$
**(b)** $x = -1 - 2\sqrt{2},\ -1 + 2\sqrt{2}$
**(c)** $x = 3 - \sqrt{11},\ 3 + \sqrt{11}$
**(d)** $x = \frac{5}{2} - \frac{1}{2}\sqrt{29},\ \frac{5}{2} + \frac{1}{2}\sqrt{29}$
**(e)** $x = -3 - \sqrt{6},\ -3 + \sqrt{6}$
**(f)** $x = \frac{5}{2} - \frac{1}{2}\sqrt{15},\ \frac{5}{2} + \frac{1}{2}\sqrt{15}$

**4 (a)** $(-1 - \sqrt{5}, 0),\ (-1 + \sqrt{5}, 0)$
**(b)** $(2 - \sqrt{3}, 0),\ (2 + \sqrt{3}, 0)$
**(c)** $(\frac{7}{2} - \frac{1}{2}\sqrt{31}, 0),\ (\frac{7}{2} + \frac{1}{2}\sqrt{31}, 0)$

**5 (a)** $(x + 2)^2 + 6$
**(b)** You end up with the square root of a negative number. So the equation has no real roots, indicating that the graph doesn't cross the $x$-axis.

## G Solving quadratic equations by using the formula

**Exercise G** (p 49)

**1 (a)** $x = \dfrac{-5 - \sqrt{13}}{6}, \dfrac{-5 + \sqrt{13}}{6}$
**(b)** $x = 1 - \sqrt{3},\ 1 + \sqrt{3}$
**(c)** $x = \dfrac{4 - \sqrt{10}}{2}, \dfrac{4 + \sqrt{10}}{2}$ or $x = 2 - \frac{1}{2}\sqrt{10},\ 2 + \frac{1}{2}\sqrt{10}$

**2 (a)** $x = -5.541, 0.541$  **(b)** $x = 0.634, 2.366$
**(c)** $x = -0.540, 0.740$

**3** $(1.55, 0),\ (6.45, 0)$

**4 (a)** You end up with an expression that involves $\sqrt{-16}$ so the equation has no real roots.
**(b)** The graph does not cross the $x$-axis.

**5 (a)** You end up with an expression that involves $\sqrt{0}$ so the equation has just one (repeated) root.
**(b)** The graph just touches the $x$-axis.

**6** $c$ must be less than 9.

**7** $c$ must be equal to 1.

**8** $b$ must be greater than $-8$ but less than 8.

## H Using the discriminant (p 50)

**H1** If the discriminant is the square of a whole number or a fraction, then the expression will factorise. The roots of the equation are rational numbers.

**Exercise H** (p 50)

**1** The discriminant is 52 which is larger than 0 so the equation has real roots.

**2** Equations B, C and F have real roots. The values of the discriminants are 13, 40 and 21 respectively.

**3** Equations A and B can be solved by factorising. The values of the discriminants are $49\ (= 7^2)$ and $169\ (= 13^2)$ respectively.

**4 (a)** $x = 2, 7$      **(b)** $x = 4 - \sqrt{2}, \ 4 + \sqrt{2}$

**(c)** $x = \frac{1}{3}$      **(d)** No real solutions

**(e)** $x = \frac{1}{2}, 2$      **(f)** $x = -5 - \sqrt{22}, \ -5 + \sqrt{22}$

**5 (a)** Crosses the $x$-axis at two points

**(b)** Touches the $x$-axis at one point

**(c)** Crosses the $x$-axis at two points

**(d)** Crosses the $x$-axis at two points

**(e)** Does not cross the $x$-axis

**(f)** Crosses the $x$-axis at two points

**6 (a)** $k = -20, 20$    **(b)** $k = 36$      **(c)** $k = -4, 4$

**7** $k = 2, 6$

**8 (a)**
$$x^2 - 4kx + 9 = 0$$
$$\Rightarrow (x - 2k)^2 - (-2k)^2 + 9 = 0$$
$$\Rightarrow (x - 2k)^2 - 4k^2 + 9 = 0$$
$$\Rightarrow (x - 2k)^2 = 4k^2 - 9$$
$$\Rightarrow x - 2k = \pm \sqrt{4k^2 - 9}$$
$$\Rightarrow x = 2k \pm \sqrt{4k^2 - 9}$$

**(b)** When $k = \frac{3}{2}$, the discriminant
$$4k^2 - 9 = 4 \times \left(\frac{3}{2}\right)^2 - 9$$
$$= 4 \times \frac{9}{4} - 9 = 0$$
So the equation has equal roots.
Another value for $k$ is $-\frac{3}{2}$.

**9 (a)**
$$x^2 + 2kx - 7 = 0$$
$$\Rightarrow (x + k)^2 - k^2 - 7 = 0$$
$$\Rightarrow (x + k)^2 = k^2 + 7$$
$$\Rightarrow x + k = \pm \sqrt{k^2 + 7}$$
$$\Rightarrow x = -k \pm \sqrt{k^2 + 7}$$
are the roots of the equation.

**(b)** $k^2 \geq 0$ for all values of $k$, so the discriminant $k^2 + 7$ is greater than 0 and hence the roots are real and different.

**(c)** $-\sqrt{2} + 3$ and $-\sqrt{2} - 3$

**10 (a)** $(2(a - 3))^2 = 2(a - 3) \times 2(a - 3)$
$$= 4(a - 3)^2 = 4(a^2 - 6a + 9)$$
$$= 4a^2 - 24a + 36$$

**(b)** $k = 1, 10$

**Test yourself** (p 52)

**1 (a)** $(x - 7)^2 + 1$      **(b)** 1

**2 (a)** $(x + 5)^2 - 5$

**(b)** Sketch of a parabola with a vertex of $(-5, -5)$ and $y$-intercept of 20

**3 (a)** $3(x - 1)^2 + 7$, so $a = 3$, $b = -1$, $c = 7$

**(b)** $x = 1$

**4 (a)** $\left(x + \frac{5}{2}\right)^2 - \frac{21}{4}$      **(b)** $\begin{bmatrix} -\frac{5}{2} \\ -\frac{21}{4} \end{bmatrix}$

**5 (a)** $(x - 4)^2 - 12$

**(b)** $x = 4 - 2\sqrt{3}, \ 4 + 2\sqrt{3}$

**6** $x = \dfrac{-7 - \sqrt{17}}{4}, \dfrac{-7 + \sqrt{17}}{4}$

**7 (a)** $y = x^2 + 6x + 10$      **(b)** $y = x^2 - 4x + 4$

**(c)** $y = x^2 - 2x + 6$

**8** $2 + \frac{3}{2}\sqrt{2}, \ 2 - \frac{3}{2}\sqrt{2}$

**9 (a)** $3(x + 4)^2 - 8$      **(b)** $-8$

**10 (a)** $4(x - 4)^2 - 60$      **(b)** $(4, -60)$

**(c)** Sketch of a parabola with a vertex of $(4, -60)$ that cuts the axes at $(4 - \sqrt{15}, 0)$, $(4 + \sqrt{15}, 0)$ and $(0, 4)$

**11 (a)** $-31$      **(b)** No real roots

**12 (a)** $4$

**(b)** Sketch of a parabola with a vertex of $(5, 4)$ that cuts the axes at $(3, 0)$, $(7, 0)$ and $(0, -21)$

**13 (a)**
$$x^2 + 2kx + c = 0$$
$$\Rightarrow (x + k)^2 - k^2 + c = 0$$
$$\Rightarrow (x + k)^2 = k^2 - c$$
$$\Rightarrow x + k = \pm \sqrt{k^2 - c}$$
$$\Rightarrow x = -k \pm \sqrt{k^2 - c}$$

**(b)** $k = 9, -9$

**14** $y = -\frac{1}{2}x^2 - 4x - 7$

# 4 Indices

## A Positive and negative indices

### Exercise A (p 55)

1 (a) $243$    (b) $-32$    (c) $\frac{1}{32}$    (d) $1$    (e) $-\frac{1}{10}$

2 (a) $0.09$      (b) $0.25$      (c) $0.125$
   (d) $0.0001$      (e) $0.000\,001$

3 (a) $\frac{1}{27}$    (b) $\frac{16}{49}$    (c) $\frac{3}{2}$    (d) $\frac{16}{9}$    (e) $\frac{8}{125}$

4 (a) $2^5$    (b) $2^{-3}$    (c) $2^{-1}$    (d) $2^0$    (e) $2^{-6}$

5 (a) $2^8$    (b) $5^{-3}$    (c) $2^{-4}$    (d) $3^{-4}$    (e) $5^{-1}$

6 (a) $3^3$    (b) $3^{-2}$    (c) $3^{-7}$    (d) $3^{10}$    (e) $3^{10}$

7 (a) $2^4$    (b) $2^9$    (c) $2^9$    (d) $2^{-4}$    (e) $2^{-13}$

8 (a) $5^{-2}$
   (b) $\left(\frac{1}{25}\right)^{-4} = (5^{-2})^{-4} = 5^{-2 \times -4} = 5^8$

9 (a) $2^{-10}$    (b) $2^{-6}$    (c) $2^4$    (d) $2^3$    (e) $2^{10}$

10 (a) $n^{-1}$ or $\frac{1}{n}$    (b) $3n^{-2}$ or $\frac{3}{n^2}$    (c) $n^8$
   (d) $5n^6$      (e) $n^{20}$      (f) $2n^7$
   (g) $\frac{1}{2}n$ or $\frac{n}{2}$    (h) $\frac{1}{3}n^5$ or $\frac{n^5}{3}$    (i) $\frac{5}{3}n^{-2}$ or $\frac{5}{3n^2}$
   (j) $\frac{4}{3}n^5$ or $\frac{4n^5}{3}$

11 (a) $5^5 + 5^4$    (b) $5 + 5^2$    (c) $5^6 - 5$
   (d) $5^{-1} + 5$    (e) $5^2 - 5^{-1} + 5^{-5}$

12 (a) $x^2 + x^5$    (b) $x^7 - x$    (c) $x^{-4} + x^{-2}$
   (d) $x + x^{-3} - x^{-4}$    (e) $x^{-4} - x$

13 (a) $x = 9$    (b) $x = -2$    (c) $x = -2$
   (d) $x = -5$    (e) $x = -4$

14 (a) $x = \frac{5}{2}$    (b) $x = \frac{5}{2}$    (c) $x = \frac{10}{3}$
   (d) $x = 2$    (e) $x = \frac{4}{3}$

## B Roots and fractional indices

### Exercise B (p 58)

1 (a) $6$    (b) $5$    (c) $2$    (d) $2$    (e) $1$

2 (a) $27$    (b) $16$    (c) $243$    (d) $27$    (e) $4$

3 $125^{\frac{2}{3}} = \left(\sqrt[3]{125}\right)^2 = 5^2 = 25$, so $125^{-\frac{2}{3}} = \frac{1}{25}$

4 (a) $\frac{1}{3}$    (b) $\frac{1}{4}$    (c) $\frac{1}{32}$    (d) $\frac{1}{9}$    (e) $\frac{1}{8}$

5 $\left(\frac{1}{9}\right)^{\frac{3}{2}} = \left(\sqrt{\frac{1}{9}}\right)^3 = \left(\frac{1}{3}\right)^3 = \frac{1}{27}$

6 $\left(\frac{4}{9}\right)^{\frac{3}{2}} = \left(\sqrt{\frac{4}{9}}\right)^3 = \left(\frac{2}{3}\right)^3 = \frac{8}{27}$
   so $\left(\frac{4}{9}\right)^{-\frac{3}{2}} = \frac{1}{\left(\frac{8}{27}\right)} = \frac{27}{8}$

7 (a) $\frac{1}{9}$    (b) $\frac{3}{2}$    (c) $\frac{1}{32}$    (d) $\frac{4}{25}$    (e) $16$

8 (a) $a^{\frac{5}{2}}$    (b) $a^{\frac{5}{2}}$    (c) $a^{\frac{3}{4}}$    (d) $a$    (e) $a^{\frac{3}{2}}$
   (f) $a^{-2}$    (g) $a^{-\frac{2}{3}}$    (h) $a^{-\frac{1}{8}}$

9 (a) $2^{\frac{1}{2}}$    (b) $2^{\frac{1}{5}}$    (c) $2^{-\frac{1}{2}}$    (d) $2^{\frac{1}{2}}$    (e) $2^{\frac{3}{2}}$
   (f) $2^{\frac{9}{2}}$    (g) $2^{\frac{3}{2}}$    (h) $2^{-\frac{1}{2}}$    (i) $2^{-\frac{9}{2}}$    (j) $2^{\frac{1}{6}}$
   (k) $2^4$    (l) $2^{\frac{3}{2}}$    (m) $2^2$    (n) $2^3$    (o) $2^{\frac{15}{2}}$

10 $x^{\frac{9}{2}}$

11 (a) $x + x^{\frac{9}{2}}$    (b) $x^{\frac{3}{2}} - x^{\frac{7}{2}}$    (c) $x^{\frac{5}{2}} - x$
   (d) $x^{-\frac{1}{2}} + x^{\frac{1}{2}}$    (e) $x^3 + x^{\frac{11}{2}}$

12 (a) $4x$      (b) $5x^{\frac{3}{2}}$      (c) $2x^{\frac{1}{2}}$
   (d) $\frac{1}{2}x^{\frac{3}{2}}$      (e) $\frac{4}{3}x^{-\frac{1}{2}}$

13 (a) $6x - 8x^{\frac{1}{2}}$    (b) $5x^3 + 2x^2$
   (c) $2x^{\frac{1}{2}} + 3x^{\frac{7}{2}}$    (d) $\frac{1}{9}x^{\frac{3}{2}} - \frac{2}{3}x^{-\frac{1}{2}}$

14 (a) $x = 27$    (b) $x = \frac{1}{49}$    (c) $x = 1$
   (d) $x = 32$    (e) $x = \frac{8}{125}$

15 (a) $x = 25$    (b) $x = 16$    (c) $x = \frac{8}{27}$    (d) $x = 1$
   (e) $x = 27$    (f) $x = 32$    (g) $x = 81$    (h) $x = 9$
   (i) $x = \frac{1}{27}$    (j) $x = \frac{1}{4}$

## C Further problems

### Exercise C (p 61)

1 (a) $x = 1$    (b) $x = \frac{2}{3}$    (c) $x = -\frac{1}{2}$
   (d) $x = 2$    (e) $x = -2$

2 (a) $3^{2x}$    (b) $3^{x+1}$    (c) $3^{3x+2}$
   (d) $3^{x-2}$    (e) $3^{\frac{x}{2}}$

3 (a) $2^{2x}$    (b) $2^{3x}$    (c) $2^{-4x}$    (d) $2^{5x-1}$
   (e) $2^{x-\frac{1}{2}}$    (f) $2^{3x-2}$    (g) $2^{10-x}$    (h) $2^{\frac{x}{2}}$
   (i) $2^{4x-\frac{3}{2}}$    (j) $2^x$

**4** (a) $x = \frac{1}{2}$    (b) $x = -\frac{1}{2}$    (c) $x = -\frac{1}{3}$    (d) $x = \frac{2}{3}$

    (e) $x = \frac{1}{3}$    (f) $x = -\frac{3}{5}$    (g) $x = \frac{2}{3}$    (h) $x = -\frac{3}{4}$

    (i) $x = -2$    (j) $x = -\frac{3}{4}$

**5** (a) $x = \frac{1}{5}$    (b) $x = \frac{1}{6}$    (c) $x = \frac{3}{2}$    (d) $x = -\frac{3}{2}$

    (e) $x = \frac{5}{2}$    (f) $x = -\frac{1}{2}$    (g) $x = -6$    (h) $x = \frac{1}{2}$

    (i) $x = -\frac{1}{2}$    (j) $x = -3$

**6** (a) $y = \frac{1}{2}$    (b) $x = \frac{1}{3}$    (c) $p = 6$    (d) $n = -\frac{3}{5}$

**7** $3^{2x} = (3^x)^2 = y^2$

**8** $8^x = (2^3)^x = 2^{3x} = (2^x)^3 = u^3$

**9** $5^{n+2} = 5^n \times 5^2 = 25 \times 5^n = 25x$

**10** (a) $\quad 2^{2x} - 5 \times 2^x + 4 = 0$

$\Rightarrow \quad (2^x)^2 - 5 \times 2^x + 4 = 0$

$\Rightarrow \quad\quad y^2 - 5y + 4 = 0$ where $y = 2^x$

    (b) $x = 0, 2$

**11** (a) $\quad 25^x - 6 \times 5^x + 5 = 0$

$\Rightarrow \quad (5^2)^x - 6 \times 5^x + 5 = 0$

$\Rightarrow \quad 5^{2x} - 6 \times 5^x + 5 = 0$

$\Rightarrow \quad (5^x)^2 - 6 \times 5^x + 5 = 0$

$\Rightarrow \quad\quad n^2 - 6n + 5 = 0$ where $n = 5^x$

    (b) $x = 0, 1$

**12** (a) $\quad 9^x - 4 \times 3^{x+1} + 27 = 0$

$\Rightarrow (3^2)^x - 4 \times 3^1 \times 3^x + 27 = 0$

$\Rightarrow \quad 3^{2x} - 12 \times 3^x + 27 = 0$

$\Rightarrow \quad (3^x)^2 - 12 \times 3^x + 27 = 0$

$\Rightarrow \quad\quad u^2 - 12u + 27 = 0$ where $u = 3^x$

    (b) $x = 1, 2$

**13** (a) $y^2 - 4y + 3 = 0$    (b) $x = 0, \frac{1}{2}$

**14** (a) $\quad 5^{2x+1} - 6 \times 5^x + 1 = 0$

$\Rightarrow \quad 5^1 \times 5^{2x} - 6 \times 5^x + 1 = 0$

$\Rightarrow \quad 5 \times (5^x)^2 - 6 \times 5^x + 1 = 0$

$\Rightarrow \quad\quad 5n^2 - 6n + 1 = 0$ where $n = 5^x$

    (b) $x = -1, 0$

**15** (a) $\quad 4^{x+1} - 33 \times 2^x + 8 = 0$

$\Rightarrow (2^2)^{x+1} - 33 \times 2^x + 8 = 0$

$\Rightarrow \quad 2^{2x+2} - 33 \times 2^x + 8 = 0$

$\Rightarrow \quad 2^2 \times 2^{2x} - 33 \times 2^x + 8 = 0$

$\Rightarrow \quad 4 \times (2^x)^2 - 33 \times 2^x + 8 = 0$

$\Rightarrow \quad\quad 4u^2 - 33u + 8 = 0$ where $u = 2^x$

    (b) $x = -2, 3$

**16** (a) $\quad\quad 4^{x-1} - 2^x + 1 = 0$

$\Rightarrow \quad\quad (2^2)^{x-1} - 2^x + 1 = 0$

$\rightarrow \quad\quad 2^{2x-2} - 2^x + 1 = 0$

$\Rightarrow \quad 2^{-2} \times 2^{2x} - 2^x + 1 = 0$

$\Rightarrow \quad \frac{1}{4} \times (2^x)^2 - 2^x + 1 = 0$

$\Rightarrow \quad\quad \frac{1}{4}y^2 - y + 1 = 0$ where $y = 2^x$

$\Rightarrow \quad\quad y^2 - 4y + 4 = 0$

    (b) $x = 1$

**17** (a) $\frac{1}{4}u^2 - u + 1 = 0$ or $u^2 - 4u + 4 = 0$    (b) $x = \frac{1}{2}$

## Test yourself (p 63)

**1** (a) $\frac{1}{16}$    (b) $7$    (c) $\frac{1}{2}$    (d) $125$    (e) $\frac{1}{8}$

**2** (a) $x = 0$    (b) $x = 3$    (c) $x = -2$

    (d) $x = 25$    (e) $x = -\frac{2}{3}$

**3** $a$

**4** $x^{-\frac{1}{2}} + x^{\frac{3}{2}}$

**5** A proof such as

$$\frac{\sqrt{x}(5 - 6x^3\sqrt{x})}{10x} = \frac{5\sqrt{x} - 6x^4}{10x}$$

$$= \frac{5\sqrt{x}}{10x} - \frac{6x^4}{10x}$$

$$= \frac{\sqrt{x}}{2x} - \frac{3x^4}{5x}$$

$$= \frac{x^{\frac{1}{2}}}{2x^1} - \frac{3x^4}{5x^1}$$

$$= \frac{1}{2}x^{\frac{1}{2}-1} - \frac{3}{5}x^{4-1}$$

$$= \frac{1}{2}x^{-\frac{1}{2}} - \frac{3}{5}x^3$$

**6** (a) $x = -\frac{1}{2}, y = \frac{5}{2}$    (b) $8$

**7** $9^{y-1} = (3^2)^{y-1} = 3^{2(y-1)} = 3^{2y-2}$

   Hence $3^x = 9^{y-1} \Rightarrow x = 2y - 2$.

**8** $x = \frac{1}{3}$

**9** (a) $5^{x+\frac{1}{2}}$    (b) $x = \frac{3}{2}$

**10** (a) $k = 3$    (b) $x = \frac{6}{5}$

**11** (a) $x = -6$    (b) $x = \frac{1}{2}$

**12** (a) $\quad\quad 7^{2x+1} - 8 \times 7^x + 1 = 0$

$\Rightarrow \quad 7^1 \times 7^{2x} - 8 \times 7^x + 1 = 0$

$\Rightarrow \quad 7 \times (7^x)^2 - 8 \times 7^x + 1 = 0$

$\Rightarrow \quad\quad 7u^2 - 8u + 1 = 0$ where $u = 7^x$

    (b) $x = -1, 0$

# 5 Further equations

## A Rearranging to solve equations: revision

### Exercise A (p 65)

1 (a) $x = 0, 8$

(b) $x = -5, 3$

(c) $x = -2, 6$

(d) $x = \frac{30}{7}$

(e) $x = 2, 3$

(f) $x = \frac{3}{5}, 4$

(g) $x = \frac{-1-\sqrt{61}}{6}, \frac{-1+\sqrt{61}}{6}$

(h) $x = -1, \frac{5}{12}$

(i) $x = \frac{5-\sqrt{33}}{4}, \frac{5+\sqrt{33}}{4}$

2 (a) $x = -3, 2$

(b) $x = -3-\sqrt{14}, -3+\sqrt{14}$

(c) $x = -9, 1$

(d) $x = -5, \frac{3}{2}$

(e) $x = 2-\sqrt{6}, 2+\sqrt{6}$

(f) $x = -9, -\frac{1}{4}$

(g) $x = 7$

(h) $x = 5$

(i) $x = -3-\sqrt{2}, -3+\sqrt{2}$

(j) $x = \frac{9}{2}, -5$

(k) $x = -8$

(l) $x = \frac{9-\sqrt{57}}{4}, \frac{9+\sqrt{57}}{4}$

3 (a) $x = -1.732, 1.732$    (b) $x = -1.207, 0.207$

(c) $x = -0.434, 0.768$    (d) $x = -2.220, -0.180$

(e) $x = 0.316$    (f) $x = -8.243, 0.243$

## B Solving problems

### Exercise B (p 67)

1 $38.627\,\text{m}$

2 $(-1, -\frac{3}{2}), (6, 2)$

3 $(-4, 28), (\frac{1}{2}, 1)$

4 (a) A proof such as:

'Where the graphs intersect the $x$-values satisfy the equation $x^2 - x - 1 = x + 1$. This rearranges to give $x^2 - 2x - 2 = 0$. Completing the square leads to $(x-1)^2 - 3 = 0$ and $x = 1 \pm \sqrt{3}$. So $x = 1 - \sqrt{3}$ is one solution and the corresponding value of $y$ is $1 - \sqrt{3} + 1 = 2 - \sqrt{3}$. Hence one of the points is $(1 - \sqrt{3}, 2 - \sqrt{3})$.'

(b) $(1 + \sqrt{3}, 2 + \sqrt{3})$

5 $x = \dfrac{1 + \sqrt{5}}{2}$

6 (a) $p(60 - 6p)$  or  $60p - 6p^2$

(b) Solving the equation $60p - 6p^2 = 80$ leads to two solutions which correspond to profits per radio of £8.42 and £1.58. She could choose either. The lower profit might give more reliable sales. Alternatively, if she had limited space on her stall, she might prefer to sell fewer at a higher margin.

(c) No, she couldn't. One way to show that this is not possible is to show that there are no real solutions to the equation $60p - 6p^2 = 200$. The equation rearranges to $3p^2 - 30p + 100 = 0$ and the discriminant is $-300$ which is less than zero. Hence there are no real solutions to the equation.

## C Solving simultaneous equations by substitution

### Exercise C (p 69)

1 (a) $x = -7, y = 49$
   $x = 1, y = 1$

(b) $x = -2, y = -1$
   $x = 5, y = 6$

(c) $x = \frac{3}{4}, y = 5\frac{9}{16}$
   $x = -1, y = 6$

(d) $x = -3, y = -1$
   $x = 1, y = 3$

(e) $x = -3, y = -6$
   $x = -1, y = -4$

(f) $x = -1, y = 2$
   $x = 4\frac{3}{5}, y = -\frac{4}{5}$

**2** $(-5, 4)$, $(1, 10)$

**3 (a)** Accurate graphs of $y = \frac{1}{2}x^2 - 2x + 1$ and
   $y = 4 - x$

   **(b)** Estimates such as: $(-1.6, 5.6)$, $(3.6, 0.4)$

   **(c)** $(-1.646, 5.646)$, $(3.646, 0.354)$

**4 (a)** $x = 1, y = 5$;  $x = 2, y = 4$

   **(b)** $x = -4, y = -1$;  $x = 1, y = 4$

   **(c)** $x = -3, y = 4$;  $x = 5, y = 0$

**5 (a)** $x = 2 + 2\sqrt{2}, y = 7 + 2\sqrt{2}$
      $x = 2 - 2\sqrt{2}, y = 7 - 2\sqrt{2}$

   **(b)** $x = \dfrac{1 - \sqrt{13}}{2}, y = 2 + \sqrt{13}$

      $x = \dfrac{1 + \sqrt{13}}{2}, y = 2 - \sqrt{13}$

   **(c)** $x = 2 - \sqrt{3}, y = 3 - 2\sqrt{3}$
      $x = 2 + \sqrt{3}, y = 3 + 2\sqrt{3}$

**6** $\sqrt{11} - 1$, $\sqrt{11} + 1$

**7** The length is $5 + \sqrt{2}$
   and the width is $5 - \sqrt{2}$.

**8** $\left(\sqrt{5} + 2, \sqrt{5} - 2\right)$, $\left(\sqrt{5} - 2, \sqrt{5} - 6\right)$

**9** $(-2.407, 1.791)$, $(-1.099, -2.791)$, $(1.099, -2.791)$,
   $(2.407, 1.791)$

## D Counting points of intersection

### Exercise D (p 72)

**1** One way to show that they do not intersect is to
   show that there are no real solutions to the
   equation $x^2 + 2x + 4 = 3x + 2$. The equation
   rearranges to $x^2 - x + 2 = 0$ and the discriminant
   of $x^2 - x + 2$ is $-7$ which is less than zero. Hence
   the equation has no real roots and the graphs do
   not intersect.

**2** One way to show that the line is a tangent is to
   show that there is only one real solution to the
   equation $x^2 - 6x + 5 = 1 - 2x$ by using the
   discriminant. The equation rearranges to
   $x^2 - 4x + 4 = 0$ and the discriminant of $x^2 - 4x + 4$
   is 0. Hence the equation has one real root and the
   line is a tangent.

**3 (a)** One way to show that the line is a tangent is to
   show that there is only one real solution to the
   equation $2x^2 + 13x + 23 = 5 + x$ by
   completing the square. The equation
   rearranges to $x^2 + 6x + 9 = 0$ which is
   equivalent to $(x + 3)^2 = 0$. Hence the equation
   has one real root and the line is a tangent.

   **(b)** $(-3, 2)$

**4 (a)** Meet at two points   **(b)** Meet at one point

   **(c)** Do not meet

**5** One argument is that substituting $x = -1$ into
   $y^2 = 4x$ leads to $y^2 = -4$ which has no real solutions.

**6** $k = -7$

**7** $k = -\frac{1}{2}$

**8** One way to show this is to let the two numbers be
   $x$ and $y$. Then $x + y = 4$ (giving $y = 4 - x$) and
   $xy = 5$. Substitution gives $x(4 - x) = 5$ which
   rearranges to $x^2 - 4x + 5 = 0$. The discriminant of
   $x^2 - 4x + 5$ is $-4$ which is less than zero. So no real
   solution exists and hence it is impossible to find
   two such numbers.

**9** $k = -7, 17$

### Test yourself (p 73)

**1** The length is $\sqrt{5} + 2$ and the width is $2\sqrt{5} - 4$.

**2 (a)** $x = -1, y = 8$;  $x = 3, y = 16$

   **(b)** $(-1, 8)$ $(3, 16)$

**3** $x = 1, y = 0$;  $x = 3, y = 2$

**4** $x = 4, y = 3$;  $x = -2\frac{2}{3}, y = -\frac{1}{3}$

**5 (a)** $x = 4, y = 7$

   **(b)** The straight line is a tangent to the parabola
      because they meet at only one point, $(4, 7)$.

**6** $x = -1, y = 1$;  $x = \frac{3}{2}, y = -\frac{1}{4}$

**7** One way to show that they do not intersect is to
   show that there are no real solutions to the
   equation $y^2 + 7(2 - y) = 0$. The equation
   rearranges to $y^2 - 7y + 14 = 0$ and the
   discriminant of $y^2 - 7y + 14$ is $-7$ which is less
   than zero. Hence the equation has no real roots
   and the graphs do not intersect.

# 6 Inequalities

## A Linear inequalities: revision (p 74)

**A1** (a) (i) T  (ii) F  (iii) T  (iv) F  (v) F

(b) $t > 3$

**A2** (a) 5

(b) At $x = 2$, the graph of $y = 2x + 1$ is below the graph of $y = x + 6$.

(c) $x \geq 5$

(d) $x < 5$

**A3** (a) $-2$  (b) $x < -2$  (c) $x > -2$

**A4** (a) (i) F  (ii) T  (iii) T  (iv) T  (v) T

(b) $p \leq 2.5$

**A5** $<$

**A6** Adding or subtracting a positive or a negative leaves the solution set unchanged, as does multiplying or dividing by a positive. However, multiplying or dividing by a negative reverses the direction of the inequality sign.

### Exercise A (p 76)

**1** (a) $x \geq 3$  (b) $y < 2$  (c) $z < 1$

(d) $p > 3$  (e) $q \geq 3$  (f) $a < -2$

(g) $b \geq -2$  (h) $x > -1$  (i) $y > -9$

(j) $z \leq 2\frac{2}{3}$  (k) $w < \frac{1}{2}$  (l) $d \leq -\frac{2}{7}$

**2** (a) $x < 1$  (b) $x < 3\frac{1}{2}$  (c) $x \leq 4$

(d) $y > -\frac{2}{5}$  (e) $y \leq 3$  (f) $y < -8$

**3** (a) $x > 4$  (b) $x > -3\frac{1}{7}$  (c) $x \leq 6\frac{1}{4}$

## B Linear inequalities: solving problems

### Exercise B (p 77)

**1** Using $h$ for the number of hours gives $8h + 11 > 73$ and so $h > 7\frac{3}{4}$.
So National Insurance needs to be paid if the number of hours worked is greater than $7\frac{3}{4}$.

**2** Using $d$ for the number of days gives $2d + 10 < 3.5d + 5$ and so $d > 3\frac{1}{3}$.
So Cutting Edge is less expensive if the chain saw is hired for more than 3 days.

**3** (a) (i) Each shorter edge is $(l - 6)$ cm so the total length of the two shorter edges is $(2l - 12)$ cm. Now, in a triangle, the total length of the two shorter edges must be greater than the length of the longest edge. So $2l - 12 > l$ which leads to $l > 12$.

(ii) The total length of wire is $2l - 12 + l = 3l - 12$. Now $l > 12$ so we know that $3l > 36$ and that $3l - 12 > 24$ as required.

(b) $3l - 12 \leq 100$
$\Rightarrow \quad 3l \leq 112$
$\Rightarrow \quad l \leq 37\frac{1}{3}$ as required

**4** (a) If $w \geq 20$ then the length of the edge parallel to the wall would be zero or negative. So $w$ must be less than 20.

(b) $40 - 2w$

(c) (i) The length of the edge parallel to the wall is $40 - 2w$. Hence the total perimeter of the rectangle is $2w + 2(40 - 2w) = 2w + 80 - 4w = 80 - 2w$. The total perimeter cannot be more than 60 metres so $80 - 2w \leq 60$ as required.

(ii) The solution is $w \geq 10$ so the minimum value of $w$ is 10.

## C Quadratic inequalities (p 78)

**C1** (a) (i) F  (ii) T  (iii) T  (iv) F  (v) F

(b) $-3 < x < 3$

**C2** (a) $A\,(-5, 0)$, $B\,(5, 0)$  (b) $x \leq -5$, $x \geq 5$

**C3** (a) $P\,(-2, 3)$, $Q\,(1, 6)$  (b) $-2 < x < 1$

**C4** $x \leq -4$, $x \geq 7$

**C5** $-5 \leq x \leq 3$

**C6** One way is to show that the inequality can be written as $x^2 - 5 < 0$ and then work graphically to obtain $-\sqrt{5} < x < \sqrt{5}$.

**C7** One way is to show that the inequality can be written as $x^2 - 5 > 0$ and then work graphically to obtain $x < -\sqrt{5}, x > \sqrt{5}$.

### Exercise C (p 80)

**1** (a) $-5 < x < 2$  (b) $x \leq -9$, $x \geq -2$

(c) $x < 3$, $x > 6$      (d) $-2 \leq x \leq 7$

(e) $x \leq 0$, $x \geq 3$      (f) $x < -2$, $x > 2$

2 (a) $-5 < q < \frac{1}{2}$      (b) $k < -\frac{1}{3}$, $k > 4$

(c) $y \leq -4$, $y \geq 0$      (d) $-3 \leq p \leq \frac{1}{2}$

(e) $0 < a < \frac{1}{3}$      (f) $t \leq -\frac{3}{2}$, $t \geq \frac{2}{3}$

3 (a) $-\sqrt{2} < x < \sqrt{2}$      (b) $x \leq 1 - \sqrt{2}$, $x \geq 1 + \sqrt{2}$

(c) $-1 - \frac{1}{2}\sqrt{6} < x < -1 + \frac{1}{2}\sqrt{6}$

4 (a) $k < -5$, $k > 5$      (b) $-1 < k < 3$

(c) $k \leq -5$, $k \geq 2$      (d) $k < -4$, $k > \frac{1}{2}$

(e) $0 < k < 5$      (f) $-\sqrt{5} < k < \sqrt{5}$

(g) $k < 1 - \sqrt{3}$, $k > 1 + \sqrt{3}$

(h) $k < -1$, $k > \frac{1}{4}$      (i) $-\frac{3}{2} < k < \frac{3}{2}$

5 (a)      $6x - x^2 < 5$

$\Rightarrow$  $6x - x^2 - 5 < 0$

$\Rightarrow$  $x^2 - 6x + 5 > 0$ as required

(b) $x < 1$, $x > 5$

6 (a)      $(2 - x)(x - 3) > 0$

$\Rightarrow$  $2x - 6 - x^2 + 3x > 0$

$\Rightarrow$      $-x^2 + 5x - 6 > 0$

$\Rightarrow$          $5x - x^2 > 6$ as required

(b) $2 < x < 3$

7 (a) $-3 < x < 3$      (b) $x < -1$, $x > 4$   (c) $x < -7$, $x > 2$

8 (a)      $y(y + 2) < 8$

$\Rightarrow$      $y^2 + 2y < 8$

$\Rightarrow$ $y^2 + 2y - 8 < 0$ as required

(b) $-4 < y < 2$

9 (a) $3 < x < 4$      (b) $-7 < y < 1$      (c) $k < -\frac{2}{3}$, $k > 1$

10 (a) $(x + 1)^2 - 16$      (b) $-5 < x < 3$

11 (a) $x^2 + 4x + 5 = (x + 2)^2 + 1$ and so
$x^2 + 4x + 5 > 0$ for all values of $x$.

(b) $x^2 + 2x + 1 = (x + 1)^2$ which is greater than or
equal to 0 for all values of $x$. Hence
$x^2 + 2x + 1 < 0$ has no real solutions.

12 $1 < x \leq 4$

13 (a) $x < -5$, $x > -3$      (b) $-4 \leq x \leq -2$, $x \geq 1$

(c) $x < -5$, $1 < x < 6$

14 (a) $-1 < x < 6$      (b) $-13\frac{1}{2} < x < -5$

## D Inequalities and the discriminant (p 82)

D1 (a) 5      (b) $5 \geq 0$

D2 (a) $-3$      (b) $-3 < 0$

D3 (a) $k^2 - 4$      (b) $k \leq -2$, $k \geq 2$

D4 (a) $k^2 - 4k$      (b) $0 < k < 4$

### Exercise D (p 83)

1 (a) The equation has real roots so the discriminant
must be greater than or equal to 0.
The discriminant here is $k^2 - 4 \times 16 = k^2 - 64$
so $k^2 - 64 \geq 0$ as required.

(b) $k \leq -8$, $k \geq 8$

2 (a) $k \leq -10$, $k \geq 10$      (b) $k \leq 0$, $k \geq \frac{4}{9}$

(c) $k \leq -9$, $k \geq -1$

3 $k < 0$, $k > 1\frac{1}{4}$

4 (a) $k < 0$, $k > 16$  (b) $-\frac{3}{2} < k < \frac{3}{2}$    (c) $\frac{6}{7} < k < 2$

5 The equation does not have real roots when the
discriminant is less than 0.
The discriminant here is $k^2 - 8$ and
$k^2 - 8 < 0 \Rightarrow -\sqrt{8} < k < \sqrt{8}$
i.e. $-2\sqrt{2} < k < 2\sqrt{2}$ as required.

6 (a) $-\sqrt{3} < k < \sqrt{3}$      (b) $-6 < k < 2$

(c) $k < -\frac{1}{7}$, $k > 1$

7 The discriminant here is
$(-(k + 4))^2 - 4 \times k \times 4$
$= (k + 4)^2 - 16k$
$= k^2 + 8k + 16 - 16k$
$= k^2 - 8k + 16$
$= (k - 4)^2$
Now $(k - 4)^2 \geq 0$ for all values of $k$ so the equation
will have real roots for all values of $k$.

8 $k > -\frac{1}{4}$

9 $1 < k < 9$

## E Quadratic inequalities: solving problems

### Exercise E (p 85)

1 (a) $n(2n - 1) > 465$ has solution set given by
$n < -15$ and $n > 15\frac{1}{2}$. Hence the relevant value
of $n$ is 16.

(b) 496

**2** The width must be greater than or equal to 5 metres but less than or equal to 15 metres.

**3 (a)** $\dfrac{n(n+1)}{2} > 100$ has solution set

given by $n < -\frac{1}{2} - \frac{1}{2}\sqrt{801}$ and $n > -\frac{1}{2} + \frac{1}{2}\sqrt{801}$.

Now $-\frac{1}{2} + \frac{1}{2}\sqrt{801} = 13.6509\ldots$ Hence the relevant value of $n$ is 14.

**(b)** 105        **(c)** 45

**4 (a)** $2x - 5 > 16$    **(b)** $x^2 - 5x < 104$   **(c)** $10\frac{1}{2} < x < 13$

### Test yourself (p 87)

**1** Using $w$ for the number of words gives
$50w + 250 < 20w + 500$ and so $w < 8\frac{1}{3}$.
So it is cheaper to use the *Cadzow Times* for a message of 8 words or fewer.

**2 (a)** $x > 10\frac{1}{2}$      **(b)** $x < -2,\ x > 7$

**3 (a)** $y < -1\frac{1}{2}$      **(b)** $-9 < x < \frac{1}{2}$

**4** $x < -1\frac{1}{2},\ x > 4$

**5** $x < 2 - \sqrt{3},\ x > 2 + \sqrt{3}$

**6 (a)** $x < 2\frac{1}{2}$    **(b)** $\frac{1}{2} < x < 5$    **(c)** $\frac{1}{2} < x < 2\frac{1}{2}$

**7 (a)** The equation has real roots so the discriminant must be greater than or equal to 0.
The discriminant here is
$$(5k)^2 - 4 \times 2k$$
$$= 25k^2 - 8k$$
$$= k(25k - 8) \text{ so}$$
$$k(25k - 8) \geq 0 \text{ as required.}$$

**(b)** $k \leq 0,\ k \geq \frac{8}{25}$

**8** The inequality is $12t - 5t^2 < 4$ which leads to $(5t - 2)(t - 2) > 0$ and $t < \frac{2}{5}, t > 2$. So the height of the ball is less than 4 metres before 0.4 seconds and after 2 seconds.

**9** The width must be greater than or equal to 15 metres and less than or equal to 35 metres.

**10** $k < -4,\ k > 4$

**11** $-10 < k < 10$, where $k$ is the $y$-intercept of the line.

## 7 Polynomials

### A Indices: revision

#### Exercise A (p 88)

**1 (a)** 36    **(b)** 18    **(c)** 36    **(d)** 125
   **(e)** 48    **(f)** 12    **(g)** 477    **(h)** 28
   **(i)** 40    **(j)** 35

**2 (a)** $\frac{3}{2}$    **(b)** 9    **(c)** 0    **(d)** $-\frac{1}{8}$

**3 (a)** 10    **(b)** $-1$    **(c)** $-5$    **(d)** 32

**4 (a)** $5x^3$    **(b)** $12x^3$    **(c)** $10x^5$    **(d)** $2x^4$
   **(e)** $\frac{5}{3}x^3$    **(f)** $8x^3$    **(g)** $9x^4$    **(h)** $\frac{1}{4}x^6$

### B Cubic graphs (p 89)

**B1** The shape of each graph is always a curve with a 'kink' in the middle. It is always one of the three basic shapes shown below; if the value of $a$ is negative, then it will be a reflection in the $x$-axis o one of these shapes.

**B2** The graphs cross or touch the $x$-axis one, three and two times respectively.

**B3** Comments such as:
$y = x^3$ increases from left to right.
The graph has rotation symmetry about the origin.
Near the origin the curve 'wiggles', being momentarily flat at $(0, 0)$.

$y = x^3 - x$ has rotation symmetry about the origin.
Near the origin the curve has a pronounced 'wiggle', decreasing for a little while before beginning to increase again.

$y = x^3 + x$ increases from left to right like $y = x^3$ and has rotation symmetry about the origin.
The curve 'wiggles' near the origin too but doesn' flatten out like $y = x^3$.

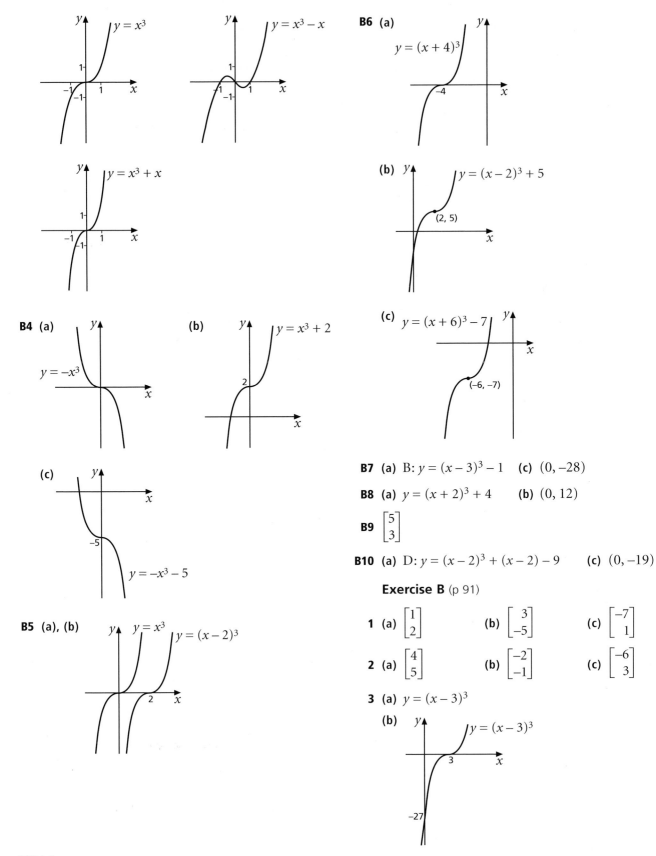

**B6 (a)** $y = (x + 4)^3$

**(b)** $y = (x - 2)^3 + 5$ $(2, 5)$

**(c)** $y = (x + 6)^3 - 7$ $(-6, -7)$

**B7 (a)** B: $y = (x - 3)^3 - 1$ **(c)** $(0, -28)$

**B8 (a)** $y = (x + 2)^3 + 4$ **(b)** $(0, 12)$

**B9** $\begin{bmatrix} 5 \\ 3 \end{bmatrix}$

**B10 (a)** D: $y = (x - 2)^3 + (x - 2) - 9$ **(c)** $(0, -19)$

**Exercise B** (p 91)

**1 (a)** $\begin{bmatrix} 1 \\ 2 \end{bmatrix}$ **(b)** $\begin{bmatrix} 3 \\ -5 \end{bmatrix}$ **(c)** $\begin{bmatrix} -7 \\ 1 \end{bmatrix}$

**2 (a)** $\begin{bmatrix} 4 \\ 5 \end{bmatrix}$ **(b)** $\begin{bmatrix} -2 \\ -1 \end{bmatrix}$ **(c)** $\begin{bmatrix} -6 \\ 3 \end{bmatrix}$

**3 (a)** $y = (x - 3)^3$

**(b)** $y = (x - 3)^3$

**B4 (a)** $y = -x^3$ **(b)** $y = x^3 + 2$

**(c)** $y = -x^3 - 5$

**B5 (a), (b)** $y = x^3$ $y = (x - 2)^3$

$y = x^3$ $y = x^3 - x$ $y = x^3 + x$

**4** $y = (x - 5)^3 - 3$

**5** $y = (x - 2)^3 + (x - 2)$

**6** (a) $y = (x - 1)^3 + x + 2$     (b) $(0, 1)$

**7** $y = (x + 3)^3 - x - 5$

## C Further graphs and manipulation (p 92)

The important elements of sketches here are the $x$- and $y$-intercepts and the general shape. There is no need to be any more precise.

**C1** $y = x^3 + 9x^2 + 27x + 27$

**C2** (a) $x^3 + 9x^2 + 23x + 15$     (b) $2x^3 - x^2 - 13x - 6$

(c) $6x^3 - 22x^2 - 8x$     (d) $15x^3 + 52x^2 - 31x + 4$

**C3** (a) $x = -3, -2, 1$

(b) It crosses the $x$-axis at $(-3, 0)$, $(-2, 0)$ and $(1, 0)$.

(c) At $(0, -6)$

(d)

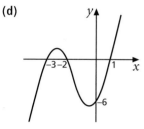

(e) $y = x^3 + 4x^2 + x - 6$

**C4** (a) $(-1, 0), (0, 0), (4, 0)$

(b)

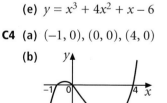

(c) $y = x^3 - 3x^2 - 4x$

**C5** (a) (i) $(-1, 0), (\frac{1}{2}, 0) (3, 0)$     (ii) At $(0, 3)$

(b)

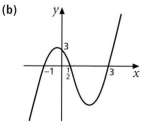

(c) $y = 2x^3 - 5x^2 - 4x + 3$

**C6** (a) $x = -3, 1$

(b) It meets the $x$-axis at two points: $(-3, 0)$ and $(1, 0)$. Since it is a cubic shape, it must just touch the $x$-axis at one of these points.

(c) At $(0, 3)$

(d)

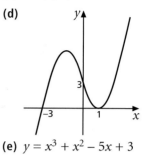

(e) $y = x^3 + x^2 - 5x + 3$

**C7** (a)  $\begin{aligned}(x + 3)^3 + 1 \\ = (x + 3)(x^2 + 6x + 9) + 1 \\ = x^3 + 9x^2 + 27x + 27 + 1 \\ = x^3 + 9x^2 + 27x + 28\end{aligned}$

(b)

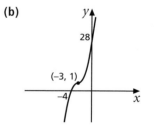

**C8** (a) $3x^3 - x^2 - 4x = x(3x^2 - x - 4)$

(b) $x(3x - 4)(x + 1)$

(c)

**C9** (a) $x = 1 + \sqrt{5}, 1 - \sqrt{5}$

(b) $x = 0, 1 + \sqrt{5}, 1 - \sqrt{5}$

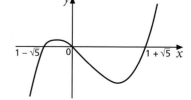

**C10** (a) $x(x - 5)(2 - x) = x(-x^2 + 7x - 10)$
$= -x^3 + 7x^2 - 10x$

(b) Q

**Exercise C** (p 95)

**1 (a) (i)** 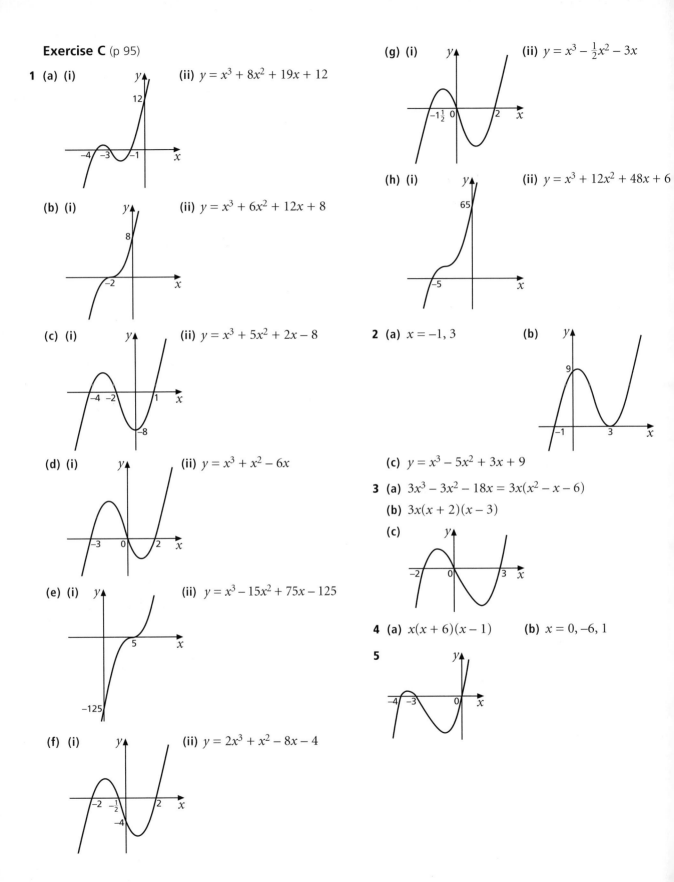 **(ii)** $y = x^3 + 8x^2 + 19x + 12$

**(b) (i)** **(ii)** $y = x^3 + 6x^2 + 12x + 8$

**(c) (i)** **(ii)** $y = x^3 + 5x^2 + 2x - 8$

**(d) (i)** **(ii)** $y = x^3 + x^2 - 6x$

**(e) (i)** **(ii)** $y = x^3 - 15x^2 + 75x - 125$

**(f) (i)** **(ii)** $y = 2x^3 + x^2 - 8x - 4$

**(g) (i)** **(ii)** $y = x^3 - \frac{1}{2}x^2 - 3x$

**(h) (i)** **(ii)** $y = x^3 + 12x^2 + 48x + 6$

**2 (a)** $x = -1, 3$ **(b)**

**(c)** $y = x^3 - 5x^2 + 3x + 9$

**3 (a)** $3x^3 - 3x^2 - 18x = 3x(x^2 - x - 6)$

**(b)** $3x(x + 2)(x - 3)$

**(c)**

**4 (a)** $x(x + 6)(x - 1)$ **(b)** $x = 0, -6, 1$

**5**

**6 (a)** −4 **(b)**

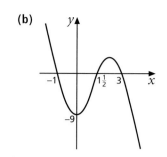

**(c)** $y = -2x^3 + 7x^2 - 9$

**7** $x = 0, 2$

**8 (a)** $x = 0, 5 - \sqrt{3}, 5 + \sqrt{3}$

**(b)**

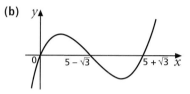

**9** C

**10**

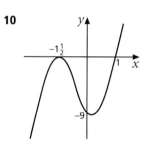

## D Polynomial functions

### Exercise D (p 97)

**1** $x^3 - x^2 + 11x - 2$

**2 (a)** 30 **(b)** 43 **(c)** 0

**3 (a)** $x^5 + 2x^4 + 3x^2 + 7x + 2$

**(b)** $x^4 + 12x^2 + 36$

**(c)** $2x^5 + 6x^4 - x^3 + 8x^2 + 14x - 5$

**(d)** $-x^4 + x^3 + 7x - 1$

**(e)** $3x^4 - x^3 + 10x^2 - 3x$

**(f)** $x^6 - 3x^4 + 3x^2 - 1$

**(g)** $x^4 - 15x^2 + 10x + 24$

**(h)** $-6x^3 - 27x^2 + 41x - 12$

**4 (a)** 5 **(b)** 6 **(c)** 26 **(d)** 11 **(e)** 50

**5 (a)** $g(5) = 0, g(-5) = 0$ and $g(-2) = 0$

**(b)** $(5, 0), (-5, 0), (-2, 0)$

**6 (a)** $x^5$ **(b)** $-x^5 + 5x^2 + 5$

**(c)** $x^7 + x^5 - 2x^4 - 4x^2 - 2$

**(d)** $x^{10} - 4x^7 - 4x^5 + 4x^4 + 8x^2 + 4$

**7 (a) (i)** 2 **(ii)** 0 **(iii)** −20 **(iv)** 0 **(v)** 0

**(b)**

**8 (a)** $f(x) = 2x^3 + 13x^2 + 8x - 48$

**(b)**

**9 (a)** $g(x) = x(2x - 1)(x - 3)$ **(b)** $x = 0, \frac{1}{2}, 3$

**10** $c = 5$

**11** $a = 2, b = -5$

## Mixed questions (p 98)

**1 (a)** C: $y = (x - 4)^3 + 1$

**(b)** $y = x^3 - 12x^2 + 48x - 63$

**2 (a)** −6 **(b)**

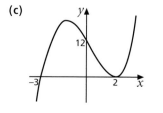

**(c)** $f(x) = 2x^3 - x^2 - 13x - 6$

**3 (a)** 12 **(b)** $x = -3, 2$

**(c)**

**4 (a) (i)** $-2$    **(ii)** $21$    **(iii)** $-9$

**(b) (i)** $-3x^3 + 9x^2 - 13$

**(ii)** $3x^5 - 3x^4 - 2x^3 + 11x^2 - 6$

**(iii)** $9x^4 - 12x^2 + 4$

**5 (a)** $p(x) = 2x(x + 3)(x - 3)$

**(b)**

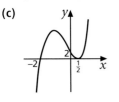

**6 (a)** $f(x) = x(x + 1)(x + 2)$

**(b)** The factorisation shows that $f(a)$ can be written as the product of three consecutive integers when $a$ is an integer. One of these must be a multiple of 3 so the product $f(a)$ must also be a multiple of 3.

**Test yourself** (p 99)

**1 (a)** $y = x^3 - 6x^2 + 13x - 11$    **(b)** $(0, -11)$

**2 (a)** P    **(b)** R    **(c)** Q    **(d)** S

**3 (a)** $g(0) = 2, g(2) = 36$    **(b)** $x = \frac{1}{2}, -2$

**(c)**

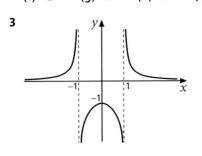

**(d)** $g(x) = 4x^3 + 4x^2 - 7x + 2$

**4 (a) (i)** $x^3 + x^2 - 2x$    **(ii)** $x^5 + x^4 - 8x^3 - 12x^2$

**(b)** $x = -2, 0, 3$    **(c)** $x = -2, 0, 4$

**5 (a)** $f(x) = x(x + 1)(x + 6)$

**(b)** The factorisation shows that, when $a$ is an integer, $f(a)$ can be written as the product of two consecutive integers and one other integer.
One of the consecutive integers must be even so the product $f(a)$ must also be even.

# 8 Graphs and transformations

## A Further graphs (p 100)

**A1 (a) (i)**    **(ii)**

**(iii)**    **(iv)**

**(v)**    **(vi)**

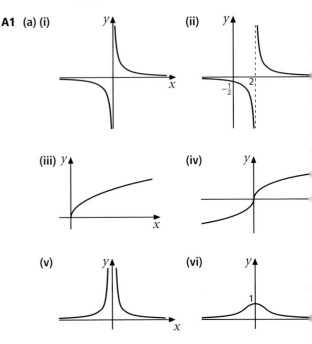

## Exercise A (p 101)

**1 (a) (i)** The value of $y$ gets closer and closer to 1.

**(ii)** $y = 1$

**(b)** $x = 2$

**(c)** $\frac{1}{2}$

**(d)** 1

**2 (a)** B    **(b)** F    **(c)** H    **(d)** A    **(e)** I

**(f)** C    **(g)** G    **(h)** D    **(i)** E

**3**

## B Translating

### Exercise B (p 103)

**1 (a)** $y = \dfrac{1}{x-5} - 1$

**(b)**

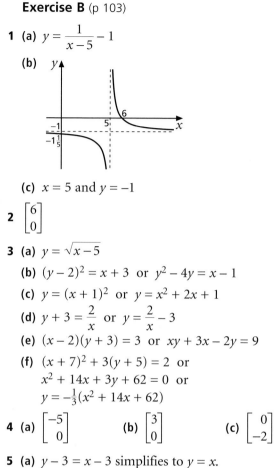

**(c)** $x = 5$ and $y = -1$

**2** $\begin{bmatrix} 6 \\ 0 \end{bmatrix}$

**3 (a)** $y = \sqrt{x-5}$

**(b)** $(y-2)^2 = x+3$ or $y^2 - 4y = x - 1$

**(c)** $y = (x+1)^2$ or $y = x^2 + 2x + 1$

**(d)** $y + 3 = \dfrac{2}{x}$ or $y = \dfrac{2}{x} - 3$

**(e)** $(x-2)(y+3) = 3$ or $xy + 3x - 2y = 9$

**(f)** $(x+7)^2 + 3(y+5) = 2$ or
$x^2 + 14x + 3y + 62 = 0$ or
$y = -\tfrac{1}{3}(x^2 + 14x + 62)$

**4 (a)** $\begin{bmatrix} -5 \\ 0 \end{bmatrix}$  **(b)** $\begin{bmatrix} 3 \\ 0 \end{bmatrix}$  **(c)** $\begin{bmatrix} 0 \\ -2 \end{bmatrix}$

**5 (a)** $y - 3 = x - 3$ simplifies to $y = x$.

**(b)** The image is the graph itself.

The vector $\begin{bmatrix} 3 \\ 3 \end{bmatrix}$ makes an angle of 45° with
the $x$-axis, as does the straight line $y = x$.
Hence the vector will not change the position
of the line.

**6 (a)** $y - 1 = x$ simplifies to $y = x + 1$.

**(b)** $y - 4 = x - 3$ simplifies to $y = x + 1$.

**(c)** The translations give the same image.
Both translations have the form $\begin{bmatrix} k \\ k+1 \end{bmatrix}$.
So the image of $y = x$ will be of the form
$y - (k+1) = x - k$, simplifying to $y = x + 1$.

## C Reflecting (p 104)

**C1 (a)** Each reflection is shown by a dotted graph.

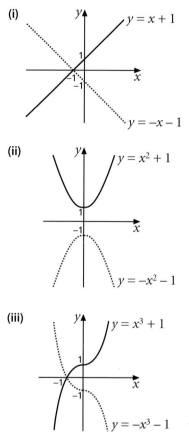

**(b)** A comment such as: The equation of each
image can be found by multiplying the
right-hand side by –1.

**(c)** $y = -x^4 - 1$

**C2 (a) (i)**

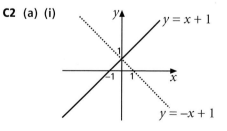

**(ii)** The image here is the same as the original
graph.

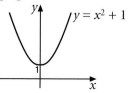

**(iii)**

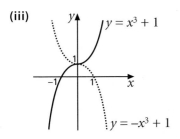

$y = x^3 + 1$

$y = -x^3 + 1$

**(b)** A comment such as: The equation of each image can be found by replacing $x$ with $-x$.

**(c)** $y = x^4 + 1$

**C3 (a)**

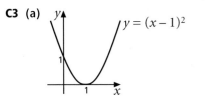

$y = (x - 1)^2$

**(b)** $y = -(x - 1)^2$  or  $y = -x^2 + 2x - 1$

**(c)** $y = (x + 1)^2$  or  $y = (-x - 1)^2$
or  $y = x^2 + 2x + 1$

**C4 (a)** $y = -x^2 - x$

**(b)**

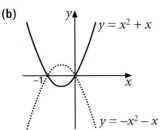

$y = x^2 + x$

$y = -x^2 - x$

**C5** Using notation similar to that on page 105, on any curve the image of $(x_1, y_1)$ is $(x_2, y_2) = (-x_1, y_1)$, which implies that $x_1 = -x_2$ and that $y_1 = y_2$. So the equation of the image can be found by replacing $x$ by $-x$.

**C6 (a)** $y = x^2 - x$

**(b)**

$y = x^2 + x$

$y = x^2 - x$

**C7 (a)** Replace $x$ by $y$ and replace $y$ by $x$.

**(b) (i)** $x = y + 6$  or  $y = x - 6$

**(ii)** $y + x = 10$  or  $x + y = 10$

**(iii)** $y^2 + (x - 3)^2 = 9$

### Exercise C (p 106)

**1 (a)** $y = -x + 5$

**(b)** $y = -\dfrac{1}{x} - 3$

**(c)** $y = -x^3 - x$

**(d)** $x - y = 10$  or  $y = x - 10$

**(e)** $-xy = 10$  or  $y = -\dfrac{10}{x}$

**(f)** $x^2 + y^2 = 5$

**2 (a)** $y = -x + 2$  **(b)** $y = -\dfrac{1}{x} - 1$

**(c)** $y = x^2 - 2x$  **(d)** $y = 2x^2 + 5x$

**(e)** $x^2 - y^2 = 4$  **(f)** $y = x^2 + 3x + 5$

**3** Replacing $x$ by $-x$ gives $y = (-x)^4 + (-x)^2 - 9$ which simplifies to give the original equation $y = x^4 + x^2 - 9$. Since the graph is unchanged after reflection in the $y$-axis, it must have the $y$-axis as a line of symmetry.

**4** Replacing $y$ by $-y$ gives $(x + 2)^2 + (-y - 3)^2 = 1$. Now $(-y - 3)^2 = (-(y + 3))^2 = (y + 3)^2$ so the equation can be written as $(x + 2)^2 + (y + 3)^2 = 1$.

## D Stretching (p 106)

**D1 (a), (b)** The image is shown by dotted lines.

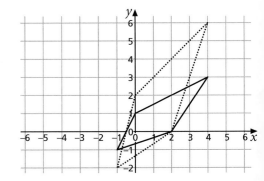

**D2** **(a), (b)** The image is shown by dotted lines.

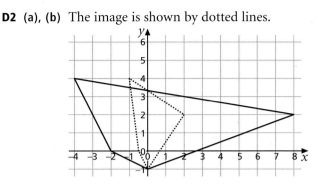

**D3** **(a)** Each image is shown by a dotted graph.

**(i)**

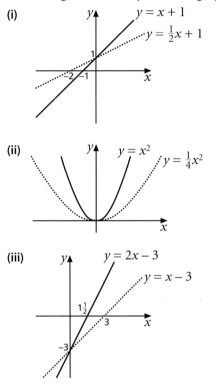

$y = x + 1$

$y = \frac{1}{2}x + 1$

**(ii)**

$y = x^2$

$y = \frac{1}{4}x^2$

**(iii)**

$y = 2x - 3$

$y = x - 3$

**(b)** A comment such as: The equation of each image can be found by replacing $x$ by $\frac{1}{2}x$.

**D4** **(a)** Each image is shown by a dotted graph.

**(i)**

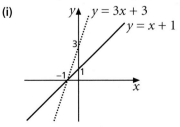

$y = 3x + 3$

$y = x + 1$

**(ii)**

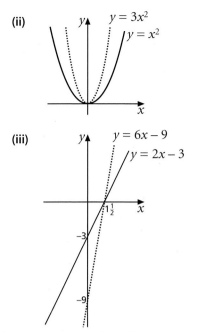

$y = 3x^2$

$y = x^2$

**(iii)**

$y = 6x - 9$

$y = 2x - 3$

**(b)** A comment such as: The equation of each image can be found by multiplying the right-hand side by 3.

**D5** **(a)** $y = \frac{1}{3}x$      **(b)** $y = \frac{1}{4}x^2 - 4$

    **(c)** $y^2 + \frac{1}{25}x^2 = 7$      **(d)** $y = 3x + 6$

    **(e)** $y = 4x^2 + 3$

**D6** **(a)** $\frac{1}{3}y + x = 4$ or $y = -3x + 12$

    **(b)** $y = x^2 + \frac{3}{4}$ or $4y = 4x^2 + 3$

**D7** **(a)** Factor 3 in the $y$-direction

    **(b)** Factor $\frac{1}{3}$ in the $x$-direction

    **(c)** Factor $\frac{1}{3}$ in the $x$-direction

### Exercise D (p 108)

**1** **(a)** $y = \frac{1}{2}x + 3$      **(b)** $y = 2x - 1$

    **(c)** $y = \frac{1}{4}x^2 - 2$      **(d)** $y = \frac{1}{4}x^2 + x + 1$

    **(e)** $\frac{1}{2}xy = 4$ or $xy = 8$    **(f)** $\frac{1}{4}x^2 + y^2 = 1$

**2** **(a)** $y = 3x - 1$      **(b)** $y = 27x^3 + 5$

    **(c)** $y = \dfrac{1}{3x}$

**3** **(a)** $\frac{1}{4}y = x + 6$ or $y = 4x + 24$

    **(b)** $\frac{1}{4}y = 3x - 2$ or $y = 12x - 8$

    **(c)** $\frac{1}{2}y + x = 10$ or $y + 2x = 20$ or $y = -2x + 20$

**4** **(a)** Factor 5 in the $y$-direction

    **(b)** Factor $\frac{1}{5}$ in the $x$-direction

(c) Factor 5 in the $x$-direction

(d) Factor $\frac{1}{2}$ in the $x$-direction

(e) Factor 4 in the $y$-direction

# E Function notation

## Exercise E (p 111)

**1 (a)** A translation of $\begin{bmatrix} 0 \\ 6 \end{bmatrix}$ **(b)** A translation of $\begin{bmatrix} -6 \\ 0 \end{bmatrix}$

**(c)** A translation of $\begin{bmatrix} 0 \\ -1 \end{bmatrix}$ **(d)** A translation of $\begin{bmatrix} 1 \\ 0 \end{bmatrix}$

**(e)** A stretch of factor 2 in the $y$-direction

**(f)** A stretch of factor $\frac{1}{2}$ in the $x$-direction

**(g)** A stretch of factor $\frac{1}{3}$ in the $y$-direction

**(h)** A stretch of factor 3 in the $x$-direction

**2 (a)**

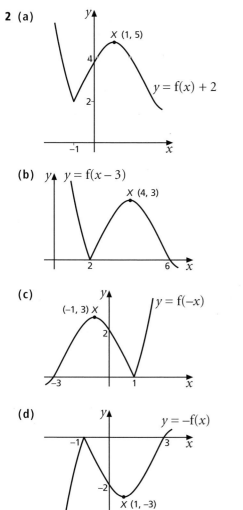

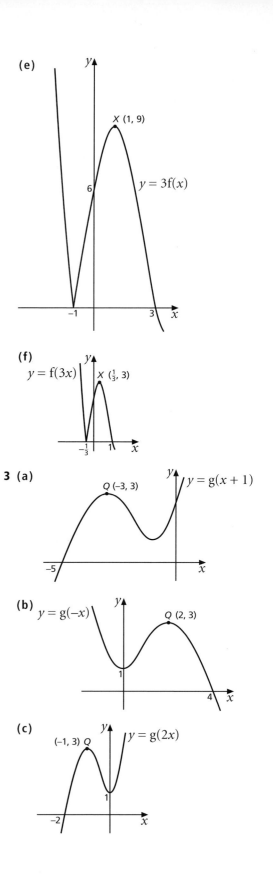

**(e)**

**(b)** $y = f(x - 3)$

**(f)**

**3 (a)**

**(b)** $y = g(-x)$

**(c)**

**(d)**

**(d)**

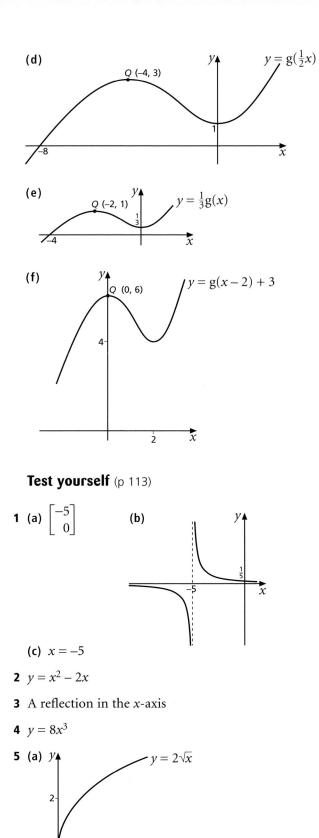

$y = g(\tfrac{1}{2}x)$

$Q\ (-4, 3)$

1

$-8$

$x$

**(e)**

$Q\ (-2, 1)$

$y = \tfrac{1}{3}g(x)$

$\tfrac{1}{3}$

$-4$

$x$

**(f)**

$y = g(x - 2) + 3$

$Q\ (0, 6)$

4

2

$x$

### Test yourself (p 113)

**1 (a)** $\begin{bmatrix} -5 \\ 0 \end{bmatrix}$

**(b)**

$\tfrac{1}{5}$

$-5$

$x$

**(c)** $x = -5$

**2** $y = x^2 - 2x$

**3** A reflection in the $x$-axis

**4** $y = 8x^3$

**5 (a)**

$y = 2\sqrt{x}$

2

1

$x$

**(b)** $y = 6\sqrt{x}$ **(c)** A translation of $\begin{bmatrix} 1 \\ 0 \end{bmatrix}$

**6 (a)**

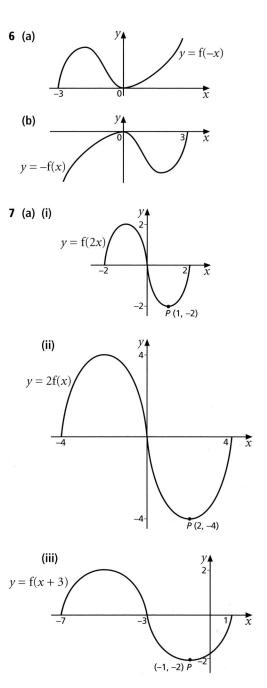

$y = f(-x)$

$-3$ 0 $x$

**(b)**

0 3 $x$

$y = -f(x)$

**7 (a) (i)**

2

$y = f(2x)$

$-2$ 2 $x$

$-2$

$P\ (1, -2)$

**(ii)**

4

$y = 2f(x)$

$-4$ 4 $x$

$-4$

$P\ (2, -4)$

**(iii)**

2

$y = f(x + 3)$

$-7$ $-3$ 1 $x$

$(-1, -2)\ P$ $-2$

**(b)** A stretch by scale factor $\tfrac{1}{2}$ in the $x$-direction

**8** A stretch by scale factor 2 in the $y$-direction

# 9 Sequences and series

## A Using a rule for the $n$th term (p 114)

Values are given to four significant figures where appropriate.

**A1** (a) (i) $5, 11, 17, 23, 29, 35$

(ii) $a_{10} = 59, a_{25} = 149, a_{100} = 599$

(iii) The terms increase at a steady rate.

(b) (i) $2, -1, -4, -7, -10, -13$

(ii) $b_{10} = -25, b_{25} = -70, b_{100} = -295$

(iii) The terms decrease at a steady rate.

(c) (i) $5, 7, 11, 19, 35, 67$

(ii) $c_{10} = 1027, c_{25} = 33\,554\,435,$
$c_{100} = 1.268 \times 10^{30}$

(iii) The terms increase at a faster and faster rate.

(d) (I) $-1, 3, 9, 17, 27, 39$

(ii) $d_{10} = 107, d_{25} = 647, d_{100} = 10\,097$

(iii) The terms increase at a faster and faster rate (though not as fast as the sequence in part (c)).

(e) (i) $5.1, 5.01, 5.001, 5.0001, 5.000\,01, 5.000\,001$

(ii) $e_{10} = 5 + 1 \times 10^{-10}, e_{25} = 5 + 1 \times 10^{-25},$
$e_{100} = 5 + 1 \times 10^{-100}$

(iii) The terms get closer and closer to 5.

(f) (i) $4, 2.5, 2, 1.75, 1.6, 1.5$

(ii) $f_{10} = 1.3, f_{25} = 1.12, f_{100} = 1.03$

(iii) The terms get closer and closer to 1.

(g) (i) $1, 1.333, 1.5, 1.6, 1.667, 1.714$

(ii) $g_{10} = 1.818, g_{25} = 1.923, g_{100} = 1.980$

(iii) The terms get closer and closer to 2.

(h) (i) $-2, 4, -8, 16, -32, 64$

(ii) $h_{10} = 1024, h_{25} = -33\,554\,432,$
$h_{100} = 1.268 \times 10^{30}$

(iii) The terms get larger and larger in size, alternating between positive and negative values.

(i) (i) $-0.1, 0.01, -0.001, 0.0001, -0.000\,01,$
$0.000\,001$

(ii) $i_{10} = 1 \times 10^{-10}, i_{25} = -1 \times 10^{-25},$
$i_{100} = 1 \times 10^{-100}$

(iii) The terms get closer and closer to 0, alternating between positive and negative values.

## Exercise A (p 115)

**1** (a) $u_1 = 5, u_2 = 9, u_3 = 13$　　(b) $u_{100} = 401$

(c) $n = 20$　　(d) 24

**2** (a) $a_1 = 37, a_2 = 34, a_3 = 31$　　(b) $a_{16} = -8$

(c) 13

**3** (a) $p_1 = 6, p_2 = 18, p_3 = 54, p_{10} = 118\,098$

(b) The terms increase at a faster and faster rate.

**4** (a) $h_{30} = 9.7 \times 10^{-15}$ (to 2 s.f.)

(b) The terms get closer and closer to 0.

**5** (a) B: The terms increase at a faster and faster rate.

(b) A: The terms decrease at a steady rate.

(c) D: The terms increase but at a slower and slower rate, converging to a limit of 2.

(d) E: The terms decrease but converge to a limit of 2.

(e) C: The terms go up and down but get closer and closer to a limit of 2.

**6** (a) B　　(b) C　　(c) A

**7** (a) $u_n = \dfrac{1}{n}$　　(b) $u_n = \dfrac{n+1}{n}$ or $u_n = 1 + \dfrac{1}{n}$

**8** (a) $u_n = 3.007$　　(b) $\dfrac{3n+7}{n} = \dfrac{3n}{n} + \dfrac{7}{n} = 3 + \dfrac{7}{n}$

(c) As $n$ gets larger $\dfrac{7}{n}$ converges to 0 so $3 + \dfrac{7}{n}$ converges to 3.

**9** $(-1)^n \times \left( \dfrac{n+5}{n} \right)$

## B Inductive definition

### Exercise B (p 117)

**1** $2, 1, -2, -11, -38, -119$

**2** (a) $6, 5, 4.5, 4.25$　　(b) $10, 9, 7.7, 6.01$

**3** $n = 6$

**4 (a)** $u_2 = pu_1 + q$ so $4 = 2p + q$
$u_3 = pu_2 + q$ so $7.2 = 4p + q$

**(b)** $p = 1.6$, $q = 0.8$; $u_{n+1} = 1.6u_n + 0.8$

**5** $a = 2$, $b = -5$; $u_{n+1} = 2u_n - 5$

**6 (a)** $k = 0.4$; $u_{n+1} = 0.4u_n + 0.4$

**(b)** $u_4 = 1.2$

**7** $p = 4$

**8 (a) (i)** $u_2 = 8 + k$      **(ii)** $u_3 = 16 + 3k$

**(b)** $16 + 3k = 20.5$, $k = 1.5$

**9 (a) (i)** $u_2 = 2p + 1$      **(ii)** $u_3 = 2p^2 + p + 1$

**(b)** $2p^2 + p - 10 = 0$, $p = -2\frac{1}{2}, 2$

**10 (a)** $u_2 = 4p + 7$
So $u_3 = p(4p + 7) + 7 = 4p^2 + 7p + 7$
Hence, $4p^2 + 7p + 7 = 9 \Rightarrow 4p^2 + 7p - 2 = 0$
$\Rightarrow (4p - 1)(p + 2) = 0 \Rightarrow p = \frac{1}{4}, -2$

**(b)** $p = \frac{1}{4}$: $u_1 = 4$, $u_2 = 8$, $u_3 = 9$, $u_4 = 9\frac{1}{4}$
$p = -2$: $u_1 = 4$, $u_2 = -1$, $u_3 = 9$, $u_4 = -11$

## C Inductive definition and limits (p 119)

**C1 (a) (i)** 3, 8, 13, 18, 23, 28

**(ii)** The terms increase at a steady rate.

**(b) (i)** 0, 0, 0, 0, 0, 0

**(ii)** The terms are all the same.

**(c) (i)** −2, −6, −18, −54, −162, −486

**(ii)** The terms decrease at a faster and faster rate.

**(d) (i)** $3, 1, \frac{1}{3}, \frac{1}{9}, \frac{1}{27}, \frac{1}{81}$

**(ii)** The terms decrease at a slower and slower rate, converging towards a limit of 0.

**(e) (i)** 5, 9, 17, 33, 65, 129

**(ii)** The terms increase at a faster and faster rate.

**(f) (i)** 3, 2.5, 2.25, 2.125, 2.0625, 2.03125

**(ii)** The terms decrease at a slower and slower rate, converging to a limit of 2.

**(g) (i)** 0.9, 0.9487, 0.9740, 0.9869, 0.9934, 0.9967

**(ii)** The terms increase at a slower and slower rate, converging to a limit of 1.

**(h) (i)** 2, 5.5, 5.1818, 5.1930, 5.1926, 5.1926

**(ii)** The terms increase at a slower and slower rate, converging to a limit of 5.192 582 403 6 (to 10 d.p.)

**(i) (i)** 3, 3, 3, 3, 3, 3

**(ii)** The terms are all the same.

**(j) (i)** −5, −5, −5, −5, −5, −5

**(ii)** The terms are all the same.

**C2** 1

**C3 (a)** If the sequence is constant then $u_{n+1} = u_n = c$. So the recurrence relation gives $c = 3c - 10$.

**(b)** $c = 5$

**C4 (a)** $c = \frac{c}{3} + 6$      **(b)** $c = 9$

**C5 (a)** $u_1 = 4$   **(b)** $u_1 = -3$   **(c)** $u_1 = -2$   **(d)** $u_1 = 5$

**C6** For all values of $a$, the sequences converge to 6. $u_1 = 6$ is the only starting value that gives a constant sequence.

**C7** For all values of $b$, the sequences converge to $-1\frac{1}{3}$. $u_1 = -1\frac{1}{3}$ is the only starting value that gives a constant sequence.

### Exercise C (p 121)

Where appropriate, values are given correct to 4 d.p.

**1** The letter $l$ is used for the limit in each equation. Any letter may, of course, be used.

**(a)** $l = \frac{l}{3} + 5$ gives $l = 7.5$
6, 7, 7.3333, 7.4444, 7.4815, 7.4938, 7.4979, ... is converging to 7.5.

**(b)** $l = 0.5l - 1$ gives $l = -2$
−8, −5, −3.5, −2.75, −2.375, −2.1875, −2.0938, −2.0469, ... is converging to −2.

**(c)** $l = \frac{l}{8} + 1$ gives $l = 1\frac{1}{7}$
0.6, 1.075, 1.1344, 1.1418, 1.1427, 1.1428, 1.1429, ... is converging to $1\frac{1}{7}$.

**(d)** $l = 0.6l + 2$ gives $l = 5$
10, 8, 6.8, 6.08, 5.648, 5.3888, 5.2333, 5.1400, 5.0840, 5.0504, 5.0302, 5.0181, 5.0109, 5.0065, ... is converging to 5.

Answers |

**2 (a)** $p_2 = 43.4375$ so about 43 birds

   **(b)** 80

**3 (a)** A value for $a$ that generates a constant sequence must satisfy the equation $a = \frac{6}{a} + 1$ which rearranges to give the quadratic equation $a^2 - a - 6 = 0$.
This factorises to $(a - 3)(a + 2) = 0$ and has two solutions, $a = 3$ and $a = -2$.

   **(b) (i)** $u_2 = \frac{6}{5} + 1 = 1.2 + 1 = 2.2$

   **(ii)** $u_3 = 3.7273$, $u_4 = 2.6098$, $u_5 = 3.2991$, $u_6 = 2.8187$, $u_7 = 3.1286$, $u_8 = 2.9178$, $u_9 = 3.0564$, $u_{10} = 2.9631$

   **(iii)** 3

   **(c) (i)** An hypothesis about the limit

   **(ii)** $-1.9, -2.1579, -1.7805, -2.3699, -1.5318,$ $-2.9170, -1.0569, -4.6769, -0.2829,$ $-20.2081, 0.7031, 9.5338$ are the first twelve terms.
It doesn't appear to be converging to $-2$. In fact, it converges to 3.

**4** This investigation yields many interesting results. For example, if $1 < r < 3$ then the sequences converge to a limit $1 - \frac{1}{r}$.

## D Arithmetic sequences (p 121)

**D1 (a)** 10, 13, 16, 19, 22

   **(b)** $u_{10} = 37$, $u_{100} = 307$, $u_{1000} = 3007$

   **(c)** $u_n = 10 + 3(n - 1)$ or $u_n = 7 + 3n$

**D2 (a)** $x_{10} = -17$, $x_{100} = -287$, $x_{1000} = -2987$

   **(b)** $x_n = 10 - 3(n - 1)$ or $x_n = 13 - 3n$

**D3 (a)** $x_n = 6 + 7(n - 1)$ or $x_n = 7n - 1$

   **(b)** $x_{100} = 699$

**D4** The $n$th term is $11 + 3(n - 1)$ or $3n + 8$.

### Exercise D (p 123)

**1 (a)** 5, 14, 23, 32

   **(b)** $u_n = 5 + 9(n - 1)$ or $u_n = 9n - 4$

   **(c)** $u_{50} = 446$

**2 (a)** 61.5

   **(b)** The $n$th term is $90 - 1.5(n - 1)$ or $91.5 - 1.5n$.

   **(c)** $n = 33$

**3** 8

**4 (a)** 47    **(b)** 19    **(c)** 31    **(d)** 100

**5** 402

**6** $-2 + 0.5(n - 1)$ or $0.5n - 2.5$

**7** $-134$

**8** First term 7; common difference $2\frac{1}{2}$

**9** $2 + 3(n - 1)$ or $3n - 1$

**10** $-71$

## E Arithmetic series (p 124)

**E1 (a)** 10    **(b)** 5050

**E2** 1275

**E3 (a) (i)** 20 100    **(ii)** 11 325

   **(b)** 8775

**E4** 29 605

**E5 (a)** 210    **(b)** $210 \times 7 = 1470$

**E6 (a)** 329    **(b)** 15 250

### Exercise E (p 126)

**1** 20 100

**2** 10 962

**3** 60 300

**4** 166 833

**5** 5820

**6** $a = 10$, $d = \frac{1}{2}$, $n = 100$ and so the sum is
$\frac{1}{2} \times 100 \times (2 \times 10 + (100 - 1) \times \frac{1}{2})$
$= 50 \times (20 + 49.5)$
$= 3475$

**7 (a)** 24    **(b)** $-150$

**8** The first term is 1 so $a = 1$.
The tenth term is 7 so $a + 9d = 7 \Rightarrow 1 + 9d = 7$ $\Rightarrow d = \frac{2}{3}$.
$n = 40$ and so the sum is
$\frac{1}{2} \times 40 \times (2 \times 1 + (40 - 1) \times \frac{2}{3}) = 20 \times (2 + 26) = 560$

**9** 5040

**10** $4\frac{1}{2}$

**11** 9

**12 (a)** 255 m   **(b)** 31 seconds

**13 (a)** £2450   **(b)** £59 000   **(c)** 30

**14** $n^2$

**15** 118.8 m$^2$

**16** 587 full turns

## F Sigma notation

### Exercise F (p 128)

**1 (a)** 30   **(b)** 36   **(c)** 36   **(d)** 21

  **(e)** 33   **(f)** 126   **(g)** 68   **(h)** $1\frac{1}{12}$

**2 (a)** 1081   **(b)** 2460   **(c)** 615   **(d)** 4080

  **(e)** 290   **(f)** 362.5   **(g)** −2325   **(h)** 6360

**3 (a) (i)** 1275   **(ii)** 465

  **(b)** 810

**4 (a)** 28

  **(b)** The first term is 23 and the last term is 77.
  The number of terms is 28 so the sum is
  $\frac{1}{2} \times 28 \times (23 + 77) = 14 \times 100 = 1400$.

**5 (a)** 473   **(b)** 1324.6   **(c)** −9637

**6 (a)** The first term is 2 and the last term is 59.
  The number of terms is 20 so the sum is
  $\frac{1}{2} \times 20 \times (2 + 59) = 10 \times 61 = 610$.

  **(b)** The first term is 2 and the last term is $3n - 1$.
  The number of terms is $n$ so the sum is
  $\frac{1}{2} \times n \times (2 + 3n - 1) = \frac{1}{2}n(3n + 1)$.

### Mixed questions (p 130)

**1** $-2.6 + 0.4(n - 1)$ or $0.4n - 3$

**2** −0.525

**3** $k = 0.2k + 4$ gives $k = 5$

**4** 11 325

**5** 80 100

**6 (a)** 3.8   **(b)** 897

**7** 41 200

**8 (a)** $\frac{3}{4}$; $176\frac{1}{4}$ or 176.25   **(b)** 74

**9 (a) (i)** 455   **(ii)** 13 230

  **(b)** 11

**10** −13, −10

**11** First term −1.35; common difference 0.3

### Test yourself (p 131)

**1** $u_2 = pu_1 + 5$
  $= 2p + 5$

  So $u_3 = pu_2 + 5$
  $\Rightarrow u_3 = p(2p + 5) + 5$
  $= 2p^2 + 5p + 5$

  Hence $\quad 2p^2 + 5p + 5 = 8$
  $\Rightarrow \qquad 2p^2 + 5p - 3 = 0$
  $\Rightarrow \quad (2p - 1)(p + 3) = 0$
  $\Rightarrow \qquad\qquad p = \frac{1}{2}, -3$

**2 (a)** $u_3 = 13$   **(b)** $l = \frac{3}{5}l - 2$ gives $l = -5$

**3 (a)** $u_1 = 96, u_2 = 92, u_3 = 88$   **(b)** 24

**4** 1275

**5** 4840

**6** 590

**7 (a)** $k = 4$   **(b)** 1751.5

**8** 250

**9 (a)** 62   **(b)** 290

**10 (a)** One proof is:
  'With $l$ as the last term we have
  $S = a + (a + d) + (a + 2d) + \dots + (l - 2d) +$
  $(l - d) + l$
  and reversing gives
  $S = l + (l - d) + (l - 2d) + \dots + (a + 2d) +$
  $(a + d) + a$
  Adding gives
  $\qquad 2S = n(a + l)$
  so $\quad S = \frac{1}{2}n(a + l)$
  As $\quad l = a + (n - 1)d$ then
  $\qquad S = \frac{1}{2}n(a + a + (n - 1)d)$
  $\qquad\quad = \frac{1}{2}n(2a + (n - 1)d)$

  **(b)** $d = 3700$   **(c)** 91 000

**11 (a)** 71 071   **(b)** 71 355

# 10 Differentiation

## A Gradient as rate of change (p 132)

**A1** (a) $3\,°C$

(b) $7\,°C$

(c) (i) $37\,°C$      (ii) $46\,°C$      (iii) $82\,°C$

(d) $2000\,m$

**A2** (a) $-0.007$ degrees per metre; the negative sign shows a rate of decrease.

(b) $0.7\,°C$

(c) $-14\,°C$

**A3** (a) 2

(b) (i) 2      (ii) 5      (iii) $\frac{1}{2}$      (iv) 4

**A4** (a) $-3$

(b) (i) $-2$      (ii) $-1$      (iii) $-\frac{1}{2}$      (iv) $\frac{7}{2}$

**A5** (a)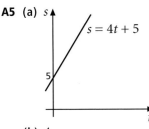

(b) 4

(c) The speed of the vehicle.

**A6** (a) It is of the form $y = 3x + c$.

(b) $y = 3x - 1$

**A7** 0 (with a sketch of $y = 5$)

### Exercise A (p 134)

**1** (a) 3    (b) $-7$    (c) 1    (d) 0    (e) $\frac{3}{2}$

**2** (a) $C = 900 + 5n$

(b) $\dfrac{dC}{dn} = 5$; the cost per unit, in pence

**3** $y = 5x + 7$

**4** $y = -2x + 8$

**5** $\dfrac{dy}{dx} = 2$; $y = 2x + 3$

**6** $\dfrac{dy}{dx} = -\frac{1}{2}$; $y = -\frac{1}{2}x + 9$

---

**7** (a) (i) $C = 30 + 20t$      (ii) 20

(b) $\dfrac{dC}{dt} = 25$; this plumber's charge for labour is £25 per hour.

## B Gradient of a curve (p 135)

**B1** (a) 8

(b) The gradient represents the speed in m/s when $t = 3$.

**B2** At $(2, 2)$ gradient $= 1$; at $(5, 2.75)$ gradient $= -\frac{1}{2}$

**B3** (a) 3

(b)

| $x$ | $-2$ | $-1.5$ | $-1$ | 0 | 1 | 1.5 | 2 |
|---|---|---|---|---|---|---|---|
| $\dfrac{dy}{dx}$ | $-4$ | $-3$ | $-2$ | 0 | 2 | 3 | 4 |

(c)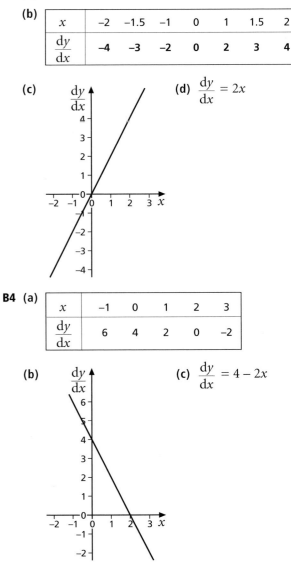

(d) $\dfrac{dy}{dx} = 2x$

**B4** (a)

| $x$ | $-1$ | 0 | 1 | 2 | 3 |
|---|---|---|---|---|---|
| $\dfrac{dy}{dx}$ | 6 | 4 | 2 | 0 | $-2$ |

(b) 

(c) $\dfrac{dy}{dx} = 4 - 2x$

**B5 (a)**

| $x$ | −3 | −2 | −1 | 0 | 1 | 2 | 3 | 4 |
|---|---|---|---|---|---|---|---|---|
| $\dfrac{dy}{dx}$ | 1.7 | 0.2 | −0.7 | −1 | −0.7 | 0.2 | 1.7 | 3.8 |

**(b)**

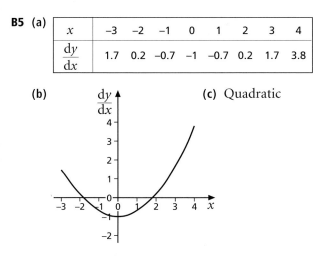

**(c)** Quadratic

## Exercise B (p 138)

**1**

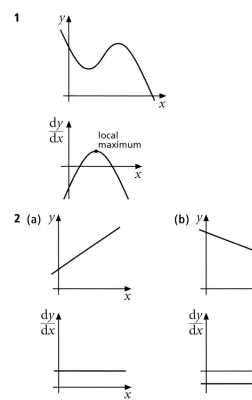

**2 (a)** **(b)**

**(c)** **(d)**

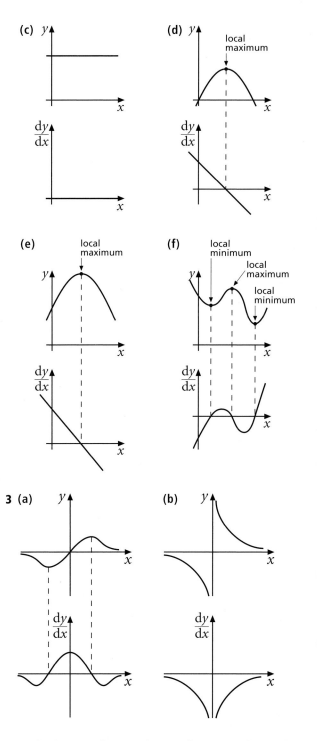

**(e)** **(f)**

**3 (a)** **(b)**

## C Calculating the gradient of a curved graph
(p 139)

**C1 (a)** Gradient of $AB = 6.001$      **(b)** 6

**C2** Gradient of tangent at $(4, 16) = 8$

Answers | **197**

**C3 (a)**

| $x$ | 0 | 1 | 2 | 3 | 4 | 5 | 6 |
|---|---|---|---|---|---|---|---|
| $\dfrac{dy}{dx}$ | 0 | 2 | 4 | 6 | 8 | 10 | 12 |

(b) $\dfrac{dy}{dx} = 2x$

**C4 (a)** The gradient is as shown in this table.

| $x$ | 0 | 1 | 2 | 3 | 4 | 5 |
|---|---|---|---|---|---|---|
| $\dfrac{dy}{dx}$ | 5 | 7 | 9 | 11 | 13 | 15 |

(b) $\dfrac{dy}{dx} = 2x + 5$

**C5** The graph of $y = x^2$ is stretched in the $y$-direction by a factor of 3, making the gradient 3 times as large.

**C6 (a)** Gradients are 0, 3, 12, 27, 48, 75.

(b) 3, 12, 27, 48, 75

(c) A quadratic function

(d) $\dfrac{dy}{dx} = 3x^2$

**Exercise C** (p 143)

**1** $6x^2 - 5$

**2 (a)** $8x - 1$      **(b)** $12x^3 - 15x^2$

**(c)** $4 - 12x + 21x^2$

**3** $-3$

**4 (a)** $-12$      **(b)** 31

**5 (a)** $8x^3 - 3$      **(b)** $5x^4 + 9x^2 - 2$

**(c)** $4x^3 - 9x^2 + 1$

**6**

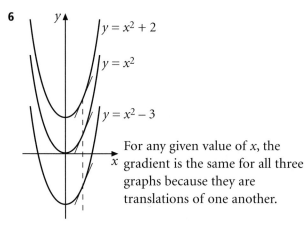

For any given value of $x$, the gradient is the same for all three graphs because they are translations of one another.

**7** 88

**8 (a)** $(0, 0)$, $(2, 0)$, $(3, 0)$

**(b)**

**(c)** Gradient at $(0, 0)$ is 6
Gradient at $(2, 0)$ is $-2$
Gradient at $(3, 0)$ is 3

**9** $p = 8$

**10** $a = 2$, $b = 7$

**11 (a)** $t = 0$ and $t = 8$      **(b)** $h$

**(c)** 10. The stone is travelling upward at 10 m/s.

**(d)** $-20$. It is travelling downward at speed 20 m/s.

**12** $a = 3$, $b = -5$

## D Differentiating $x^n$, where $n$ is negative or a fraction

**Exercise D** (page 144)

**1 (a)** $-3x^{-4}$    **(b)** $-\dfrac{1}{x^2}$    **(c)** $\tfrac{1}{3}x^{-\frac{2}{3}}$

**(d)** $\dfrac{1}{2\sqrt{x}}$    **(e)** $\tfrac{3}{4}x^{-\frac{1}{4}}$

**2 (a)** $\tfrac{3}{2}\sqrt{x}$    **(b)** $1 + \dfrac{1}{x^2}$    **(c)** $-\dfrac{6}{x^3}$

**(d)** $-\tfrac{3}{4}x^{-4}$    **(e)** $-\tfrac{1}{3}x^{-\frac{3}{2}}$

**3 (a)** $5x + 5x\sqrt{x}$      **(b)** $5 + \tfrac{15}{2}\sqrt{x}$

**4 (a)** $\tfrac{3}{2}x^{-\frac{1}{2}} - \tfrac{5}{2}x^{\frac{3}{2}}$      **(b)** $2x + \tfrac{5}{2}x^{\frac{3}{2}}$

**(c)** $6x - \tfrac{9}{2}x^{\frac{1}{2}}$      **(d)** $\tfrac{3}{2}x^{\frac{1}{2}} + \tfrac{3}{2}x^{-\frac{1}{2}} - 1$

**5 (a)** $-\dfrac{1}{x^2}$      **(b)** $1 + \dfrac{3}{x^2}$

**(c)** $\tfrac{3}{2}x^{-\frac{1}{2}} - x^{-\frac{3}{2}}$      **(d)** $-2x^{-3} - \tfrac{3}{2}x^{-\frac{5}{2}} - x^{-2}$

**6 (a)** $x^{\frac{3}{2}}$      **(b)** 4.5

**7** (a) $x + 2 + \dfrac{1}{x}$      (b) $1 - \dfrac{1}{x^2}$

## E Tangents and normals

### Exercise E (p 146)

**1** $y = 6x - 9$

**2** Tangent: $y = 3x + 2$     Normal: $y = -\frac{1}{3}x - \frac{4}{3}$

**3** Tangent: $y = 2x - 15$     Normal: $y = -\frac{1}{2}x - 10$

**4** Tangent: $y = 16x - 64$    Normal: $y = -\frac{1}{16}x + \frac{1}{4}$

**5** $y = 7x - 16$

**6** $y = \frac{1}{8}x - \frac{1}{2}$

**7** (a) $y = x - 12$      (b) $y = -x - 12$

**8** (a) $y = 2x + 2$

   (b) $y = -\frac{1}{2}x + \frac{9}{2}$   or   $x + 2y - 9 = 0$

**9** (a) $y = -3x + 9$

   (b) $y = \frac{1}{3}x + \frac{7}{3}$   or   $x - 3y + 7 = 0$

**10** (a) $y = 2x - 5$      (b) $(0, -5)$ and $(2\frac{1}{2}, 0)$

**11** (a) $\dfrac{dy}{dx} = 1 - \dfrac{12}{x^2}$

   At $A$, $\dfrac{dy}{dx} = 1 - \dfrac{12}{16} = \dfrac{1}{4}$

   Equation of a tangent at $A$ is

   $y - 7 = \frac{1}{4}(x - 4)$   or   $y = \frac{1}{4}x + 6$

   (b) $y = \frac{2}{3}x + 4$

   (c) $(4.8, 7.2)$

   (d) Gradient of normal at $A = -\dfrac{1}{\frac{1}{4}} = -4$

   Equation of normal is

   $y - 7 = -4(x - 4)$   or   $y = -4x + 23$

   (e) $y = -\frac{3}{2}x + 17$

   (f) $(2.4, 13.4)$

## F Second order derivative

### Exercise F (p 148)

**1** (a) $6x - 4$      (b) $12x^2$

   (c) $6x - 2$      (d) $12x^2 + 4$

**2** $3$

**3** (a) $-x^{-\frac{3}{2}}$      (b) $2 - \frac{3}{4}x^{-\frac{1}{2}}$

   (c) $-\frac{2}{9}x^{-\frac{4}{3}}$      (d) $2x^{-3} + \frac{15}{4}x^{-\frac{7}{2}}$

## Mixed questions (p 149)

**1** (a) $4x^3 - 6x + 5$      (b) $25$

**2** (a) $4$

   (b) It is travelling at $4\,\text{m/s}$ after 5 seconds from the start.

**3** $3x^2 - 6x + 4$

**4** $-9$

**5** (a) $y = 7x - 5$

   (b) $y = -\frac{1}{7}x + \frac{15}{7}$   or   $y = \dfrac{15 - x}{7}$

**6** (a) $y = 2x - 6$      (b) $y = -\frac{1}{2}x - 1$

**7** (a) $y = x + 3$      (b) $(1, 4)$

**8** $k = 17$

**9** $y = -\frac{3}{8}x + \frac{9}{2}$   or   $3x + 8y - 36 = 0$

**10** $y = -0.8x + 3.1$   or   $8x + 10y - 31 = 0$

**11** $\dfrac{dy}{dx} = -\frac{1}{2}$, $\dfrac{d^2y}{dx^2} = 4$

**12** $\frac{3}{4}x^{-\frac{5}{2}} - \frac{3}{4}x^{-\frac{1}{2}}$

**13** $a = 2$, $b = -7$

**14** (a) $\dfrac{dy}{dx} = 2x$. At $(k, k^2)$, $\dfrac{dy}{dx} = 2k$.

   The equation of the tangent at $(k, k^2)$ is
$$y - k^2 = 2k(x - k)$$
$$\Rightarrow \qquad y = 2kx - k^2$$
   which cuts the $y$-axis at $(0, -k^2)$.

   (b) The gradient of the normal at $(k, k^2)$ is $-\dfrac{1}{2k}$.

   The equation of the normal is
$$y - k^2 = -\frac{1}{2k}(x - k)$$
$$\Rightarrow \quad y = -\frac{1}{2k}x + k^2 + \frac{1}{2}$$
   which cuts the $y$-axis at $(0, k^2 + \frac{1}{2})$.

**15** $p = -4$, $q = -3$, $r = 14$

**16 (a)** $(x + \delta x)^3 = x^3 + 3x^2\,\delta x + 3x(\delta x)^2 + (\delta x)^3$

**(b)** $\dfrac{\delta y}{\delta x} = \dfrac{3x^2\,\delta x + 3x(\delta x)^2 + (\delta x)^3}{\delta x} = 3x^2 + 3x\,\delta x + (\delta x)^2$

**(c)** $\dfrac{\delta y}{\delta x}$ gets closer and closer to $3x^2$. (So $\dfrac{dy}{dx} = 3x^2$.)

## Test yourself (p 150)

**1 (a)** $3x^2 - 4x + 3$      **(b)** $y = 2x - 6$

**2** $6x^2 + \dfrac{1}{2\sqrt{x}} - \dfrac{2}{x^2}$

**3** $y = \frac{1}{2}x - 26$

**4** $-\frac{1}{16}$

**5 (a)** $x + 2y - 12 = 0$      **(b)** $(12, 0)$

**(c)** $2x - y - 4 = 0$      **(d)** $(2, 0)$

**6** $\frac{21}{16}$

**7 (a)** $3x^2 - 10x + 5$      **(b)** $\frac{1}{3}$

**(c)** $y = 2x - 7$      **(d)** $\frac{7}{2}\sqrt{5}$

# 11 Integration

## A Thinking backwards (p 152)

**A1** $t^2$

**A2** $\frac{5}{2}t^2$

## B Integration as the reverse of differentiation
(p 153)

**B1** The derivative of each of them is the same, $2x$.
The function $x^2 + c$, where $c$ is a number, has
derivative $2x$.

**B2 (a)** $10x$      **(b)** $5x^2 + c$

**B3 (a) (i)** $6x$      **(ii)** $8x$      **(iii)** $8$

       **(iv)** $3x^2$      **(v)** $6$

**(b) (i)** $4x^2 + c$      **(ii)** $x^3 + c$      **(iii)** $6x + c$

       **(iv)** $3x^2 + c$      **(v)** $8x + c$

**B4** $\frac{1}{4}x^4 + c$

### Exercise B (p 154)

**1 (a)** $2x^2 + c$      **(b)** $6x^2 + c$

   **(c)** $10x^2 + c$      **(d)** $\frac{1}{2}x^2 + c$

**2 (a)** $2x^3 + c$      **(b)** $5x^3 + c$

   **(c)** $\frac{1}{3}x^3 + c$      **(d)** $\frac{2}{3}x^3 + c$

**3 (a)** $x^4 + c$      **(b)** $2x^5 + c$

   **(c)** $\frac{5}{3}x^3 + c$      **(d)** $\frac{3}{2}x^2 + c$

**4 (a)**

| Function | $x$ | $x^2$ | $x^3$ | $x^4$ |
|---|---|---|---|---|
| Indefinite integral | $\dfrac{x^2}{2} + c$ | $\dfrac{x^3}{3} + c$ | $\dfrac{x^4}{4} + c$ | $\dfrac{x^5}{5} + c$ |

**(b)** $\dfrac{x^{n+1}}{n+1} + c$

## C Integrating polynomials (p 154)

**C1 (a)** $\displaystyle\int 3x^2\,dx = x^3 + c$      **(b)** $\displaystyle\int 4x\,dx = 2x^2 + c$

**C2** $\displaystyle\int 5x\,dx = \frac{5}{2}x^2 + c$

**C3** $\displaystyle\int 6x^2\,dx = 2x^3 + c$

**Exercise C** (p 155)

**1** (a) $\frac{1}{4}x^4 + c$  (b) $\frac{4}{3}x^3 + c$  (c) $3x^2 + c$  (d) $x^5 + c$

**2** (a) $y = \frac{1}{2}x^2 - 4x + c$

(b) $y = x^3 + \frac{1}{2}x^2 + c$

(c) $y = \frac{1}{3}x^3 + \frac{1}{2}x^2 + x + c$

(d) $y = x^5 + 3x + c$

**3** $f(x) = \frac{5}{2}x^2 + \frac{3}{4}x^4 + c$

**4** (a) $2x - \frac{3}{2}x^2 + \frac{1}{3}x^3 + c$  (b) $\frac{5}{4}x^4 + \frac{1}{3}x^6 + c$

**5** (a) $y = \frac{1}{2}x^4 - \frac{7}{2}x^2 + 3x + c$

(b) $y = \frac{1}{3}x^3 - \frac{1}{2}x^2 - 2x + c$

**6** (a) $3x^2 - 4x + c$  (b) $x^3 + 6x^2 + c$

(c) $\frac{4}{3}x^3 - 2x^2 + x + c$

**7** $f(x) = \frac{1}{4}x^4 + \frac{5}{3}x^3 + x^2 - 8x + c$

**8** (a) $\frac{1}{3}x^3 - \frac{3}{2}x^2 - 10x + c$  (b) $\frac{1}{2}x^4 + \frac{1}{3}x^3 + c$

## D Integrating $x^n$, where $n$ is negative or a fraction

**Exercise D** (p 157)

**1** (a) $-\frac{1}{2}x^{-2} + c$  (b) $\frac{4}{7}x^{\frac{7}{4}} + c$

(c) $\frac{2}{3}x^{\frac{3}{2}} + c$  (d) $4x^{\frac{1}{4}} + c$

**2** (a) (i) $x^{\frac{5}{2}}$  (ii) $\frac{2}{7}x^{\frac{7}{2}} + c$

(b) $\frac{2}{9}x^{\frac{9}{2}} + c$

**3** (a) $x^3 + x\sqrt{x}$  (b) $\frac{1}{4}x^4 + \frac{2}{5}x^{\frac{5}{2}} + c$

**4** (a) $x^2 + x^{-2}$  (b) $\frac{1}{3}x^3 - x^{-1} + c$

**5** (a) $\frac{1}{2}x^2 + \frac{2}{5}x^{\frac{5}{2}} + c$  (b) $x + \frac{1}{x} + c$

(c) $2x^{\frac{1}{2}} + x + c$  (d) $2x^{\frac{1}{2}} + \frac{2}{3}x^{\frac{3}{2}} + c$

(e) $2x^{\frac{1}{2}} + \frac{2}{5}x^{\frac{5}{2}} + c$  (f) $x + \frac{4}{3}x^{\frac{3}{2}} + \frac{1}{2}x^2 + c$

## E Finding the constant of integration

**Exercise E** (p 158)

**1** $f(x) = 2x^3 + 4x + 1$

**2** (a) $y = x^3 + 2x^2 + 2$  (b) $y = \frac{1}{3}x^3 + \frac{1}{2}x^2 + x + 3$

**3** $y = x^2 + \dfrac{6}{x} - 6$

**4** (a) $f(x) = 3x^3 - 3x^2 + 2$  (b) $f(x) = 5x - 2x^{\frac{3}{2}} + 3$

**5** (a) $y = \frac{2}{3}x^3 - \frac{1}{2}x^2 - 3x + c$

(b) $5\frac{1}{2}$

**6** $k = 16$

**7** $P = t^3 + 3t^2 + 96$

**8** (a) $p = -6$  (b) $y = 2x^2 - 6x + 7$

**9** (a) $y = 5x - \dfrac{1}{x} + c$  (b) $12\frac{1}{2}$

**10** (a) $a = 6, b = 8, c = 5$  (b) $y = 2x^3 + 4x^2 + 5$

## Mixed questions (p 159)

**1** (a) $\frac{2}{3}x^3 + \frac{3}{2}x^2 - x + c$  (b) $\frac{5}{6}x^6 + x^2 + c$

(c) $\frac{1}{2}x^4 - \frac{8}{3}x^3 + \frac{3}{2}x^2 - 12x + c$

**2** $f(x) = \frac{1}{4}x^4 + 4x^3 - 2x - 32$

**3** $y = \frac{1}{6}x^3 - \frac{3}{2}x^2 + 14$

**4** $s = \frac{1}{3}t^3 + t^2 - 3t + 1$

**5** (a) $a = 10$  (b) $f(x) = x^3 + 5x^2 - 4$

**6** (a) $P = 20t - \frac{1}{2}t^2 + 100$  (b) 10 and 30

**7** $f(x) = \frac{1}{2}x^2 + \frac{2}{3}x^{\frac{3}{2}} - \frac{1}{6}$

**8** (a) $y = 4x^{\frac{3}{2}} - \dfrac{4}{x} + 5$  (b) $y = 10x - 5$

**9** (a) $y = 3x - 2\sqrt{x} - 3$  (b) $\left(\frac{1}{9}, -\frac{10}{3}\right)$

**10** (a) $7\frac{31}{32}$

(b) $f(x) = \frac{1}{3}x^3 - 2x - \dfrac{1}{x} - 2\frac{2}{3}$

(c) $f'(x) = \left(x - \dfrac{1}{x}\right)^2 \geq 0$

(because it's a square)

**11** (a) $N = 5t - \frac{2}{9}t^2 - \frac{1}{27}t^3 + 36$

(b) 48

(c) After 5 weeks

(d) $\dfrac{dN}{dt} = -\frac{1}{9}(t+9)(t-5)$

When $t > 5$, $\dfrac{dN}{dt} < 0$, so $N$ is decreasing.

When $t = 12$,

$N = 5 \times 12 - \frac{2}{9} \times 12^2 - \frac{1}{27} \times 12^3 + 36 = 0$

**Test yourself** (p 161)

1 (a) $\frac{1}{4}x^4 + \frac{2}{3}x^3 - \frac{1}{2}x^2 + c$  (b) $\frac{1}{5}x^5 + \frac{7}{2}x^2 - x + c$

  (c) $\frac{1}{9}x^9 + \frac{5}{7}x^7 + c$

2 (a) $\frac{3}{4}x^4 - 2x^3 + c$        (b) $3x^4 + x^3 - 2x^2 - x + c$

  (c) $3x^3 - 6x^2 + 4x + c$

3 $y = 2x^3 - x + 5$

4 $y = 2x^3 - \frac{1}{2}x^2 - 5x + \frac{7}{2}$

5 (a) $f(x) = 2x^5 - 3x^4 - 4x + 2$

  (b) $-102$

6 $f(x) = x^3 - x^2 - 5x + 3$

7 $y = 3x^3 - 3x^2 + x + 40$

8 (a) $y = x^3 - 10x^2 + 29x - 20$

  (b) When $x = 4$, $y = 64 - 160 + 116 - 20 = 0$

  (c) $y = x + 4$

  (d) $\frac{14}{3}$

# Index